Treason of the Heart

Previous titles by the author

Nonfiction

Next Generation: Travels in Israel
The Hungarian Revolution
The Face of Defeat
Unity Mitford
Paris in the Third Reich
Cyril Connolly: Journal and Memoir
The Closed Circle: An Interpretation of the Arabs
The War That Never Was: The Fall of the Soviet Empire 1985–1991
Betrayal: France, the Arabs and the Jews

Fiction

Owls and Satyrs
The Sands of Summer
Quondam
The Stranger's View
Running Away
The England Commune
Shirley's Guild
The Afternoon Sun
Inheritance
Safe Houses

Treason of the Heart
From Thomas Paine to Kim Philby

David Pryce-Jones

ENCOUNTER BOOKS
NEW YORK · LONDON

First American edition published in 2011 by Encounter Books, an activity of Encounter for Culture and Education, Inc., a nonprofit, tax exempt corporation.

Encounter Books website address: www.encounterbooks.com

Manufactured in the United States and printed on acid-free paper. The paper used in this publication meets the minimum requirements of ANSI/NISO Z39.48 1992 (R 1997) (Permanence of Paper).

FIRST AMERICAN EDITION

LIBRARY OF CONGRESS CATALOGING-IN-PUBLICATION DATA

Pryce-Jones, David, 1936–
Treason of the heart : from Thomas Paine to Kim Philby / by David Pryce-Jones.
p.   cm.
Includes bibliographical references and index.
ISBN-13: 978-1-59403-528-9 (hardcover : alk. paper)
ISBN-10: 1-59403-528-8 (hardcover : alk. paper)
1. Treason—Great Britain—History.   2. Spies—Great Britain—History.   I. Title.
HV6295.G7P79   2011
364.1'31—dc22
2010043466

for Clarissa

Contents

Introduction

*T*reason of the Heart is about British people who have taken up foreign causes. They offer a running commentary on the history of the nation. Treason involves the repudiation of loyalties to country and to kith and kin. Radicals in one generation after another repeatedly reject their own nation and countrymen, transferring their loyalties on to some other model in impressive instances of wishful thinking and ignorance of the true state of things. Treason of this kind exemplifies hatred and contempt for whoever has any claim to their loyalties, as well as a sense of superiority, and often plain brutality. Rogue aristocrats and intellectuals, so-called "treasonable clerks," have had the freedom and the means to abuse the very privileges they enjoy, leaving humbler folk to pay for it, often with their lives. First comes the language of commitment and incitement, then come the corpses. Treating opposition and an adversarial stance as a necessary virtue, they may go to the extreme length of making common cause with their country's enemies even in times of national danger and war.

The British excelled at prescribing for others what is right and what is wrong because their own political arrangements were stable for so long. They could feel complete confidence about anything and everything they might be thinking and doing. In the course of their lives, often by chance, men and women in all stations of British life came across foreigners whom they judged to be victims of oppression and injustice. A cause was born. To help and protect people and nations singled out in this way, to agitate on their behalf, to sponsor them and, if the possibility arose, to enroll in a legion of volunteers and fight for them, became a duty, a compelling moral obligation. The element of condescension implicit in reorganizing the lives of others could be ignored. The overthrow of despotism and the triumph of liberty were the declared objectives, even though the outcome might very well be a stronger despotism and a compromised liberty.

A foreign cause that engaged the imagination of any part of the British public put government on the spot. Those with the requisite rhetorical and literary skills or influential social connections could mobilize opinion. Time and again, British government ministers had to decide whether pressure was so intense that they had to adjust policy. British governments were quite willing to deploy force in a good cause, such as the suppression of slavery and piracy. Safeguarding the monopoly of force and at the same time dampening expectations, Foreign Enlistment Acts were passed to prevent persons living in England from adventuring abroad in a foreign cause. But the law could not check those in the grip of self-righteous passions.

Tom Paine, the subject of Chapter One, is the original model of the disaffected intellectual. Promotion of the independence of the United States was his way of getting his own back on an England that he made no secret of hating. Chapter Two and Chapter Three account for those who identified first with the French Revolution and then Napoleon. Eagerly they expected England to be defeated, and after its downfall the social and political system would be refashioned to align with that of France. The Philhellenes of Chapter Four saw themselves rescuing victimized Greeks. Chapters Five and Six are devoted to the next generation of radicals caught up in the wave of nation-building in Europe. Chapters Seven and Eight turn to the ethnic, national, and religious clashes unleashed in the decades when the

Ottoman Empire crumbled at long last. Those who took up Zionism are described in Chapter Nine and those who concocted Arabism in Chapter Ten. The final two chapters deal with those who betrayed the national interest, the entire society and its culture, by subscribing to the alien ideologies of Fascism and Communism.

"When hopes and dreams are loose in the streets," wrote Eric Hoffer, the author of *The True Believer,* and a wise and experienced observer of human behavior, "it is well for the timid to lock doors, shutter windows and lie low until the wrath is past." Not only the timid, for that matter. Whether a cause concerns foreigners or ultimately the political disposition of England, those associated with it are almost invariably indifferent to the implicit violence and killing—that is, if they are not active participants. Only the greatest novelists could do justice to the complex bundle of Utopian or millenarian fantasies, the twinned hatred and self-hatred, the narcissism, guilt, sanctimoniousness, hunger for power, fanaticism, and nihilism that are on display in *Treason of the Heart.*

CHAPTER ONE

The Revolution
of the World

Many contemporaries, and posterity too, have taken Thomas Paine at his word that he was a champion of liberty to whose writings much is owed, as though he were one of the stars of the Enlightenment, so to speak an English Voltaire. "My motive and object in all my political works," he claimed on his own behalf, "has been to rescue Man from tyranny and false systems and false principles of government, and enable him to be free." His famous pamphlets, *Common Sense* and *Rights of Man,* sold hundreds of thousands of copies, an astonishing feat in that age, and they remain documents of the American and French Revolutions into both of which Paine had thrown himself. Undoubtedly he had a gift for phrases with a grandiose ring, such as "The cause of America is, in great measure, the cause of all mankind," and the often quoted "We have it in our power to begin the world over again." Not surprisingly, patriotic Americans have been eager to praise someone who took up the cause of their independence with such commitment, and seemingly was the first to call their country the United States of America.

The pursuit of liberty was not genuine, however, as it was in the cases of Voltaire or Paine's intellectual rival Edmund Burke. Paine hated England and everything to do with it with a passion that was consistent, and so all-consuming that he did not care how many might fall victim so long as he had his way. For him, liberty was not a desirable end in itself but simply the tool most fitted for pulling down the existing order. He was naturally "a disturber of things as they are,"[1] wanting, as one historian has expressed it, "to tear the world apart."[2] What might be put in place after the desired destruction did not concern him, and the inhuman indifference to the consequences of his polemics gives him a thoroughly contemporary significance.

Paine was born in 1737 in the small market town of Thetford in Norfolk. His father, a Quaker, was a maker of corsets who tried unsuccessfully to persuade his son to work with him. Instead Paine joined the Customs and Excise, but was dismissed apparently for trying to organize a strike. William Cobbett, a free though unpredictable spirit, at first took violently against him (later reversing this hostility), and put his finger on what was surely the prime source of Paine's revengeful animus against his native country: "it appears to me very clear that some beastly insults, offered to Mr. Paine while he was in the Excise in England, was the real cause of the Revolution in America." Personal failings, boasting, drunkenness, an unconsummated marriage—all suggest someone who found it hard to get on with other people.

Furnished with a letter from Benjamin Franklin, he was on his own when he reached America in December 1774, settling in Philadelphia. Soon Franklin's daughter, Sarah, was writing, "there never was a man less loved in a place than Paine in this, having at different times disputed with everyone."[3] A great deal of testimony shows how adept this cantankerous man was at quarrelling and complaining. Even John Keane, a writer who admires him without reservation, concedes that Paine had "an extraordinary knack for making enemies."[4]

The cause of American independence might well have developed differently under another monarch and ministers in London far-sighted enough to realize that the issue of taxation was open to accommodation without resort to armed conflict. As it was, George III was essentially a country gentleman out of his depth in this crisis of the empire. When he could see no resolution except through military means, he expressed sorrow rather than anger, writing to Secretary of State Edward Conway: "I am more and more grieved at the accounts in America. Where this spirit will end is not to be said."[5] The King could count on support from Tories, including Dr. Johnson, but the Whigs, much of the aristocracy, William Pitt, Burke, Horace Walpole who described himself as "a hearty American," intellectuals like the great scholar of Asiatic languages Sir William Jones, Dr. Richard Price and the Dissenters, the bluestocking author Catherine Macaulay and her brother John Sawbridge, the Lord Mayor of London, and John Cartwright the indefatigable publicist swung informed public opinion in favor of American independence. The colonists themselves were slow to divide into camps corresponding to those in England. John C. Miller writes, "In spite of radical outbursts, conservatism still characterized the American mind."[6] But as things worsened, Miller continues, "Americans who stood out loyally in support of the mother country were obliged to face the mobs without protection. Violators of the [Non-importation] Agreement were tarred and feathered, hounded from colony to colony, and forced to take refuge, when they could, on board British men-of-war." Those who opposed independence or sought to betray it, Paine warned with an ominous modern touch, "must expect the more rigid fate of the jail and the gibbet."

Published as soon after Paine's arrival as April 1776, *Common Sense* forced the issue by imagining a polarization that sounded urgent but was factitious, quite false. The colonists were to choose between independence and slavery. George Washington immediately noticed that the pamphlet was "working a wonderful change . . . in the minds of men."[7] The rights of the colonists were wrapped in the wrongs of England. In the summary judgment of one historian, the pamphlet "breathes an extraordinary hatred of English governing institutions." Americans had fled "not from the tender embraces of the mother, but from the cruelty of the monster." America was virtuous, England was corrupt, a tyranny, a despotism, originally founded by "a French bas-tard," and since then an extended monarchical racket that had pro-duced "no less than eight civil wars and nineteen rebellions" in England alone while laying the world in "blood and ashes." George III was "the Royal Brute of Great Britain," the "royal criminal," "his Mad-jesty," a "hardened, sullen-tempered Pharoah," "a full-blooded Nero," "the sceptered savage," "Mr Guelph," and Paine rendered the nobility as "no-ability." These war-cries were a travesty of the ordi-nariness of the hapless king, and of the rather civilized British consti-tutional reality which Voltaire, for one, had recently observed at first hand and praised as a model for others. Nor was the intimation of slavery anything more than a smear, and as a matter of fact the colonists practiced it, with no intention of extending independence to their slaves—something Paine conveniently overlooks.

After the Declaration of Independence in July 1776, Paine joined a group of armed volunteers, took part in military campaigns that autumn, was appointed ADC to General Nathaniel Greene and watched from a New Jersey hilltop the British being driven out of Fort Washington. The following year he acquired an official position as Secretary of the Committee for Foreign Affairs for Congress, directed against Britain. A favorite fantasy was that a few thousand men landed in England would be enough to depose the King and bring his ministers to trial. In 1781, the year of Cornwallis's fateful surrender at Yorktown, Paine made his first journey to France in the hope of persuading the authorities there to support American inde-pendence. He was instrumental in obtaining a subsidy of two and a half million silver livres. The dispatch of British troops to America, he further anticipated, would expose Britain to conquest by France.

In a letter to George Washington in his inimitably surly style of complaint, boastfulness and threat, he was to plead for financial help. He had been of service to America, he wrote, but she was "cold and inattentive" in return. He might leave for France or Holland, where "I have literary fame, and I am sure I cannot experience worse fortune than I have here." The administration took care of him. In a formal agreement in 1782 he was hired as a propagandist and paid eight hundred dollars a year for "secret services," in other words subsidized to write for his paymasters. After further intensive lobbying, he received a congressional grant of three thousand dollars, which was half the sum he had demanded. Frederick Devoe was a farmer who owned 277 acres at New Rochelle, some thirty miles from New York. Because this man had remained loyal to the British, his property was requisitioned and given to Paine who retained it, rented it out in his absence, and was to return to live there at the end of his life. So war-profiteering was a consummation of Paine's vaunted pursuit of liberty.

Charles Inglis was an Anglican clergyman and a Tory who attacked *Common Sense* for appealing to "the passions of the populace"[8] and giving vent to Paine's "private resentment and ambition." Colonists who shared that view, and remained loyal to the King, were victimized: "Terror was employed . . . speech was controlled, the newspapers censored, and dissent crushed."[9] Some were murdered, others fled to Canada; many were expropriated of everything they owned, their property simply stolen. Paul Johnson writes that loyalists who had escaped to England filed 3,225 claims for compensation, of which 2,291 awards were granted—"a miserable total compared with the vast numbers who lost all."[10] Paine had contributed to the hardship and dispossession of people who had done nothing worse than remain loyal to their political conceptions rather than adopt his.

In April 1787 Paine returned to England where he was something of a celebrity, "never beneath dining with a nobleman,"[11] for instance the Duke of Portland, Lord Lansdowne, and Charles James Fox. Fired by events in France, he lived there from November 1789 to March 1790 when he published *Rights of Man,* the republican counterpart to Burke's conservative *Reflections on the French Revolution.* "The Revolution in France is certainly a forerunner of other revolutions in Europe," Paine wrote to taunt Burke in January 1790. Allegiance to the French offered the opportunity to do damage to England from a position closer than America, moreover capitalizing on historic enmity between the two countries. Gillray spoke for conservatives when he drew one of his barbed cartoons with the caption, "Tommy Paine, the little American tailor, taking the measure of a new pair of revolutionary breeches."

As relations deteriorated and war loomed, Pitt's government decided to prosecute Paine for *Rights of Man*. The case came before a special jury, and Paine in absentia was found guilty of sedition. From Paris he had written to the Attorney General that his duties there were "of too much importance to permit me to trouble myself about your prosecution." The government of England, the letter also declared with customary hyperbole, was "the greatest perfection of fraud and corruption that ever took place since government began." The verdict meant that he faced life imprisonment and even execution if he set foot in England again.

Feted in France, he was granted citizenship and in 1792 elected to the National Convention amid cries of "*Vive* Thomas Paine." Astonishingly, he could neither speak nor read French. Etienne Dumont, a Frenchman who knew England well and was politically much like an English Whig, had met Paine at Bowood, Lord Lansdowne's country house. He left a description of Paine in Paris: "I could easily excuse, in an American, his prejudices against England. But his egregious conceit and presumptuous self-sufficiency quite disgusted me. He was drunk with vanity. If you believed him, it was he who had done everything in America. He was an absolute caricature of the vainest of Frenchmen. . . . He knew all his own writings by heart, but he knew nothing else."[12] Here again, Paine was dining with noblemen, the Duc de la Rochefoucauld (murdered by the mob in 1792), the Marquis de Chastellux (died in the Revolution), Condorcet (suicide in prison), and Lafayette (proscribed, exiled).

A less self-centered man than Paine might have been alerted to reality on the morning in June 1791 when he and Thomas Christie, a young businessman, were walking to the Tuileries. The news reached them that the royal family had fled. Paine and his colleague did not have tricolor cockades on their hats and the crowd mistook them for aristocrats. To shouts of *"à la lanterne!,"* three men were preparing to hang them when someone who may have been a government agent saved them by pleading they were American. In the aftermath of the royal family's aborted flight to Varennes, Paine scorned Louis XVI much as he had George III. "On the Propriety of Bringing Louis XVI to Trial" was an address to the Convention that wrote the King off: "whether fool or hypocrite, idiot or traitor, he has proved himself equally unworthy of the important functions that had been delegated to him. . . . We see in him no more than an indifferent person; we can regard him only as Louis Capet."[13] This time, his words carried mortal danger. When the Convention voted narrowly for the King's execution, however, Paine at least voted against it. Eleven days after the King was guillotined, Paine drafted a call to the British to revolt.

"The moment of any great change," Paine wrote in September 1792 in an address "To the People of France," is "unavoidably the moment of terror and confusion." This is one of the earliest formulations of what was to be the crude but standard apology for Communism, that you cannot make an omelette without breaking eggs. Some months later, he offered his services to the Committee of Public Safety. He and David Williams, another British associate of the Gironde faction, were appointed to a committee of nine members to draft a new constitution—they were the only two of the nine to survive the Terror. During that time of senseless blood-letting, Paine busied himself with a fantastic plan to occupy the island of Saint Helena, already within the British empire. But Jacobins and so-called *enragés* were denouncing Girondins for lack of true revolutionary zeal, and accordingly dispatching them to the guillotine. Paine wrote to Danton, himself soon to be executed, "There ought to be some regulation with respect to the spirit of denunciation that now prevails," but this was wishful thinking. Paine's association with leading Girondins was enough to compromise him. In the Convention a Jacobin deputy accused him of treason to the republic—a remarkable pendant to the accusation in London of treason to the British monarchy. Conducting the Terror in the name of the Committee of Public Safety, Robespierre scribbled a note, "Demand that a decree of accusation be passed against Thomas Paine for the interests of America and France as well." White's Hotel was the meeting-place for foreign revolutionaries, and Paine had often welcomed guests with the toast, "The Revolution of the World." On Christmas Eve 1793 Paine dined and spent the night there. Next day, the police woke him at four in the morning but left, and on December 28 five policemen and two agents of the Committee of Public Safety arrested him, taking him to the Luxembourg prison. He had promoted, and brought upon himself, this foretaste of totalitarian politics.

For the ten months until November 1794, Paine remained in the Luxembourg under sentence of death. Robespierre signed the sentence, but four days later he was himself purged with 108 Jacobins. According to his own account, Paine was in a cell with three others: "when persons by scores and by hundreds were to be taken out of the prison for the guillotine it was always done in the night, and those who performed that office had a private mark or signal by which they knew what rooms to go to, and what number to take." This mark was put on when the door was open and flat against the wall, so that when the door was shut it was inside and not visible to the death squad as they passed. "The state of things in the prisons was a continued scene of horror," Paine was to confide to George Washington in words that might have been lifted from testimony by, say, Arthur Koestler. "No man could count upon life for 24 hours. To such a pitch of rage and suspicion were Robespierre and his committee arrived, that it seemed as if they feared to leave a man living. Scarcely a night passed in which ten, twenty, thirty, forty, fifty or more were not taken out of prison, carried before a pretended tribunal in the morning and guillotined before night." But Washington the president was no longer Washington the revolutionary, and Paine was soon angrily disappointed with him. James Monroe, the American ambassador in Paris, recorded that Paine " thinks the President winked at his imprisonment and wished he might die in gaol."[14]

This experience did nothing to teach Paine about the nature and consequences of revolution, or to moderate the hatred for England that was the central obsession of his life. At the end of 1797, a group of Irish republicans and exiles formed the Society of United Irishmen, and elected Paine an honorary member. They were plotting to invade England. In White's Hotel their leader, James Napper Tandy, proposed a toast, "May the tri-coloured flag [of France] float on the Tower of London,"[15] and Paine drank to it. Wolfe Tone, who was soon to lead this plot into disaster in Ireland, recorded how Paine defended dictatorship, had a detailed plan for invading England, and subscribed a hundred livres to a fund for invasion and the overthrow of a government that was "the plague of the human race." The true time to see Paine to advantage, Wolfe Tone also observed, "is about ten at night, with a bottle of brandy and water before him."

Seizing power, Napoleon Bonaparte pursued the war with England begun by Robespierre. He agreed that Paine should head a provisional English Revolutionary Government, and in that capacity accompany French forces as a political advisor. Invited by Napoleon to speak to a military council, Paine gave the somewhat contrary advice that "The only way to kill England is to annihilate her commerce." In a polemical tract, "To the People of England on the Invasion of England," Paine as usual over-pitched his rhetoric, calling Napoleon "the most enterprising and fortunate man, either for deep project or daring execution, the world has known for many ages." Paine paid for a thousand pairs of boots for French soldiers to wear on the projected invasion. Like Washington, Napoleon proved unable to live up to Paine's illusions. Of the French he was to say to Henry

Redhead Yorke, another English radical in Paris, "This is not a country for an honest man to live in . . . they have conquered all Europe, only to make it more miserable than it was before."[16] Old and embittered but safe once he had retired to the farm near New York seized from the unfortunate Frederick Devoe, Paine found it in him to dismiss Napoleon as "the completest charlatan that ever existed."

CHAPTER TWO

The Mighty Projects
of the Times

In the days before steam, the journey from London to Paris could be done within a week, provided the tides and the winds were favorable, and there were horses or diligences to hire on shore. Increased ease of travel fostered a stereotype, according to two historians of the relationship between the countries: "Britain stood for freedom, and France for order."[1] In 1789, Arthur Young visited France for the third year running in pursuit of his studies in agriculture. He witnessed the initial months of the French Revolution. In Besançon he was assumed by a mob to be an aristocrat in disguise: "I do not half like travelling in such an unquiet and fermenting moment, one is not secure for an hour beforehand."[2] Once home, he wrote anti-revolutionary pamphlets. A believer in both freedom and order, Young had reacted to what he had seen with the rationality to be expected of any intelligent person.

Numerous English contemporaries were skeptical or dismayed by the outbreak of the revolution. Edward Rigby was a well-known doctor in Norwich, and a Whig. In Paris for the first time in July 1789, he and three friends were swept along by the crowd at the storming of the Bastille. When they suddenly caught sight of "two bloody heads raised on pikes,"[3] they retreated in shock to their hotel. John Moore, another doctor, was in that crowd and also saw those severed heads with horror. "The present revolution in France is one of the most awful events of which history affords any record,"[4] he was later to write. "The crimes with which it has been accompanied will remain a stain on the national character . . . no rational hope of future prosperity can compensate [the misery]." Others in that crowd were William Playfair, a civil engineer, Thomas Blackwell, a medical student, and the future Tory prime minister Lord Liverpool. Daniel Hailes, described as "one of the most competent and far-sighted diplomats of the eighteenth century,"[5] was able to foresee that the revolution must end in bloodshed. Another realist was William Augustus Miles, a political writer who had lived in France since 1783. "Believe me, the French are not so enlightened as is generally thought . . . there is very little knowledge, and still less principle."[6] By 1791 he had concluded, "The people in this country have become brutal." The ferocity of the revolution varied from province to province. William Cobbett, destined for much greater recognition as a political writer, lived with a lady called Anne in the north of France in 1792 for what he said were the six happiest months of his life, presumably because personal life distracted him from paying attention to public affairs. That August he sailed for New York.

A different body of opinion quickly took shape that the French Revolution was long overdue, and France would now enjoy the liberty that was a British birthright. More than that, Rousseau had informed the educated classes that Mankind was everywhere bound in chains, and in this dazzling new era these would be broken for ever. Two days after the fall of the Bastille, the British ambassador in Paris, the Duke of Dorset, sent a dispatch exactly in character for a Whig aristocrat such as he, eager to believe that everyone was as enlightened as he thought himself to be, but who would have been a prime candidate for execution in the event that England followed the French example. Those heads on pikes were not numerous enough to shake his credulity: "The greatest revolution that we know anything of has been affected with the loss of very few lives: from this moment we may consider France as a free country; the King a very limited

Monarch, and the Nobility as reduced to a level with the rest of the Nation."[7] Charles James Fox, another grandee and dissolute man-about-town, led the Whig opposition in Parliament against the Conservative government of William Pitt. "Behind Fox's judgements," in the opinion of Sir Lewis Namier, the pre-eminent specialist of the period, "were deep obsessional hatreds, which distorted his judgement and perverted his sense of reality."[8] During the war with America, he had made a point of wearing the blue and buff colors of the rebels. That July, six weeks after the event, he celebrated the fall of the Bastille with a judgment whose exaggeration is its most memorable feature. "How much the greatest event is it that ever appeared in the world! And how much the best!" A year later, he was describing the new French constitution in the same overblown manner as, "the most stupendous and glorious edifice of liberty which has been erected . . . in any time or country." He was to decide that those really responsible for the Terror were the reactionaries and foreign despots who had forced the hand of the Jacobins. This is as early an instance as any of the inversion of reality that in future was to become a standard apologia, whereby victims are held responsible for every violence, political and otherwise, committed against them by their aggressors.

Whigs reacted with headiness to match the Duke of Dorset and Charles James Fox. Another of them was Sir Samuel Romilly, a Member of Parliament, an eminent lawyer, and a follower of Rousseau, writing to a Swiss friend: "I am sure I need not tell you how much I have rejoiced at the Revolution which has taken place. I think of nothing else . . . the Revolution has produced a very sincere and very general joy here."[9] Yet another was Sir James Mackintosh, presuming to speak for his intellectual equals by giving his pro-revolution pamphlet the Latin title *Vindiciae Gallicae.*

The Dissenters, or Non-Conformists, could not claim to be fashionable like the Whigs, but they too had their distinctive style of exhortation. As schismatics from the Church of England, they suffered from various acts of discrimination, and it is hardly anachronistic to call them an organized opposition, dedicated to reform in their own interest. A number of parallel clubs existed to promote reform, for instance the London Constitutional Society, which had branches or imitators in Manchester, Sheffield, Birmingham, Derby, and other cities. The Society of the Friends of the People, in spite of its name or perhaps because of it, was for aristocrats. Part of the business was to address motions of support to revolutionaries in Paris. Maurice Margarot, a wine merchant and president of the London Corresponding Society, signed one such (and was later transported to Botany Bay for sedition): "How well purchased will be, though at the expense of much blood, the glorious, the unprecedented privilege of saying, 'Mankind is free! Tyrants and tyranny are no more! Peace reigns on the Earth! and this is the work of Frenchmen.'"[10] With equal glibness and hypocrisy, every subsequent tyrant has claimed to be purchasing peace through the expense of blood.

Dr. Richard Price, a prominent Dissenter, had supported the rebellion in America and now saw the French Revolution as its natural successor. He advocated abolishing the monarchy and the House of Lords. Early in November 1789, Dr. Price spoke in the Revolution Society, where he moved an address to the National Assembly in Paris. The club's members could not help "expressing the particular satisfaction with which they reflect on the tendency of the glorious example given in France to encourage other nations to assert the inalienable rights of mankind, and thereby introduce a general reformation in the government of Europe, and to make the world free and happy."[11]

At the end of that November, Dr. Price preached a sermon that was even more detached from reality. "I have lived to see the rights of men better understood than ever, and nations panting for liberty which seemed to have lost the idea of it.—I have lived to see THIRTY MILLIONS [the capitals are his] indignant and resolute, spurning at slavery, and demanding liberty with an irresistible voice. . . . And now, methinks, I see the ardour for liberty catching and spreading; a general amendment in human affairs; the dominion of kings changed for the dominion of laws, and the dominion of priests [he was one] giving way to the dominion of reason and conscience. . . . Be encouraged, all ye friends of freedom and writers in its defence! The times are auspicious. . . . Behold the light you have struck out, after setting America free, reflected in France, and there kindled into a blaze that lays despotism in ashes, and warms and illuminates EUROPE!"[12]

Shocked by the publicity that Dr. Price was attracting, Edmund Burke determined to force him to face facts. His *Reflections on the French Revolution* is a statement of conservative principles and moral outrage at the commitment of violence in France or anywhere else that has no equal in the language. The revolution in his view amounted to "a system of robbery," and "It must be destroyed, or it will destroy all Europe." Ideological battle was joined. At least forty-five people chose to argue with Burke in print, among them Thomas Paine, Mary Wollstonecraft, and Catherine Macaulay, the author of a history of England in eight volumes, and mocked as "Dame Thucydides" by Horace Walpole. Joseph Priestley thought Burke had given way to "intemperate reflections." This totally new and "most wonderful" era, he informed Burke in his printed rejoinder, would see "a change from darkness to light." A Dissenter, Priestley was a linguist and scientist of distinction, the discoverer of photosynthesis and credited with isolating oxygen. The fall of the Bastille had delighted the Priestley household in Birmingham. "Hurrah! Liberty, Reason, brotherly love for ever! Down with kingcraft and priestcraft! The majesty of the people for ever!"[13] Soon afterwards he was predicting the spread of revolution to other countries. When Dr. Price died in 1791, Priestley gave the funeral oration. Ten weeks later, he was playing backgammon with his wife when a mob arrived to burn down his house and laboratory. Seventeen rioters were arrested, four were found guilty in the assizes, and three hanged. In 1792, Priestley was one of seventeen foreigners awarded honorary French citizenship, and he was elected to the Paris Convention, by then the parliamentary arm of the revolution. It was wise of him to leave the country, and in the United States he found another audience. "Dr Priestley is just arrived here from England," Cobbett was to write from Philadelphia in 1794. "He has attacked our English laws and Constitution in print, and declared his sentiments in favour of those butchers in France."

Enthusiasm for the revolution soon spread from the Whigs and Dissenters generally through the country. Robert and Isabelle Tombs have noted how the revolution appealed to those on the margin of the British political system: "self-educated small businessmen, professional men and artisans in old cities such as Norwich, Bristol, Leicester and Newcastle."[14] In Norwich in 1790, on the anniversary of the fall of the Bastille, Dr. John Taylor, deacon of the Octagon Chapel in that town, danced round a Tree of Liberty with his wife, known to her friends as "Madame Roland" (the Girondin hostess, later executed). On the same date the following year, Taylor's play *The Trumpet of Liberty* was performed in the Maid's Head Tavern, electrifying the diners. Numerous incidents were more disorderly, as when people from Cambridge had sung the revolutionary song "Ça ira" in a neighboring village, and a clergyman passing on horseback had taken into custody "persons of no consideration, an attorney and a farrier."[15] Shots were then discharged into his house. In Manchester, a prominent businessman and civic dignitary, Thomas Walker, was also the leading radical, and *The Manchester Herald,* the local newspaper, excused the Paris massacres.

The massacres in August and September 1792 of hundreds of prisoners including clergymen in Paris and other cities brought some English people face to face with the violence that had been unleashed. A secretary in the Paris embassy, William Lindsay, was dining with the Duc d'Orléans in September when they saw the head of the Queen's closest friend, the Princesse de Lamballe, carried past the window. Sir Samuel Romilly now asked the crucial question: "How could we ever be so deceived"[16] about men who boasted about liberty but were "cold instigators" of the murder of women, priests, and prisoners. A conversation with Burke was enough for Sir James Mackintosh to change his mind, and in the end to speak against what he described as the abominable principles and execrable leaders of the revolution.

For many, however, revolution had already become a movement of the imagination detached from the cruelty actually involved. Upwards of 500 "friends of liberty" were at a meeting of the London Revolutionary Society in November 1792, and more than a thousand had to be turned away. That same month saw widespread rioting and strikes in Perth, Dundee, and Aberdeen, "associated with French revolutionary slogans and the planting of Trees of Liberty."[17] In Edinburgh in December 1792 delegates at a General Convention held up their right hands and took the Jacobin oath to "live free or die." A year later, they addressed each other as "Citizen" and adopted the revolutionary timetable and vocabulary. Dugald Stewart, the influential Professor of Moral Philosophy at Edinburgh University, with Walter Scott and Henry Brougham among his students, gave revolutionary republicanism his seal of approval. Lord Daer, one of Thomas Paine's companions, also hoped to raise a revolution in Scotland.

In the theory and literary practice of the Romantic age, the purpose of poetry was to explore and heighten the emotions. For poets, the French Revolution approached the "sublime," that acme of Romantic expression. William Cowper thought the revolution was a "wonderful period in the history of mankind." Coleridge, an intelligent man, burnt the words "Liberty" and "Equality" with gunpowder on the lawns of two Cambridge colleges. "The French Revolution," a poem that William Blake never quite completed, contains the words, "Kings are sick throughout the earth!" and also "Then the valleys of France shall cry to the soldier, 'Throw down thy sword and musket,/ And run and embrace the meek peasant'" (but soon French soldiers were to kill peasants all over the continent). Frenchmen had taken to wearing red revolutionary bonnets, and Blake wore one too, openly in London. Samuel Rogers, then aged twenty-eight, went to France to enjoy the revolutionary way of life and expressly to dance the "Ça ira" with peasant girls.

According to Niall Ferguson, Robert Burns might have been Scotland's Danton. "For a'that, and a'that, / it's comin yet for a'that," as Burns excitedly foretold the revolution in his dialect style, "That Man to Man the warld o'er/ Shall brothers be for a'that."[18] Employed by the Excise, Burns was mixed up in seizing guns and equipment from smugglers. Caught out by his superiors trying to ship these spoils to France, he was lucky to escape with a reprimand. One of his friends was Dr. William Maxwell, who had been among the guards at the execution of Louis XVI, itself an act that Burns dismissed as "the delivering over [of] a perjured Blockhead . . . into the hands of the hangman." In contact with the French minister of war, Maxwell offered to equip a company of French sharp-shooters with guns, and suggested raising a special force equipped with pikes and daggers for close combat. George Monro, a government secret agent under cover in Paris, reported Maxwell to be a man of violent principles and seemingly he was kept under surveillance. Returning to England, Maxwell gave the order to a Birmingham manufacturer for arms for 3,000, anticipating a further order for 20,000. When Maxwell opened a subscription to pay for these purchases, a mob attacked the house in London where he was staying, and he had to retreat to Paris.

William Wordsworth sentimentalized the revolution with lasting effect. For him, "the naïve emotionalism of the Revolution was a source of attraction,"[19] in the dry language of one authority. Lines of his like "I saw the revolutionary power/ Tossed like a ship at anchor, rocked by storms," and of course the ever-quoted "Bliss was it in that time to be alive/ And to be young was very heaven" undoubtedly conveyed a novel and powerful charge to readers of his day. Although

Wordsworth came to regret that he had made a fool of himself, his reputation as one of England's foremost poets has always been bound up with his image as a youthful revolutionary.

When first Wordsworth visited France for a walking tour in 1790, he was twenty. He could write rhapsodically of his early life, "Fair seed-time had my soul," by which he meant that he had convinced himself "of the excellence of the created universe and of the innate goodness and perfectibility of man."[20] Nature, he wrote, "peopled my mind with beauteous forms or grand." Mary Moorman, one of his principal biographers, speaks of him as a true child of the eighteenth century, disposed to admire the "softer emotions" and easily moved to tears. As a restless undergraduate at Cambridge, he had encountered Jacobin ideas, and found that they satisfied his spiritual yearning, sublime in intention though often conventionally trite in form: "Glory and Hope to new-born Liberty! / Hail to the mighty projects of the time!"

Towards the end of 1791 he made a second journey to France, and then spent almost a year in Orleans with his mistress Annette Vallon, with whom he had a daughter. Annette's brother Paul was fortunate to escape the guillotine. Wordsworth's landlord, a royalist, was eventually executed. A Mr. Foxlowe, the only other Englishman in Orleans, was a supporter of the revolution, and he and Wordsworth watched volunteers leaving to fight. Wordsworth supposed he was witnessing "A people risen up / Fresh as the morning star." He identified completely with the revolution as a cause "which no one could stand up against / Who was not lost, abandon'd, selfish, proud, / Mean, miserable, wilfully depraved, / Hater perverse of equity and truth." Naïve emotionalism had plainly swamped his powers of observation. Here was an early example of agitprop. Instead of drawing moral conclusions from the violence happening all around him, he splurged this vocabulary of denigration all over the victims.

After the 1792 massacres Wordsworth again passed through Paris on his way home. He arrived on the very day at the end of October when the Girondins made the accusations against Robespierre for which they were arrested and executed. In the company of James Watt, younger son of the inventor of the steam engine and an enthusiast of the revolution, he visited the Assembly and the Jacobin Club and picked up a stone from the Bastille as a souvenir. The English Jacobins in Paris were in the habit of holding monthly dinners in White's hotel near the Petit Palais, and Wordsworth attended the dinner on November 18. He was experiencing "the thrill of history in the making," and it "changed his enthusiasm for the principles of the Revolution into flaming hatred for the society and monarchical government of his native land."[21] Mary Moorman goes further, attributing to him "deeply precious"[22] feelings that the revolution was the cause of all mankind.

Presiding over these dinners of the English Jacobin club in Paris was Lord Stanhope, a prototype of radical chic, that is to say someone who used the privilege of his position apparently to undermine it but in practice to extend it by securing his place among those who looked like being the new elite. Pronouncements about republicanism and the virtues of the French Revolution did not affect the lifestyle of this self-promoter and attention-seeker. He maintained a house in the fashionable part of London, owned Chevening, one of the country's greatest stately homes and estates, and had been a member of the House of Commons before entering the House of Lords. William Pitt was his cousin. His daughter, the adventurous traveller Lady Hester Stanhope, took against him: "I am an aristocrat and I make a boast of it. I hate a pack of dirty Jacobins that only want to get people out of a good place to get into it themselves."[23] A granddaughter, the Duchess of Cleveland, was grateful not to live under his roof, "for, ardently as he advocated liberty and enfranchisement abroad, he was the sternest of autocrats at home." "That mischievous lunatic, Lord Stanhope,"[24] was the opinion of Horace Walpole. A contemporary satire had the lines, "Hear Stanhope, modest Earl, proclaim/ Himself a Sans-Culotte!" His grand revolutionary gestures were to announce one evening in White's hotel that he wished in future to be known as Citizen Stanhope, and to order the removal of the coronets over the iron gates at the entrance of Chevening. It was absurd of a French writer to imagine Stanhope leading a procession through London with "the head of the tyrant of St James's"[25] on a pike.

Lord Edward Fitzgerald, son of the Duke of Leinster, a cousin of Charles James Fox, and "My Eddy" to his adoring mother, also renounced his title at a White's banquet, where he proposed the characteristic toast to "The armies of France: may the example of its citizen soldiers be followed by all enslaved countries, till tyrants and tyrannies be extinct."[26] He lodged with Thomas Paine, and they discussed how the French might support revolution in Ireland. His was the plan of a man impelled by abstract principles of equality and fraternity, writes his biographer, "but a man of violence all the same."[27] Lord Edward habitually called the British army and the officials in Dublin Castle "the enemy."[28] He designed for himself a revolutionary uniform with a green cape and a cap of liberty. Returning to Ireland, he was charged with high treason, and shot dead resisting arrest in Dublin during the abortive revolution of 1798, one among others who laid down their lives to no purpose.

One Irishman capable of appreciating that revolution had no necessary connection with liberty was Archibald Hamilton Rowan. In his autobiography he recorded a gruesome experience: "the whole commune of Paris, consisting of about sixty persons, were guillotined in less than one hour and a half, in the Place de Revolution, and though I was standing above a hundred paces from the place of execution, the blood of the victims streamed under my feet."[29] After living in France for twelve months, he wrote to his wife, his ideas of reform and revolution alike had been altered, and "I never wish to see the one or the other procured by force." He escaped to Delaware in America, where his wife joined him.

Regulars at White's included other rich men like Sir Francis Burdett and Robert Pigott and Sir Robert Smith (imprisoned in Paris for

one year); the businessman John Hurford Stone; the Reverend Jere-
miah Joyce (tutor in Lord Stanhope's household, arrested for treason
but found not guilty); Robert Merry, the husband of the actress Miss
Brunton (both fled to America); the journalist Henry RedheadYorke
who attended the King's trial (two years in prison for conspiracy);
and the Sheare brothers (executed in Dublin following the events of
1798). In official documents, the Sheares were described, perhaps by
the secret agent Monro, as "men of desperate designs, capable of setting fire to the dockyards."[30] David Williams helped draft the republican constitution of 1793 and was granted honorary French
citizenship. Irish rebels, dubious attorneys and penny-a-line journalists, and members of the London Corresponding Society who classi-
fied themselves as political refugees were among other adventurers
and conspirators attending these occasions and becoming drunk on
toasts to the Revolution. In February 1793 the club was disbanded
and closed on the orders of the Convention. In the course of four
days that October, about 250 British subjects were rounded up and
imprisoned in the Luxembourg, leaving few at liberty. According to
the secret agent Monro, at the moment of his own subsequent arrest
Robespierre had on his desk a list with 40,000 names of suspects to
be liquidated—a foretaste of Stalinism.

These Englishmen, even the most marginal of them, would have
emerged as leaders and household names in the event of a revolution
in their own country. One of the fanatics frequenting White's was
John Oswald. Born in Edinburgh in 1760, he joined the army and
sailed for India in 1781. After only a few months of active service,
"his rebelliousness crystallised into ideological dissent,"[31] and he
returned to England a rebel and early anti-imperialist "inflamed with
outrage at the violent injustice of human society."[32] Emulating Hin-
dus, he had also become a vegetarian. He turned his hand to writing
poetry, "somewhat priapic satires," and pamphlets in one of which he
called Burke "an eloquent madman." He was also a parliamentary
reporter. In his excellent biography, David Erdman quotes Oswald's

typically threatening reaction to a debate about enclosures: "The honourable House of Commons vanished from my sight; and I saw in its stead a den of thieves, plotting in their midnight conspiracies the murder of the innocent, and the ruin of the fatherless and the widow!"[33]

Moving to Paris permanently in the spring of 1791, Oswald acted as a middleman supplying money and weapons from British radicals to the French government. He was apparently the first British man to join the French Jacobin Club,[34] the body that was to appropriate the revolution and exterminate its political rivals. According to the author Tristram Stuart, Oswald found it "encouraging" that during the 1792 massacres people were willing to break into prisons and kill the aristocrats detained there. Commissioned to recruit a company of pikemen, he was appointed their colonel commandant. Joseph Haslewood, a somewhat cautious friend and witness, left a portrait of him living in a hut near Paris and sending his two sons to forage for food in neighboring gardens and the forest. Oswald could not bear to see blood spilled and thought that soldiers were butchers, but out of sheer contrariness, Haslewood continues, "He also at the head of his infernal pikemen formed the guard which closely surrounded the scaffold on which the late King of France was guillotined. Immediately after the head of the unfortunate monarch fell into the basket, he and his whole troops struck up a hymn he had composed for the occasion, and danced and sang, like so many Savages, round and round the scaffold."[35] Also present at that execution was William Maxwell, the would-be arms dealer, and he dipped his handkerchief in the King's blood.

Another friend, Henry Redhead Yorke, was present one day at a party of some members of the Convention when Oswald was dining on his usual root vegetables. He records that in the course of conversation Oswald very coolly proposed "as the most effectual way of averting civil war, to put to death every suspected man in France. I was shocked at such a sentiment coming from the mouth of an

Englishman; but Oswald had been for some time the commander of the pikemen of Paris, and in this capacity had forgotten his national character."[36] This was an early example of the future totalitarian disposition to murder the innocent to make sure they could not be enemies. The monstrosity of it was too much for Thomas Paine as well, who said to him, "you have lived so long without tasting flesh, that you now have a most voracious appetite for blood." In September 1793 Oswald led a body of pikemen, perhaps renamed as the English Legion, to suppress the Catholic and monarchist counter-revolution in the Vendée (which cost the lives of 250,000 people, mostly peasants). In various clashes in the region he and his two sons were killed.

Among these activists was an apologist, Helen Maria Williams, a literary lady proud of her "sensibility" and self-described as "a citizen of the world." She arrived in Paris in time for the 1790 Festival of the Federation, "the most sublime spectacle, which, perhaps, was ever represented on the theatre of this earth . . . the people, transported with joy, shouted and wept." (For Burke, this same spectacle was "most horrid, atrocious and afflicting.")[37] Between that year and 1796 she published her *Letters from France,* eight volumes of determined fellow-traveling that could not fail to mislead her readers. Victims of popular fury were hanged on lamp-posts. "The sight of *la lanterne* chilled the blood in my veins,"[38] she allowed, immediately recovering with the thought that acts of barbarity stain every revolution. France was an example of "enlightened freedom" that all the nations of Europe might soon emulate.

She lived with John Hurford Stone, a shady businessman who sometimes presided over the dinners at White's, and they entertained together in a *salon.* A letter to Stone from his brother William in London was intercepted, and its contents led to William's trial for treason, for which he was acquitted. From lodgings in the rue de Lille, Helen Maria Williams witnessed the storming of the Tuileries. One of the Swiss guards died on her doorstep, and when next day she came on two corpses in the street, she rushed back indoors. In

England it was rumored that she had walked unmoved among the bodies of those massacred. When Louis XVI was executed, she adopted a position of speculative detachment: "the French revolution is still in progress, and who can decide how its last page will finish?"[39] She detected an abstracted liberty "uncontaminated, pure, exalted, and sublime," disconnected from real events, and she thought Robespierre "regulates the most ferocious designs with the most calm and temperate prudence."[40] She excused the crimes of the revolutionaries, her biographer Deborah Kennedy observes, by saying they had "unhappily strayed." Madame Roland had entrusted her with some papers just before she was arrested and executed. On the night of her own arrest, Helen Maria Williams managed to burn these papers and some of her own. Commissioners of the revolutionary committee and guards with drawn swords had knocked on her door at two o'clock in the morning. They took her to the Luxembourg and then moved her to a convent converted into a prison. Released some weeks later, she and John Hurford Stone fled in the first part of 1794 to Switzerland. Twenty-five years later she had learnt nothing: "The interest I once took in the French Revolution is not chilled, and the enthusiasm I once felt for the cause of liberty still warms my bosom."[41]

Mary Wollstonecraft was far more intelligent, a genuine bluestocking eager for controversy. Dr. Price and other Dissenters had set in place her dissatisfaction with the world, especially with the rich and privileged. One of the earliest feminists, she earned her living by writing and translating. Settling in Paris towards the end of 1792, she lived with Gilbert Imlay, an American from Kentucky involved in import-export schemes that evaded the British blockade. Her baby, Françoise, was born in May 1794. At the American embassy, Imlay registered Mary as his wife though they never married. Mary soon got the measure of the posturing Helen Maria Williams: "the *simple* goodness of her heart continually breaks through the varnish." From her windows, Mary watched Louis XVI being taken in a carriage

through empty streets to his death. She wrote to Joseph Johnson, a
radical publisher in London, that she bowed to the majesty of the
people whose propriety of behavior was in unison with her own feelings and made her shed tears. She could write to one correspondent
that a revolution which cost so much blood and tears sickened her,
and yet tell Imlay in 1795 that England was a country "for which I
feel repugnance that almost amounts to horror."[42]

English men and women who had experienced at first hand the
bloody excesses of the French Revolution, then, were not inclined to
be grateful to their own country for sparing them anything of the
kind. Like Mary Wollstonecroft, Wordsworth felt repugnance that
England was not following the French example but on the contrary
opposing it militarily. Writing an angry open letter to the reactionary
Bishop of Llandaff, he deplored the "mulish lamentation" that had
broken out over the execution of Louis XVI. For him, it was a cause
for rejoicing that the French should defeat the English in the war now
declared between the two nations: "When Englishmen by thousands
were o'erthrown, / Left without glory in the field." Coleridge caught
a more general sense of disillusion when he called on Wordsworth to
write a poem in blank verse, "addressed to those, who, in consequence of the complete failure of the French Revolution, have
thrown up all hopes of the amelioration of mankind."

Yet shortly before his death in 1797 Burke thought that one-fifth
of the "political nation" consisted of "pure Jacobins utterly incapable
of amendment."[43] He was right. In a speech at a meeting of the
Friends of Parliamentary Reform, John Thelwell spoke for the next
generation of radicals: "I venerate, I esteem, I adore the principles
upon which the French Revolution has been established."[44] Whole
sections of the population were unable to see that many people supposed to be their elders and betters had deceived and indoctrinated
them with false hopes, and they then continued to deceive themselves of their own free will. "Principles, issues, examples, vocabulary, songs, heroes and villains, were all drawn wholesale from that

era," comments one authority. British workers flew the tricolor, called each other "citizen," and closed their meetings with the "Marseillaise."[45] "Standard rhetoric for working-class agitation came from the French revolution," and echoes of it were to be heard down the years.

CHAPTER THREE

"The God
of My Idolatry"

T hroughout the twenty-two years from 1793 to 1815, England and France were at war, with the interlude of a single year after the Treaty of Amiens in 1802. Launched by Robespierre and the Jacobins, this war seemed to many a clash between the two incompatible political systems of monarchy and republicanism, and, more than that, a struggle to the death between reaction and progress. As a matter of principle British republicans opposed Pitt, William Windham, Lord Granville, the Duke of Wellington, and whoever else was perceived as a defender of the Tory status quo. Seizing power in a coup in 1799, Napoleon Bonaparte soon mobilized France to become the world's leading military power. The war now acquired the much more open and dangerous dimension of national rivalry. The winner could expect to enjoy supremacy throughout the continent of Europe, with imperial repercussions in the Middle East and India. The loser might well be overwhelmed. Shortly before the Brumaire coup that brought him to power, Napoleon had command of an "Army of England" and in the Channel harbors of France assembled flat-bottomed boats and landing craft in preparation to invade England. This would have been a hazardous operation at the best of times, and Nelson's destruction of the French fleet, first at Aboukir Bay and finally at Trafalgar, put paid to it in practice. Nonetheless Napoleon never lost his determination to defeat England, and a decade had still to pass before he committed the strategic blunder of invading Russia, and England could put together the coalition necessary to defeat France on land. And still the final victory at Waterloo was "a damned nice thing," as the Duke of Wellington expressed it, "the nearest run thing you ever saw in your life."

E. Tangye Lean's *The Napoleonists* describes in absorbing detail the way politicians of the Whig opposition and the leading writers and journalists of the period created an image of Napoleon as a man of destiny, the agent of progressive change in the world. He was presented as everything that the reactionary Tories were not. Those in the habit of excusing and praising Napoleon took such pride in renouncing patriotism that they were perceived as agents of a mortal enemy, indeed traitors. Lord Holland might have been a Whig prime minister. He considered Napoleon "the greatest statesman and the ablest general of ancient or modern times."[1] Holland House, the family's magnificent seat in London, was set in an estate large enough to pass as the countryside. Here was also one of the finest libraries. Lord Stanhope, William Godwin the radical who thought Napoleon "an auspicious and beneficent genius" and whose daughter Mary married Shelley, Samuel Whitbread the possessor of a brewing fortune and a member of Parliament, Elizabeth Inchbald who wrote plays, dukes and peers—a whole swarm of ambitious politicians and scribblers, met and plotted at dinners and receptions there.

Charles James Fox, Lord Holland's uncle, was as quick to excuse and flatter Napoleon as he had been to hail the French Revolution. Here was the George Washington of France, a moderate man as well. In no circumstances would Napoleon seize power by force, and when he did so, Fox whitewashed it as the kind of reorganization of the state that military men are apt to go in for. Napoleon had made good the past, Fox told Lord Holland, he had "thrown a splendour even over the violence of the Revolution."[2] After the Treaty of Amiens, Fox declared, "the Triumph of the French government over the English does in fact afford me a degree of pleasure which it is very difficult to disguise."[3] At that same moment, he traveled to Paris and attended a huge dinner given by Napoleon in the Tuileries. The two met for talks, Napoleon complimented Fox extravagantly, and Fox thought Napoleon was "sincere in his desire for peace."[4]

Lord Whitworth, the British ambassador in Paris, had to shut his doors because the many hysterical admirers of the First Consul appeared to justify a belief current in France that a strong pro-Bonaparte party existed in England. Carola Oman has described some of these hero-worshippers advocating that "France required the vigorous hand of a Dictator,"[5] something they would not have wanted for themselves. Mary Berry, an authoress, said that Napoleon had ended the Revolution and seemed so simple and unaffected that she hoped he would not be assassinated. Other ladies "could not shut their eyes to the superiority of his talents and the amazing ascendancy of his genius." On account of her many amours including Byron, the Countess of Oxford was known as the Harleian Miscellany (a pun on her husband's family name of Harley). She considered Napoleon her ideal of manly beauty. According to scandal sheets, the daughter of the Duchess of Gordon saw herself as Lady Georgina Bonaparte. Mary Linwood was doing a remarkable portrait of him in woolwork. Meeting Napoleon, Amelia Alderson, married to the painter John Opie, "shook with excitement."[6] When Napoleon seized Spain, she changed her mind, suspecting that he was "a sort of Dictator." This made her friend Mrs. Inchbald most indignant.

Fears of an invasion revived in Britain after the revocation of the Treaty of Amiens. 10,000 British subjects in France were arrested. The novelist Fanny Burney, married to a French émigré, was held for ten years. Helen Maria Williams had written an "Ode to Peace" which so annoyed Napoleon that he had her arrested, to experience her second spell in a French prison. When Napoleon then set the style for future Third World tyrants by having himself declared First Consul for life, Wordsworth and Southey were among intellectuals who gave up on him. On a visit to France in 1802 in the brief interim of peace, Wordsworth thought that the former greeting of "citizen" sounded hollow, "as if a dead man spoke it." Coleridge admitted that he was another victim of self-deception, lamenting all in his own circumlocution "the having hoped proudly of an individual and the having been so miserably disappointed."[7]

In a very well researched book, *Napoleon and the British,* Stuart Semmel has described how Britain then divided into loyalists who were anti-Napoleon, and radicals who were either pro-Napoleon or whose "anti-anti-Napoleonism,"[8] as he terms it, could make them flat-out fellow-travelers. In the British imagination, Semmel finds, the place of Napoleon was complex, on a scale between hatred and admiration, and in any case a lens through which to examine British identity and performance. People were not consistent either. William Burden, a Cambridge don, a republican, and a political writer, could enthuse at first, then criticize, and finally return to his first opinion, judging Napoleon after his downfall as potentially "the greatest man the world ever saw." Lewis Goldsmith, a journalist, praised Napoleon only to condemn him vociferously, but he seems to have been a double agent, paid to write propaganda by both sides. For William Cobbett, almost everything to do with Napoleon was a stick with which to beat England.

Among admirers of Napoleon were veterans from White's hotel such as the liberal Sir Francis Burdett and Capel Lofft, a perpetual busybody who welcomed the new violence as "the most sublime and bloodless of revolutions,"[9] (although after imprisonment Henry Redhead Yorke had become a Conservative, and William Playfair, present at the fall of the Bastille, now thought the French were "unfit for freedom").[10] William Roscoe, a well-known banker in Liverpool and a friend and correspondent of Mary Wollstonecraft, became unpopular locally for supporting Napoleon.[11] The famous Latin scholar Dr. Samuel Parr said that he never failed to pray for Napoleon's success every night when he went to bed. Leigh Hunt founded a weekly review, *The Examiner,* and was denounced and put on trial by the Attorney General as a Bonapartist who was preparing the way for Britain's invasion.[12]

In 1810 Anne Plumptre published in three volumes *A Narrative of a ThreeYears' Residence in France.* Hatred of her own country and its perceived weaknesses found full expression in her devotion to Napoleonic France and its perceived strengths. This woman hit upon the argument destined for a flourishing future in totalitarian times, that any restraints on liberty were excusable because they would ultimately end in the freedom of all. Though absolute, Napoleon's government increased liberty and he could not be called a tyrant. She excelled at false equivalents, comparing Napoleon's burning of an Italian village to the British burning a Connecticut town, and the judicial execution of the Duc d'Enghien to the price put on the head of the Old Pretender, the Stuart claimant to the throne. In his diary Henry Crabb Robinson, a close observer of his contemporaries, recalled her remarking that Britain would "be all the happier if Buonaparte were to effect a landing and overturn the Government. He would destroy the Church and the aristocracy, and his government would be better than the one we have."[13]

"For my part," wrote William Hazlitt, "I set out in life with the French revolution."[14] In his last essay, in 1830, he was repeating how in his youth, "the light of the French Revolution circled my head like a glory, though dabbled with drops of crimson gore." Typical of this most over-rated and equivocal of writers, the fake poeticism of these phrases prettifies brutal reality. His father was a Dissenter, and as a child Hazlitt had spent a few years in America seemingly learning contempt for his own country. Coleridge observed that Hazlitt was "easily roused to Rage and Hatred." Hazlitt smoothly generalized these emotions: "the English population is the only one to which the epithet *blackguard* is applicable." De Quincey thought, "His inveterate misanthropy was constitutional." Byron, not so different in his impulses, had a rather brilliantly visualized image of Hazlitt "who *talks pimples*—a red and white corruption rising up—, but containing nothing, and discharging nothing, except their own humours."

Hazlitt welcomed Napoleon's coup, and thought of him as "the god of my idolatry," the conqueror who would liberate Europe. Hearing the news of his hero's victory at Austerlitz, he says with that fake poeticism of his that he saw the evening star with "other thoughts and feelings than I shall ever have again." Napoleon, he said, destroyed "the grand conspiracy of Kings." In fact, Napoleon made kings of three of his brothers and his brother-in-law. If Napoleon was arbitrary and a tyrant, he went on, this was because France was "on garrison duty," blockaded by England. But in perpetual reversal of garrison duty, France was steadily occupied in far-flung military campaigning from the Atlantic to Moscow. "Tyranny in him was not sacred," that is to say not sanctioned by divine right, but again in fact Napoleon made sure to have himself crowned Emperor in a religious ceremony in Rheims cathedral.

With insight, the diarist Henry Crabb Robinson, a man at the center of intellectual circles, observed that Hazlitt always vindicated Napoleon for reasons springing from class-consciousness, "not because he is insensible to his enormous crimes, but out of spite to the Tories of this country and the friends of the war of 1792."[15] Hazlitt was frank about this at least: "I hate the sight of the Duke of Wellington for his foolish face. . . . I cannot believe that a great general is contained under such a paste-board vizor." Personalized spite of the kind was very much in the idiom of the day, as in Shelley's lines against another dignitary, then Foreign Secretary, "I met Murder in the way—He had a mask like Castlereagh." All the same, here was a body of like-minded intellectuals and aristocrats wishing for France to defeat England, indifferent to the consequences with a frivolity bordering on mindlessness, if not treason.

1814 was the crucial year whose series of battles forced Napoleon to abdicate. Already notorious, Byron was a foremost spokesman for those who glorified Napoleon as a superman redesigning the world on progressive lines. That January, he told his long-suffering publisher John Murray that Napoleon "has my best wishes to manure the fields of France with an invading army," a jaunty way of expressing his contempt for British purposes and British soldiers. Next month, he was writing, "Napoleon! This week will decide his fate. All seems against him; but I believe and hope he will win." That April, Paris capitulated. "I mark this day!" Byron commented on hearing the news, "I am utterly bewildered and confounded." Immediately, in a matter of hours and in a spirit of distress at events, he wrote the ten stanzas of his "Ode to Napoleon Bonaparte." (Shelley was to write a poem in a similar vein, "Feelings of a Republican on the Fall of Bonaparte.") A few days later Byron wrote to the even more long-suffering Annabella Milbanke whom he was soon to marry so disastrously, "Buonaparte has fallen—I regret it—& the restoration of the despicable Bourbons—the triumph of tameness over talent—and the utter wreck of a mind which I thought superior even to Fortune—it has utterly confounded and baffled me." Invited to view the procession up Piccadilly of the Prince Regent and Louis XVIII, now the restored Bourbon King of France, Byron wrote (again to Murray), "You know I am a jacobin [sic], and could not wear white [i.e. Bourbon colours], nor see the installation of Louis the Gouty." Exile to the island of Elba seemed to Napoleon's admirers an ending too inglorious to be tolerated. Whig politicians, Lord John Russell among them, visited Elba to pay their respects as though to an Emperor in a miniature court. Napoleon's escape from captivity thrilled them. Byron exulted, "It is impossible not to be dazzled and overwhelmed by his character and career. Nothing ever so disappointed me as his abdication, and nothing could have reconciled me to him but some such revival as his recent exploit."

The battle of Waterloo in June 1815 marked the end of the protracted upheaval caused by the French Revolution and Napoleon's subsequent coup. These years had seen the first attempt to impose some form of absolute rule over the entire continent, and the dead

were numbered in millions, a foretaste of the subsequent century.
During the Hundred Days preceding the battle, the diarist Crabb
Robinson called on William Godwin, that pathfinder of political cor-
rectness, and found him "passionate in his wishes for the success of
the French." On the night of the decisive final battle, Major-General
Sir Robert Wilson and Lord Grey, the future prime minister, were in
Brooks's club in elegant St. James's demonstrating to a large audience
that Bonaparte had 200,000 men across the river Sambre in northern
France and by now must be in Brussels. Wilson was reading aloud a
letter spreading disinformation that the British population of Brussels
was fleeing to Antwerp when in the words of one of his sceptical
bystanders, "the shouts in the street drew us to the window"[16] to hear
the crowds celebrating the news of British victory. Wilson went to
Paris where he helped a friend of Napoleon's to escape justice. The
Duke of Wellington himself was to recall the reaction to Waterloo of
two other figures from the highest society: "when the truth came out
of our having won, Lord Sefton went to Lady Jersey and said to her
'Horrible news! They have gained a great victory!'"[17]

Hearing this same news, Hazlitt "was like a man shot through the
heart." The artist Benjamin Robert Haydon (himself the painter of a
famously poignant picture entitled "Napoleon Musing at St. Helena")
wrote of Hazlitt, "It is not to be believed how the destruction of
Napoleon affected him; he seemed prostrated in mind and body, he
walked about unwashed, unshaven, hardly sober by day, and always
intoxicated by night, literally, without exaggeration, for weeks."[18]
Some dozen years later, Hazlitt wrote a biography in several volumes
of Napoleon, and it became clear that although he might claim to
hate tyranny in the abstract he had nevertheless spent a lifetime promoting to the best of his ability this particular form of it.

Samuel Whitbread had consistently opposed the war, and tried to
make the Duke of Wellington out to be a greater enemy than
Napoleon. The latter, he thought, had been wronged, "aggran-
dized,"[19] forced to be aggressive by the refusal of legitimate sover-

eigns to accept him. He spoke often and at length in Parliament, in an early outlining of what was to become in the next century the classic defense of totalitarianism, that the victim of aggression is in the wrong and has only himself to blame for it. Seven weeks before Waterloo he moved a formal motion in Parliament against the war, and three weeks before the battle he voted against subsidies for the Allies. To him, the war was "an insane project, especially as to the calculations upon its speedy conclusion."[20] The day after Napoleon had capitulated, Whitbread committed suicide. His Whig colleagues then did their best to hide that he had killed himself because the Waterloo victory was unbearable. Whitbread's "appetite for applause"[21] had been so great, in Lord Holland's particularly oily falsehood, that he had killed himself at the prospect of it ending.

When the ship taking Napoleon to exile in Saint Helena anchored briefly in Plymouth, Byron told his friend John Cam Hobhouse that he thought there was no alternative but to commit suicide like Whitbread. When he added the name Noel to his and started signing his letters NB, he took childish pleasure in sharing Napoleon's initials. Leaving England in 1816, and as it turned out going into exile himself, Byron visited the battlefield of Waterloo and cut his name into the wall of the farmhouse at Hougoumont where hand-to-hand fighting had been at its fiercest. In *Don Juan,* he taunted the Duke of Wellington, wondering, "And I shall be delighted to learn who,/ Save you and yours, have gained by Waterloo." Wellington's revenge was to say, "There never existed a more worthless set than Byron and his friends."

Yet as Stuart Semmel shows, soon "nostalgia for Napoleon began creeping in."[22] Lady Holland sent him parcels of books with her devoted inscription to the "Emperor," and in his will he was to leave her a snuff-box. Charles James Napier, who had been wounded at Corunna during the Peninsular wars, and was later the general commanding the campaign to conquer the Indian province of Sind, expressed an attitude that was becoming increasingly popular:

"Millions of men sigh at his captivity and curse his gaolers."[23] The doctor in Saint Helena, Barry O'Meara, published a memoir, *Napoleon in Exile,* presenting him as a victim rather than a dictator obliged to pay the penalty for ambitions that had cost so many their lives. Napoleon had shaped the age, and once safely out of the way he could be considered a great man, exceptional, a genius among mediocrities everywhere else. Those who had believed in him could be forgiven as romantics. They might have been wrong, but only for the right reason that their emotions and hopes for the betterment of mankind had been so elevated. That specious line of exculpation was destined to last.

CHAPTER FOUR

"We Are All Greeks"

"**N**ationalism is a doctrine invented in Europe at the beginning of the nineteenth century"[1] is the lapidary opening sentence of Elie Kedourie's book on the topic. The French Revolution and then the supremacy of Napoleon had impelled peoples all over the continent to evolve a new primary definition of themselves not as subjects of some ruler or bound together because of a shared language or religion but as members of their nation, and on that account citizens of it. This appeal to a novel identity was irresistible, destined to spread far and wide, mobilizing and politicizing equally aristocrats and the masses who had previously known little or nothing of this kind. Nationalism has proved the most powerful secular concept of the modern age, and perhaps of all ages.

Radical doctrine laid down that every nation has the right to govern itself, and that self-government is a sufficient and necessary condition of liberty. "Without nationality, neither liberty nor equality is possible," said Mazzini, whose attempt to unite the Italian nation on these lines was an outstanding example of nationalism in action. For many a radical, many an adventurer, many an innocent, the equation of nationality and liberty might be revolutionary but it also contained a universal truth, and anyone struggling to embody it deserved support. Foreign Secretaries had to deal with the consequences, and one of them, George Canning, took issue in a pointed couplet mocking whoever threw himself into foreign causes, "A steady patriot of the world alone / The friend of every country but his own." Here were the origins of what Elie Kedourie in another of his lapidary judgments criticized as "fashionable Western sentimentality which holds that Great Powers are nasty and small Powers virtuous."[2]

The dilemma facing each awakening nation was how to become a state. By definition, the small, inconsequential, poorly educated, agricultural nation was at the mercy of any larger, influential, inventive and industrializing neighbor, or, more dangerous still to the prospect of independence, overlord. In the quest for a state, the weak, the minority, had no choice but to make normal life a misery for the strong, or the majority, by means of national liberation movements, uprisings, revolutions, fomenting the chaos that could not fail to draw in great powers and lead to congresses and treaties and the realignment of frontiers. Violence was bound to accompany the birth of the state, condemning many to lose control of what had been a settled existence, and worse, to become cannon-fodder. Those willing to sacrifice themselves for the cause were elevated to heroes, and in due course a few of their representatives and spokesmen would have statues erected to them in the main square of their capital city, preferably in front of a brand-new parliament building with impressive classical columns. Nationalism was to prove the structural flaw of empires, cracking them open and bringing them down piecemeal one after another. Soviet Communism put into practice the alternative of reducing by force every nation within reach to a common identity based on ideology. Nationalism was well able to endure this pointlessly cruel experiment, and in the end strangled to death its one serious rival in the field of ideology.

The Ottoman Empire was first in line to have to deal with this challenge of nationality. Since the capture of Constantinople, the Ottoman sultans had been masters of conquered Christian lands, and in what were then Muslim-governed provinces the tenets of Islam discriminated against Christians, decreeing for them a lower or second-class status. Over time, the empire succumbed to the inertia inherent in centralized and absolute rule and a religious faith that stood against change. Pashas, officials appointed as so many viceroys within the empire, took advantage of plenary powers to acquire land and to extort taxes from the Christian peasants forming the bulk of the population in the provinces in Europe. The ambitious among them, for instance Ali Pasha of Jannina or Muhammad Ali in Cairo, wrested a degree of independence for themselves. As standards of administration declined, the Christians had no means to obtain redress for injustice. Nonetheless, the unique Ottoman blend of corruption, backwardness, laisser-aller, and custom might well have lasted more or less indefinitely, except for the winds beginning to blow in from Europe. Constitutionalism and republicanism, never mind nationhood, were unfamiliar concepts, but violence as a means of relieving grievance at least had precedence and authority. Violence was an uncertain tool, for on one hand it condemned the Christian provinces to years of Ottoman backlash, but on the other it necessarily drew the European powers into what became known as the Eastern Question, the international rivalry that was to bedevil chancelleries for decades to come, and keep Europe under the shadow of war for a century. The Serbs in their province were still too far out of touch to attract attention, let alone support, and when they began a nationalist movement the Turks simply drowned it in blood.

Greece was another matter. There were a few cosmopolitan Greeks, who could write pamphlets about liberty and propose a constitution on the approved French model. The first Greek newspaper had appeared in Vienna in 1784. In Odessa a secret society of Greek exiles began to conspire and prepare for an uprising against the Ottomans, eventually enrolling just over a thousand members. As a political movement coalesced, men with often self-appointed and honorific titles appeared to lead it and to jockey for position. Well-placed in Saint Petersburg and prepared for military leadership,

Prince Alexander Ypsilanti expected to be able to persuade Russia to intervene on behalf of Greece once the war of liberation was under way. Alexander Mavrogordato was a Phanariot, that is to say, born and brought up in the privileged Greek elite of Istanbul. "A cultured man, thoroughly Europeanised,"[3] speaking several languages, he was the friend of Byron and Shelley, the former considering him "the Washington of Greece." Count Capodistria, the first president of an independent Greece, was murdered at the orders of a rival by two thugs, one of whom was shot on the spot and the other hanged. Botsaris, Colocotronis, and others became household names promoted in radical circles in Europe, but they were warlords unscrupulously on the make. Their followers, the rank-and-file Greeks known as klephts, were a scratch lot of brigands under arms, for whom the concepts of the state and independence were understood as openings for killing and plundering.

And then there were the British, who first came to Greece in order to explore a landscape made familiar by their education in the great public schools where modern Greeks were idealized as descendants of Pericles. E. D. Clarke was one of them, a civilized travel writer with an eye for the picturesque. Sponsored by the avant-garde Society of Dilettanti, the artist James "Athenian" Stuart revived an interest in classical antiquity. Lord Elgin bought the Parthenon frieze from the Turks still forming the garrison on the Acropolis. Dr. Lemprière wrote a dictionary of classical antiquities that is still a standard work. But for the informed majority, Turkish rule was intolerably primitive and unjust, fully responsible for the sad condition of the Greeks. William Eton was convinced that Greece "can no longer submit to the Turkish yoke; she pants for emancipation, and already aspires to be ranked among the independent states of Europe."[4] Thomas Hughes, a Cambridge priest and High Tory, had a view of Islam as "hatched and matured in falsehood, hypocrisy and blood."[5] Rather than dwelling on the glories of Salamis and Thermopylae, he went on, "the cause I plead is that of suffering Christians." For this advocate of violence, Turks were "weak, contemptible, vice-stained tyrants"[6] fit to be exterminated. Almost everyone in England who was following the issue would have agreed with Canning, the Foreign Secretary, when he said that he saw simply the desire of an oppressed Christian people to cast off the Turkish yoke.

Lord Byron's involvement in Greek affairs was fortuitous, the function of a character so spoiled that he believed he could do as he pleased with no need to explain or apologize for anything to anyone. It was his good fortune to have been born in 1788, at a moment when England was on the threshold of riches and imperial power, and a British peer could take for granted the respect of the rest of the world. Byron was ten when he inherited his title, as well as Newstead Abbey, a huge but dilapidated house with an estate of 3,000 acres near Nottingham, as well as another property in Lancashire with valuable coal mines. The outward show was misleading. The Byrons had "bad blood," in a phrase of the era. The previous Lord Byron, the poet's great-uncle, had murdered his neighbor at Newstead in the course of a quarrel about how to hang game. The poet's father had married for money, squandered his wife's fortune, and died alone in poverty and exile in France. Byron never knew his father, and was brought up by a fond, feckless, and financially ruined mother.

Educated at Harrow and Cambridge, he had a habit of embellishing his letters with a suitable quotation from the classics. Even when young he seemed to others to be striking a pose, world-weary, superior because opposed to everything conventional. He was twenty-one in 1809 when he set off to Greece. "I shall enter the Austrian or Russian service, perhaps the Turkish, if I like their manners," he had written to his mother, "the world is all before me, and I leave England without regret." And again, "I dislike England and the farther I go, the less I regret leaving it." His companion on that first journey was John Cam Hobhouse who reported that at the time Byron lectured him about not caring enough for the English nobility. At Tepelene, Byron called on the celebrated Ali Pasha, finding that he possessed "that

dignity which I find universal among the Turks." Ali Pasha was certainly "a remorseless tyrant" but also "the Mohametan Buonaparte,"
which from Byron was a compliment. In Greece, he carved his name
on a pillar of the ruined temple at Sunion and measured himself
against the heroic standards of antiquity by swimming the Helle-
spont. "I like the Greeks who are plausible rascals," he informed a
Harrow school friend with the light touch of someone above the fray,
"with all the Turkish vices, but without their courage. However, some
are brave, and all are beautiful." He and Hobhouse also sailed on a
sloop to Turkey, tourists as they would be called today.

The first cantos of *Childe Harold's Pilgrimage,* published in 1812,
carried elegiac echoes of the long-lost glories of Greece. "Fair
Greece! Sad relic of departed worth! Immortal, though no more;
though fallen, great!" After this lament Byron asked, "Who now shall
lead thy scatter'd children forth?" No new poem had ever been so
successful; it hit the taste of the age, as he put it. He had a natural gift
for story-telling and for rhyming, and this was immediately obvious:
"I awoke one morning and found myself famous." *The Giaour* was an
Oriental poem begun in late 1812, based on the story of a Turkish
girl whom he had supposedly saved from being thrown into the sea in
Athens. Another spectacular success, *The Corsair,* his long poem of
1814, sold 10,000 copies in a single day, and seven editions in four
weeks. Of course, verses in *Don Juan* in 1821 were destined to shape
public opinion and become anthology pieces for generations of
schoolchildren: "The mountains look on Marathon——/ And
Marathon looks on the sea;/ And musing there an hour alone,/ I
dreamed that Greece might still be free;/ For standing on the Persian's grave,/ I could not deem myself a slave." Affairs with women
added to a reputation in which admiration, envy, scandal, and censure were hard to disentangle. It was common knowledge that he had
committed incest with his half-sister, and that his wife Annabella had
left him because he had indecently assaulted her. One among the
women in his career as a seducer was Lady Caroline Lamb, wife of

William Lamb, later Lord Melbourne and prime minister, and she earned immortality with her description of him as "mad—bad—and dangerous to know."

Byron's poetry, as William St. Clair explains in his admirable book *That Greece Might Still Be Free,* galvanized literary Philhellenism into an international movement: "Few, if any, Englishmen have had such a widespread influence or aroused such interest among their contemporaries at home and abroad." [7] Shelley, his friend, rival, and in the end his victim, enthused in the preface to his rhapsodic *Hellas,* "We are all Greeks"—a formula that President Kennedy was to echo with his "We are all Berliners." Pushkin, Stendhal, Lamartine, Schumann, and Mazzini were among Byron's admirers. He corresponded with Goethe, the most eminent public figure in the Europe of the day, and who sent him a poem in his own hand. To Eckermann, however, Goethe expressed political reservations: "Lord Byron is only great as a poet; as soon as he reflects he is a child." Altogether about 1,200 Philhellenes were to take part in the Greek War of Independence, the majority men of education and status in their own countries, but volunteering out of a feeling that they were "selflessly joining an honourable cause."[8] Of these, St. Clair is able to identify 940 Philhellenes coming from twelve countries, the contingents from Germany and France forming just over half the total. The death-rate was high, about a third of the total. Sixty-seven known Philhellenes from eight different countries were killed in the one disastrous battle of Peta. Gary J. Bass, it should be said, gives overall numbers that are significantly lower.

What had its origins in the salon emotions of Philhellenism ended in what today would qualify as ethnic cleansing. From the spring of 1821 onwards, Greeks and Turks indulged in mutual atrocities and massacres either in Turkey itself or on the Greek mainland, in Crete, and other islands. In a first-hand account published in 1827, Philip Green, the British consul in Patras, deplored the war between "these two semi-barbarian people."[9] Numbers are uncertain, but in just the first year of the fighting, more than 50,000 Turks, Greeks, Albanians, Jews, and others had lost their lives.[10] During the siege of Tripolitsa alone, St. Clair writes, "Upwards of ten thousand Turks were put to death. European officers who were present described the scenes of horror." The dead were mutilated and dogs' heads stuck between their legs. One British officer was Thomas Gordon, a professional soldier and a man of means with an estate in Scotland. Disgusted by what he had witnessed and catching the plague that followed the massacre, he left Tripolitsa, but was to return to Greece in his yacht. Eventually he settled in Argos and wrote a history of the war. 1822 was the year of the massacre of the Greek inhabitants on the island of Chios. Tens of thousands were butchered, and the customs authorities gave official certificates for 41,000 slaves, mainly women and boys, 5,000 of whom were sold for trivial sums in Istanbul. In that capital, "Sacks of human heads, noses and ears from Chios were strewn around the streets."[11] Delacroix's paintings of atrocities on Chios and elsewhere retain their power to horrify to this day.

About thirty British Philhellenes published accounts of their experiences. George Finlay, a lawyer at the Scottish bar, is the best of them. He and two friends, Lieutenant Caulfield and Mr. Sams, had travelled in Turkey dressed in Turkish costume. At an audience at the Sublime Porte the reigning Sultan Mahmud struck him as "nothing more than an obstinate madman,"[12] and he thought that before the Ottoman Empire could hope for improvement the Turks "must cease to be Turks." The two colleagues of whom Finlay wholly approved were Byron and Frank Abney Hastings. The son of a baronet, well off, Hastings had been a naval officer and fought at Trafalgar, only to quarrel with his superiors. He spent a huge sum of his own money on a steam ship for the Greek navy. Technical difficulties ensued, and he was killed before this innovation could contribute to success. Lord Cochrane was another naval officer who had been in many engagements during the Napoleonic wars, and afterwards had commanded the navies first of Chile, then of Brazil, in their wars of liberation.

"There is no man I envy so much," was Byron's opinion of him. The Greeks invited him to command their embryonic navy, and "as a mercenary for hire, he demanded what he considered he was worth."[13] General Sir Richard Church accepted the invitation from the Greeks to command their soldiers. He had served in the British army throughout the Napoleonic wars and afterwards commanded the forces of the counter-revolutionary King of Naples. "Oh, how I hate the Turks,"[14] he wrote to his mother, and many years later, to his sister-in-law about his commitment to Greece, "I do not regret having sacrificed everything in the world to the cause which I embraced." Finlay called him, "the liege lord of all true Philhellenes."[15] Church had a high enough rank to be able to plead with Canning, the foreign secretary, to lend his powerful hand to "the sublime task of emancipating Greece."[16] W. J. Humphreys had been through Sandhurst to train as an officer, and in common with others he believed himself "about to taste the reality of the fantasies he had acquired from reading Byron."[17] John Hane became a colonel in the Greek army, and Edward Masson, a Scottish schoolmaster, served the new state as Attorney General. One Haldenby is described as a rich young man, and some others remain even more anonymous. Of the ninety-nine recorded British Philhellenes, twenty-one died.

The Greek revolution, comments the historian Douglas Dakin, was a vast conspiracy organized by intellectuals, financed by the merchant classes, and eventually extended to the military classes. Formalizing conspiracy, so to speak, the London Greek Committee met in March 1823 for the first time in the Crown and Anchor tavern in the Strand. The original membership was twenty-six, though this rose to over eighty. Many were Members of Parliament or public personalities like Lord John Russell, Sir John Bowring, Hobhouse, and the philosopher Jeremy Bentham. With the sole exception of Thomas Hughes, the bloodthirsty Tory clergyman, they were all radicals, in a sense reminiscent of the group that had gathered thirty years previously in White's hotel in Paris. The Committee liaised with Greek emissaries and planted propaganda in the press. By means of subscriptions, loans, and Greek bonds, the Committee also raised money for the cause. Incompetence and corruption completed the sense of conspiracy.

A former sea captain who had seen service in the Mediterranean, and a prolific publicist, Edward Blaquiere was one of the more assiduous members of the Greek Committee. A cynic, he recognized the publicity value of Byron. Still, he could hardly have anticipated that his enrolment of Byron on behalf of the Committee would seal the false image of a great poet sacrificing his life for his beliefs, and enshrine him as a hero for posterity to admire and imitate. When Blaquiere called on him in Italy on his way to Greece in 1823, Byron was in a particularly indecisive and dissatisfied mood, fed up with moving residence from one side of the country to the other, feeling smothered by his latest mistress Teresa Guiccioli, disappointed by Italian revolutionaries to whom he had given secret support and money. He had been writing to his friend, the poet Tom Moore, that he had been fluctuating between going to South America and Greece, and would have gone if not for Teresa, "for love, in these days, is little compatible with glory." Blaquiere told Byron that the Committee was inviting him to be their representative in Greece. Byron accepted. Within weeks he was summoning the loud-mouth Trelawny, "Pray come, for I am at last determined to go to Greece; it is the only place I was ever contented in."

Byron parted with his menagerie of dogs, cats, the monkey, the peacock, the guinea-hen, and the Egyptian crane. He sold his Napoleonic snuff-box. He had introduced himself to Teresa as "Pair d'Angleterre et son plus grand poète,"[18] and to keep up the style he ordered a resplendent scarlet and gold uniform with a gilt helmet and plume and his coat of arms on it. The Inventory of his so-called Military Wardrobe and Equipage lists "Four Full Dress Uniform Coats trimmed with Gold Lace. Sword knots. Dress Hat. Cap. Epaulets. Sashes. Gold Lace Shoulder Knots. 10 swords." Arms and

ammunition were shipped. James Hamilton Browne, a Scottish Philhellene, joined the expedition, as did Trelawny and Count Piero
Gamba, Teresa's young brother. Giovanni Falcieri, a Venetian gondo-
lier familiarly known as Tita; Fletcher, the faithful valet from Not-
tinghamshire; and Lega Zambolli, the steward of Teresa's husband,
Count Guiccioli, came too. A Greek agent suggested that Byron
might become the country's king, which prompted Leslie Marchand,
the great Byron scholar, to remark that he was "at least flattered by it,
and referred to it often thereafter."[19]

Escapism had another more somber side. Byron was worldly-wise
enough to know that the Committee was exploiting his reputation and
endangering his person. Shortly before leaving, he told Lady Blessing-
ton, a spirited society writer, that he had a presentiment he would die
in Greece, indeed he hoped to die in battle because that would be a
good ending, better than on the bed of disease. Trelawny accused him
of indecision, dawdling, and self-pity. Soon after arriving in the Aegean
in September 1823, Byron was confiding to the abandoned Teresa, "Of
the Greeks I can't say much good hitherto." A month later, he wrote
just as gloomily to her, "I was a fool to come here but being here I must
see what is to be done." Once at Missolonghi, more a mud patch than a
village on the Greek mainland, he took command of Byron's Brigade,
a ragbag of Philhellenes, German officers, and undisciplined Albanians
in it for their wages. Freshly recruited from England was William
Parry, a clerk from Woolwich, the London barracks where engineers
and artillerymen trained. Risen from the ranks, he styled himself
"Major Parry of Lord Byron's Brigade, commanding officer of Artillery
and Engineer in the service of the Greeks." A heavy drinker, somewhat
crude, he was the unlikely person Byron found most congenial in the
final stage of his life. Byron had set out with 10,000 Spanish dollars and
bills of exchange for 40,000 more dollars, but he was expected to pay
for everything, on the assumption that his own fortune or the Committee's funds were available and limitless. Everyone was after him,
including the Philhellene Colonel Leicester Stanhope, the future Earl

of Harrington, who wanted money to print a paper although the Greeks and Albanians were illiterate. Byron objected. "At times," Stanhope recorded, "Lord Byron would become disgusted with the Greeks, on account of their horrid cruelties, their importuning him for money, and their not fulfilling their promises."[20] In the last letter Byron wrote, he complained that the Greeks "had many 'a strong and long pull' at my purse." Had he not fallen ill, one suspects, he would have thrown it all up and returned to Teresa. In April 1824 he seems to have had some sort of seizure. Caught in a rainstorm a few days later, he developed a fever. Too weak to prevent them, he let the doctors bleed him. This was fatal.

Reaching for the moral of the story, Harold Nicolson, a discerning critic and biographer of Byron, writes indignantly about "all this cant about Causes, and Liberty, and Adventure."[21] To him, Byron's Greek venture was the last chance in a life that had lost its meaning: "there was really nothing else for him to do." He died as he had lived, then, in a pose. E. Tangye Lean goes further, in the belief that Byron really had martyrdom in mind, and was offering "the first great example to European liberalism of suicide in the interests of a people. It was a model which established Byron's influence in the nineteenth century above any other Romantic."[22] The glamour, the legend, falsified the reality that a great poet had died to no real purpose at the age of thirty-six. The Greeks and the Philhellenes had provided the Turks with a pretext for terror and primitive slaughter. Whole areas of Greece were burnt out and depopulated. Enmity between Greeks and Turks became so uncompromising that it has lasted into the present. When the Greek cause looked like sparking a wider and more dangerous war affecting the balance of power in the world, the alliance of Britain, France, and Russia intervened. The destruction of the Turkish fleet at the battle of Navarino meant that the Turks could no longer supply a standing army in Greece. The Greeks owed their independence, perhaps even their survival as a nation, to the great powers. The Philhellenes had been a distraction.

CHAPTER FIVE

That Sound That Crashes in the Tyrant's Ear

In 1820, with the Philhellene cause still in the future, Byron was offering his services to the revolution breaking out in the Kingdom of Naples, "without any other motive than that of sharing the destiny of a brave nation defending itself against the self-called Holy Alliance, which but combines the vice of hypocrisy with despotism."

In Ravenna at the time, he was also telling his publisher John Murray in his conversational style with dashes as though taking a breath, "I shall think it by far the most interesting spectacle and moment in existence—to see the Italians send the Barbarians of all nations back to their own dens.—I have lived long enough among them—to feel more for them as a nation than for any other people in existence—but they want Union—and they want principle—and I doubt their success—however they will try probably—and if they do—it will be a good cause—no Italian can hate an Austrian more than I do—unless it be the English—the Austrians seem to me the most obnoxious race under the Sky." He was at least realistic enough to conclude this outburst of spleen by saying, "to be sure Revolutions are not to be made with Rose-water."

Sending the Barbarians back to their own dens was what every radical flattered himself that he was helping to do in the course of the nineteenth and twentieth centuries. To their dismay, radicals mostly discovered that there was little or no opportunity to take up arms and kill for the cause, so they had to make do with meetings, forming associations, lobbying, writing poems, and so forth—which is what Byron meant with that dismissive reference to Rose-water. Revolution in Spain, also in 1820, came on top of the prior upheavals of the Peninsular wars. "Spain rises, awful and sublime, / O'er slavery, error, war and crime," ran lines in *Black Dwarf,* a radical publication that indulged in this kind of flag-waving.[1]

Politics in Spain soon proved to be a struggle for power between different members of the Bourbon family. Lord Palmerston, then Foreign Secretary, gave his consent to the formation of a British Auxiliary Legion to take sides in what came to be known as the First Carlist War. The Foreign Enlistment Act was suspended for the purpose. George de Lacey Evans was given command. A soldier who had been present at the burning of the White House in 1812, and then served with Wellington, he had become a radical Member of Parliament. This Legion was 10,000 strong, and many went to Spain with their wives and children. Methods close to the press-gang rounded the men up. Told that he was going to fight for Queen Isabella against her uncle Don Carlos, one Irishman by the name of Kippeen misunderstood and answered, "Bang me if I go to fight against Donkies," and left the ranks to go home.[2] Almost half of the Legionnaires were to die out there, a high proportion of them in a typhus epidemic. Many more were maimed.

More arbitrary and reactionary than Don Carlos were the Russian and Austro-Hungarian Emperors. Opposition to these stalwarts of the Holy Alliance offered radicals of every sort the thrill of revolution, barricades, their own flags, and the vision of a new state arising from the wreckage of former tyranny. Poland was an early test case. Edmond Burke's panegyric *Appeal from the New to the Old Whigs* in 1791 had in the words of one authority, "probably done more than any other work to change the British attitude to Poland."[3] Tadeusz Kosciuszko had participated in the American War of Independence, earning a compliment from Thomas Jefferson as "one of our great revolutionary worthies." Further inspired by the French Revolution, Kosciuszko in 1794 declared a Polish National Insurrection. National self-determination, according to the Tsar's advisor Count Nesselrode, was nothing less than "the Polish disease." Putting an end to it, the Russians massacred 20,000 people in Warsaw. The eleven-year-old son of a British major stationed in Germany ran away into the Black Forest. When his family found him, he explained that he had been making his way east "to help the Poles."[4] This boy was Ernest Jones, destined to be a leading Chartist. The Polish cause, comments the historian Henry Weissar, brought together "proletarian internationalists, exiles of various nations, and foreign intellectuals," all imagining themselves in a contest between light and justice against darkness and tyranny. This was "a vague glittering thing" derived from "the threadbare clichés of the ultra-radical press." Ernest Jones grew up to shout at a public meeting his thanks to the "Heroes of Poland" for having "lavished your precious blood on the ramparts of western civilisation."

In 1800 the defeated Kosciuszko published a manifesto, "Can the Poles recover their independence by armed action?" They had to wait a century and more to find out. In his poem *The Age of Bronze,* Byron had a verse that opened "Poland! O'er which the avenging angel passed,/ But left thee as he found thee, still a waste," to conclude, "That sound that crashes in the tyrant's ear—Kosciuszko!" Thomas Campbell, a lesser poet but every bit the conventional radical of that moment, wrote almost identically, "Hope, for a season, bade the world farewell, /And Freedom shrieked—as Kosciuszko fell!" One of the Poles who fled to Paris was Jozef Sulkowski, and he captured what was to be a lasting aspiration: "Poland is wherever people are fighting for liberty."[5] Within a few years almost 700 Poles had settled in London. Leading members of the newly founded Literary Association of the Friends of Poland were Prince Adam Czartoryski, who had been the Tsar's Foreign Minister before siding with the insurrection of his fellow Poles, Stanislaus Worcell and Count Platen, supported by the poet Thomas Campbell and Lord Dudley Stuart. A son of the Marquess of Bute, one of the richest men in the country, Lord Dudley had married Christine Bonaparte, the daughter of Napoleon's brother Lucien. A Member of Parliament, he was a prototype of what was already becoming the very familiar figure of someone throwing his rank and his fortune into the promotion of a cause that could not directly affect British interests but nonetheless was bound to have repercussions on foreign policy, complicating the task of government without necessarily achieving anything for the object of his attention. Lord Dudley, a Liberal, was certainly sincere in his anger, but for him a greater priority was to use his position to embarrass political opponents. Sponsorship of the Poles in speeches in the House of Commons and subsequently published for greater effect were bound to have the subsidiary effect of painting the Conservatives as friends of the tyrannical Russia.

The Polish Literary Association had branches in Hull, Birmingham, Nottingham, Leeds, Edinburgh, and Glasgow. More conspiratorial was the rival Polish Democratic Society. What these exiles and their friends achieved was the transformation of public opinion about Russia. The influential *Westminster Review,* for instance, considered that Russia had hitherto only been thought of as the land of strange and distant barbarians: "But things are altered now; and Russia, barbarous still, has aspired to, and has obtained, a dictatorship over the states of Europe."[6] Joseph Hume, a Member of Parliament and one of the Friends of Poland, declared in the House of Commons that the Tsar was "a monster in human form."[7] When Tsar Nicholas I came on a state visit in 1844, hostile demonstrations broke out. At a huge meeting in the National Hall in High Holborn the audience held up proceedings several times with shouts that the British people should not offer hospitality to a mass murderer.

When Hungary erupted with its parallel case of "the Polish disease" of self-determination, the target of anger was Austria. Born in

1802, Lajos Kossuth began his career as a lawyer. One A. J. Blackwell, an unofficial British representative in Hungary and evidently a secret agent, warned that Kossuth was a dangerous agitator. Kossuth had been a political prisoner for four years, during which time he learnt English. He then edited a newspaper with the relatively large circulation of 5,000, and popularized the nationalist cry, "Hungary, awake!" Metternich, the Austrian Chancellor held by all right-thinking liberals throughout Europe to be the embodiment of reaction, granted him an interview. Austrian forces with Croat auxiliaries and Russian reinforcements put down the Hungarian uprising of 1848. In London, Lord Dudley Stuart became chairman of a Hungarian Committee, on which were Lord Nugent, Richard Cobden, and Charles Gilpin, all of them Members of Parliament, Professor F. W. Newman (a personal friend of Kossuth's), and a prominent lawyer, J. Toulmin Smith. Kossuth had brought bloodshed and disaster to Hungary, unsettling the relationship with Austria in a way that could never really be repaired, but he was in the hands of professionals able to present him as a freedom fighter and hero. Arriving at Southampton in October 1851, he was welcomed by the Hungarian Committee members, together with Whigs and Radicals and Chartists and émigrés. Special cheap trains were run from London. The Corporation of Southampton entertained him, and then so did the City of London. "I have political aims in view in England," said this man of the hour, "I wish to appeal to the people as the defender of my oppressed country."[8]

100,000 gathered to hear him speak in London, 200,000 in Manchester, and "the entire population" in Birmingham.[9] The Committee sponsored a slim unsigned volume: "His love of fatherland and humanity alike dictate a hatred of the Czar; of the Emperor of Austria; and he never swerves from honestly and openly expressing that hatred."[10] And much more like that at an even higher pitch of emotion. Queen Victoria had another opinion, however, writing to the King of the Belgians that the popular Kossuth-fever derived from ignorance of the man who was "an ambitious and *rapacious* humbug."[11] As it turned out, he spent the rest of his life intriguing to start a war against Austria, to be waged either by the French or the Italians. Napoleon III, this prime conspirator soon discovered, was a willing accomplice who needed no special inciting to attack the Austrians in Italy in 1859. Mobilized by Kossuth, a brigade of Hungarian exiles fought alongside the French at the battle of Solferino in yet another vain and bloody enterprise.

CHAPTER SIX

Imperishable and International Poetry

The new ideology of nationalism was an immediate threat to the patchwork of kingdoms, grand duchies, republics, and the Papal States of the Italian peninsula. Napoleon's attempt to impose his order had been conspicuously unsuccessful. His re-allocation of dynasties and territories shook the old structures irredeemably, bringing about multiple confrontations between rulers determined to fight from the instinct of self-preservation, and revolutionaries determined to wrest power and if possible weld a unitary state in the fashionable French manner. The course of history had been against the emergence of anything like an Italian identity. Even those who nominally spoke the same language often could not understand each other, so different were the dialects in the country. The multiple clashes of ideas and personalities, the rivalries of the outside powers of France and Austria, rapidly degenerated into violence and war.

In Italy there was already a class of men with the means and the literary bent to spread nationalism to the masses who as yet did not realize that their settled lives and identity were about to be changed out of all recognition. Silvio Pellico was one of the first to popularize hatred of the Austrians occupying Lombardy and the Veneto, and imposing their heavy Habsburg rule in these provinces. *My Prisons*, Pellico's account of his years of suffering and incarceration at the hands of the Austrians, was a bestseller; it is still a classic of the prison literature which is so much a part of the modern age. Another nationalist of much the same stamp was Ugo Foscolo, a poet and dramatist, and a certified revolutionary. Disappointed by Napoleon in whose honor he had written an ode, and hounded by the Austrians, he fled to London, the prototype of the political refugee, another modern familiarity. Finding soul-mates among the Whigs, he became a habitué of Holland House. The observant Emily Eden described the social and political arrangements of Lord and Lady Holland in their great Jacobean mansion in Kensington: "ten people every day at dinner, and a few in the evening, and there is always an author for the good of one's mind, and a doctor to prevent one's dropping down dead, and the rest are people who know one another well, and have the same politics."[1]

According to Lord Holland, Foscolo was the man "of greatest value he had ever met." Foscolo was taken into society as an equal, and "swept all before him with his charming manners and vivacious conversation." Lord Holland introduced him to his circle of friends: the Duke of Bedford, Lord Brougham, the poets Thomas Campbell and Samuel Rogers, Roger Wilbraham (an octogenarian and the country's foremost scholar of Italy), Lady Aberdeen, Lady Westmorland, and many more. He also arranged for the leading publishers and editors to commission books and essays from Foscolo. These people were among the grandest in the land, possessors of titles and inherited fortunes, whose continuity depended on stability. The republican and Jacobin-inspired revolution preached by Foscolo would in practice have put an end to their privileges and perhaps their lives. Such disturbance as there was in the England of that day did not rise to the bloody levels elsewhere on the continent, and therefore "for the good of one's mind" indeed, they were able to catch from someone like Foscolo the thrill of revolution without any danger that it might really sweep them away. Hypocrisy and the search for thrills on the part of the fortunate few contributed equally to the formation of public opinion.

The Milanese Count Giuseppe Pecchio, a friend of Foscolo's, was also sentenced to death and escaped to London in 1823. In that year, as he recorded it, "London was populated by exiles of all sorts and of all countries; Constitutionalists wanting one single room, Constitutionalists wanting two rooms, Constitutionalists in the French style, some in the Spanish style, others American. President-generals dismissed by republics, parliamentary presidents . . . and a [shoal] of journalists, poets and men of letters. London was the Elysium (a satirist would say the Botany Bay) of illustrious men and heroes manqués."[2] Among those fleeing the upheavals they had helped to bring about in those years were Victor Hugo and Alexander Herzen. In 1856 Felice Orsini escaped the Austrians to reach London. The way to achieve Italian independence, he believed, was to assassinate Napoleon III; he designed a bomb for the purpose and commissioned a London gunsmith to make six of them. Two years later, he threw one of these devices at Napoleon III's carriage, failed to kill him, but was himself captured and guillotined. Not least of these opponents to the European order, Karl Marx lived and wrote his books in London from 1849 until his death in 1883.

A revolutionary the equal of any in dedication, Giuseppe Mazzini was only sixteen when first he was forced into exile in 1821. He had worked to establish Young Italy, a popular nationalist model later imitated by Young Turkey, Young Egypt, Young Algeria, and others. When the Austrians declared that membership of Young Italy was high treason, Mazzini found safety in London from 1836 onwards. The conservative Thomas Carlyle sympathized with Italy because it was "dismembered, scattered asunder" and he and his wife Jane were Mazzini's rather improbable friends. A *cause célèbre* erupted in 1844 when it emerged that the authorities had been intercepting Mazzini's correspondence, the equivalent at that time of telephone tapping. That same year, however, the chief minister of the Kingdom of Sardinia spoke for most Italians when he dismissed the prospect of Italian unity as a dream of "school-boys, fifth-rate poets and stump orators."

As part of the copycat political events right across Europe in
1848, revolutionaries took over the Papal States and declared the
Roman Republic in their stead. Returning to Rome, Mazzini collaborated with Garibaldi, a member like him of Young Italy, and did
what he could to establish himself in power as one of a triumvirate.
Hitherto the private property of the Whigs and the Holland House
set, revolution in Italy and the whole cause of the Risorgimento was
now approved by mainstream public opinion with unqualified enthusiasm until Italy was indeed unified. Some saw the Jacobin spirit of
1793 reviving. "Garibaldi! Garibaldi!/ Thrills the shout through
street and square,/ While the legion of the hero/ Gathers to its thun-
der there!" was one of the verses by the Reverend John Jeffrey, a fifth-
rate poet if ever there was one, in *The Red Republican,* a paper run by
the Chartist George Harney. Although a better poet and settled in
Italy, Walter Savage Landor also failed to rise to inspiration: "Rise
Garibaldi! Rise, Mazzini! . . . Strike and spare not; strike high." In the
spirit of the times, it was evidently thrilling to the point of witless-
ness to depict violence directed against the established order as liberty and the pursuit of freedom.

As in the case of Greece, so in Italy an idealized view of the classical past of Rome took hold of educated people. Wordsworth captured the mood in his poem *Memorials of a Tour in Italy:* "Awake,
Mother of Heroes, from thy death-like sleep." Felicia Hemans felt the
same: "Though dimm'd thy brightness, riveted thy chain,/ Yet, fallen
Italy! Rejoice again!/ /Lost, lovely realm! Once more 'tis thine to
gaze/ On the rich relics of sublimer days." In August 1846 Robert
and Elizabeth Barrett Browning settled into the Casa Guidi, a slightly
gloomy house on a corner near the Palazzo Pitti in Florence. Immediately she subscribed to the cause of Italian independence and its
ideological counterpart of hating Austria. Her poem *Casa Guidi Windows* contains lines as famous as they are vapid and sentimental, "I
heard last night a little child go singing/ 'neath Casa Guidi windows,
by the church,/ 'o bella libertà, O bella!'"

In the spring of 1848 the Grand Duke of Tuscany proclaimed a constitution. In the morning when Browning went to the post and to look for a newspaper, his wife would call after him, "Bring me back news of a revolution."[3] With an echo of Paris in 1789 she would tease him when they disagreed, "A bas les aristocrates!" The revolution of 1848 and the Roman Republic in fact were crushed by a French expeditionary force. Mazzini wrote to Emilie Hawke, an English sympathizer, "as true as I am living, we shall conquer them or die in a manner that will honour Rome for ever."[4] "I offer not pay, not lodging, nor provisions. I offer hunger, forced marches, battles and death," Garibaldi exclaimed in a rhetorical trope that Winston Churchill was to adapt to his purposes in 1940. In fact Mazzini and Garibaldi resumed their former existence as political exiles, embittered but safe.

One of the defenders of the doomed Roman Republic was Hugh Forbes, a character whose flamboyance and disposition to violence is reminiscent of John Oswald in the Paris of 1793. Born in 1805, Forbes went up to Oxford and at the age of twenty-one was commissioned into the Coldstream Guards. His first wife was English; he went to live in Tuscany with his second wife, an Italian. In Palermo during the events of late 1848 he attempted to raise a "British Legion" to take part in the liberation of Sicily. In the opinion of G. M. Trevelyan, in his day the historian most fully engaged in these events, Forbes was "*italianissimo* but not *simpatico*."[5] In the summer of the following year, as Trevelyan continues, Forbes took over "the unenviable command of the last forces of the Roman Republic, rapidly dissolving before the Austrian invasion of the Marches. Forbes kept order by causing thieves to wear their coats inside out as a disgrace." In the exemplary style of a Guards officer, he himself stood out by always appearing everywhere, even in battle, dressed in a fine white cotton suit and white top hat.[6] Retiring to America for a spell, he lectured in New York about Italy, and then took up the cause of emancipating the slaves. At the request of John Brown, he went west to organize for a while military resistance to the raids of the Confederates. G. M. Trevelyan finally comes to terms with this character with the statement that by the time of his death in 1892 he had laid waste his fortune on behalf of one generous cause after another, to conclude, "He was not altogether a wise man."

The 1850s for Italy were years of turbulence and high political intrigue. In London and in other cities were branches of radical bodies, the Society of the Friends of Italy, the Emancipation of Italy Fund Committee and the Garibaldi Fund Committee. The secret Treaty of Plombières between Napoleon III and Count Cavour, the chief minister of Piedmont and future prime minister of unified Italy before his sudden and premature death from a fever in June 1861, precipitated unification. France and the Italians between them were to drive the Austrians back, reach a compromise and share the spoils— namely independence and unity for Italy under King Victor Emanuel II, and territory for France. War resumed, therefore, in 1859. Ever since the failure in the previous decade of the Roman Republic, Garibaldi had been longing for such a turn of events. Cavour and Victor Emanuel II could count on the Piedmontese army. Garibaldi commanded about 3,000 volunteers known as the Cacciatori delle Alpi, though by the time fighting was over their number seems to have risen to 12,000. What might appear outwardly to have been a united nationalist movement in fact contained a power struggle between Italians with differing ambitions, and all in the context of international realpolitik.

These complexities were much simplified in the minds of anyone English who was following them. "That spring the Italian cause became fashionable in society,"[7] writes G. M. Trevelyan. "Ladies of high position learnt the language and studied the history and literature of Italy," while their husbands in Parliament listened to William Gladstone praising the Italian exiles, and then met them in the great Whig houses. In Florence, Elizabeth Barrett Browning was ecstatic, the once helpless invalid now utterly indifferent to the fact that she would feel uplifted because others were to lose their lives in the battles ahead. "Louis Napoleon has acted—I was going to say sublimely—and why should I not? Italy stretches her arms to him as to the very angel of resurrection. Emancipation was impossible without foreign help, and he brings it at all risks to himself and to France. . . . Now we shall have a free Italy. And the Italians will fight nobly. . . . Oh, it seems to me like a beautiful dream. . . . But if it were a dream the cannons would wake me."[8] Young Pen Browning, who was never quite able to outgrow the psychological demands that came from being the child of such parents, exclaimed, "If I were a great boy and I hadn't a wife, certainly I would go and fight for dear Italy." When Elizabeth Barrett Browning finally learnt that Napoleon III had acquired territory that might have been Italian, she felt betrayed and obliged Pen to remove the Napoleon medal he had pinned on his blouse. Nonetheless poems in her last volume *Songs of Congress* were still exercises in wish-fulfilment, praising the French emperor, Cavour, and Italian patriots.

Lucy Riall is the author of an enlightening book whose title *Garibaldi: Invention of a Hero* sums up its content. According to this very detailed analysis, the cause of Italian unification needed someone to personify it and Garibaldi was eminently suitable for the role. Bearded, described romantically as a "white savage" with a gentlemanly appearance, he had a striking physical presence and did nothing to hide his compulsive womanizing. Dressing the part of a guerrilla leader, he had fought in South America, and writers from Alexandre Dumas to George Sand and eventually even Joseph Conrad naturally wove myth around his person and his exploits. Here was some sort of contemporary *beau idéal*. The popular press was then beginning to print despatches and illustrations, and Garibaldi understood publicity. His red shirts were made for him by the haberdashers Thresher and Glenny in the Strand, and were as distinctive a symbol as Che Guevara's beret. To equip his men with these red shirts, and to pick them out as his Thousand, was an example of public relations quite as eye-catching as anything in Nazi Germany or the Soviet

Union, where careful thought was also applied to the design of uniforms and the naming of units.

At the head of his Cacciatori, Garibaldi resumed campaigning first in mainland Italy, then in the spring of 1860 in Sicily, and so back again to what had been the kingdom of Naples under the Bourbons, a dynasty as fossilized as the Habsburgs further north. Prematurely in June 1860 *The Times* had an article, "We publish today news which will gladden the heart of every friend of liberty in Europe. The insurrection in Sicily is fully, and we trust finally, victorious." Algernon Swinburne was among those swept away by the enthusiasm of the moment, asking, "Is Garibaldi the greatest man since Adam, or is he not?"[9] Admirers in Glasgow contributed thousands of pounds. A club in Manchester sent four hundred rifles of "first-class quality."

Lucy Riall gives many revealing examples of the quasi-religious devotion Garibaldi was arousing. Ferdinand Eber, who started as the London *Times* correspondent and ended by becoming one of Garibaldi's officers, described him in his red flannel shirt in Palermo where "The people threw themselves forward to kiss his hands, or at least to touch the hem of his garment, as if it contained the panacea for all their past and perhaps coming sufferings. Children were brought up, and mothers asked on their knees for his blessing." Charles Forbes, an English volunteer and not to be confused with the Coldstream Colonel Hugh Forbes, published an account of these experiences in 1861. He had been present when Garibaldi arrived in Messina. "There is a sort of intimate communion of mind between Garibaldi and the masses which is perfectly electrifying. They look up to him as a sort of link between themselves and the Deity." Harriet Meuricoffre, an English Protestant with a Swiss husband, wrote to her father from Naples that here was the one man in the world you would follow blindfold to death, since his "devotion to and faith in a holy cause" were "written in letters of light" on his face.[10]

The huge fan mail that Garibaldi received from England was astonishingly credulous.[11] From India Alexander Andrews wrote all in his own syntax that he longed "to join the banner of liberty under the heaven Conferred destroyer of Tyrants." A woman signing herself Violet wrote from High Wycombe to express her "deep and earnest admiration" for "the real nobility, and the pure generosity" of his character. William Rayner from Swansea compared Garibaldi to Cromwell. Also in Wales, Margaret Davies described herself as his "profound admirer" and wished to go as a nurse to his wounded soldiers. In Dublin, John Spear, "a staunch friend of Italian freedom," proposed to organize "a noble *Irish* legion." A fifteen-year-old boy, F. Keel in Birmingham, wrote asking to be allowed to join him, "for I love you as I did my parents."

Like the Philhellenes of an earlier generation, the Cacciatori included international volunteers, usually handicapped by the inability to speak Italian. Many of them had lived through the revolution of 1848 and hoped that their action now was an extension of it. There were Frenchmen and Poles, Swiss, a Hungarian Legion, and in addition a group of Americans. The Foreign Enlistment Act prohibited Englishmen from joining in, but those who wished to do so got round the Act by calling themselves "excursionists" whose purpose was merely to visit Mount Etna. They wore uniforms, they further claimed, only in order to be able to recognize each other.

A number of British subjects were well established in Sicily, and they tended to look fearfully on the fighting about to overtake them. Benjamin Ingham, a shrewd and successful businessman originally from Yorkshire, had already put on record his doubts about the popular enthusiasm in Palermo where he lived, "the letterati [*sic*] are in reality the principal authors of revolution." Admiral Codrington and the British navy had saved the Philhellene cause, and now in a comparable representation of ultimate law and order Commander Winnington-Ingram and the Argus anchored in Palermo Bay in June 1860 "to look after British interests," as he noted in his diary.

Among those Commander Winnington-Ingram met was John Peard,[12] whom he described correctly as "a Cornish gentleman of property," present in Sicily "for the mere love of fighting." In the mixture of idealism and murder in his conduct, John Whitehouse Peard indeed exemplifies the ambiguity within almost every cause of this sort. He was born in 1811, the son of Vice-Admiral Shulman Peard who had served under Nelson. In 1859 he had left his law practice in the Inner Temple in order to enlist in the Cacciatori as a private. In that year's campaign he fought with a rifle he normally used for deer-stalking. "He was a first-class shot, " according to Christopher Hibbert, "and was said to make notes of the numbers of Austrians he killed or wounded in a little black notebook." Asked about his motives for fighting, he replied, "I have a great respect for Italian independence but I am also very fond of shooting." In the manner of Colonel Hugh Forbes, he wore distinctive civilian clothes in the field until he was warned that he might be shot as a spy, whereupon he changed into a British army uniform. At the battle of Milazzo, he was observed doing "tremendous work with his sharpshooter."

A fine, soldierly man, six feet tall and fourteen stone in weight, Peard had the beard of a patriarch, which caused him to be mistaken for Garibaldi and was to earn him the title of "Garibaldi's Englishman." The press liked to play this up. On one occasion, he entered the town of Postiglione accompanied by brass bands and hundreds of cheering people, whereupon a priest assumed him to be Garibaldi, fell to his knees and welcomed him as "the second Jesus Christ." Something like 600 volunteers and excursionists finally mustered as the British Legion on the mainland for the last part of Garibaldi's campaign, and Peard was given command of them. In the book of reportage he published in 1861, Charles Forbes proved to be a reasonably objective witness of Garibaldi's campaign, and he found Peard by temperament to be cool and dispassionate. Some of the British reacted against him, however, as a "bloodthirsty man, who, unable to gratify his penchant for murders in his own country, comes out here and gloats over his victims." Wrapping up what must have been many a quarrel and much insubordination, Peard wrote to a friend, "Defend me from ever again commanding a brigade of English volunteers in a foreign country. As to the officers, many were most mutinous and some something worse."[13]

One of these officers and colleagues was John William Dunne. Garibaldi gave him too the rank of Colonel, and appointed him the first commander of the so-called British Legion. Born in 1827, Dunne had served in the British army in the Crimea, where he had commanded Turkish infantry, or Bashi Bazouks. In that war, he "displayed his wonderful powers of disciplining rough lives,"[14] in the words of an *Illustrated London News* correspondent. To Palermitans he was known as Milord, and he seemed to like to wear a thigh-length coat with astrakhan collar and cuffs. One patriot, Alberto Mario, described how Dunne would sit in a chair in the middle of the Marina dressed in a suit of Indian silk and patiently and energetically drill his troops. Another patriot wrote (I translate), "He was a strange man, I believe rather a drunkard [*un po alcolizzato*] but brave and courageous to the point of rashness." At the battle of Milazzo, for instance, some Palermitan street boys, so-called *picciotti,* under his command were taking cover under a stone wall, until Dunne came up and threw them "like puppets" bodily over it towards enemy fire. Later, at the battle of the Volturno, he was shot in the back by one of his officers because he had refused to promote the man on grounds of cowardice. He went on to fight for Denmark in its war with Prussia and then for Poland, dying in 1906. The unfortunate *picciotti* were of course expendable. Alberto Mario and his English wife née Jessie White had cared for these boys in a foundling hospital they set up in Palermo. As republicans, the two had previously been in prison. A kind of Florence Nightingale figure, in Raleigh Trevelyan's phrase, Jessie White made herself responsible for the wounded and sick during these campaigns. The house in which she lived in Florence has a memorial plaque in her honor.

Dunne's second-in-command was Major Percy Wyndham, who had the improbable distinction of having served in the French navy and the Austrian army. Daniel Dowling from Kilkenny had been with the Royal Artillery at Sebastopol in the Crimean war, and although a captain in the British army he had enlisted as a sergeant in the service of Garibaldi. Raleigh Trevelyan calls him "the most remarkable of them all," though he rather withdrew that judgment by following up with the instant qualification, "perhaps." Garibaldi promoted Dowling to be Colonel of the artillery and attached him to his staff. With Dunne were also Lieutenants Edward and Alfred Styles and Robert Walker, Cadets Henry Archer and the seventeen-year-old Alexander Patterson, someone called Clifford, and Peter Cunningham, a sailor. Colonel Hugh Forbes had the idea of sending Edward Styles back to London to help recruit for the British Legion. Styles promoted himself captain, then major, and he fabricated and sold commissions, pocketing the money. These commissions were not recognized by Peard, and when Styles was rash enough to return to Naples after the battle of the Volturno he was arrested for misappropriation of funds.

G. M. Trevelyan speaks of the "roughs" recruited from London and Glasgow, and his namesake and relation Raleigh Trevelyan dismisses the whole British Legion as "hopelessly amateur and a great liability." Another historian, Christopher Hibbert, quotes the British Minister in Naples commenting on those who had arrived there the previous day, as it happened after the fiercest of the fighting was over. "Last night," the Minister reported, "they immediately distinguished themselves in a truly national manner by getting drunk and disorderly, and in sleeping on or under the tables in the principal cafes which have today been closed in consequence." An Italian journalist, Count Arrivabene, wrote that with the exception of Peard and Lord Seymour, son of the Duke of Somerset, the British Legion "were assuredly not very manageable fellows."

The drive towards unification involved a shifting in the balance of forces within Italy. To simplify, at the end of 1860 Victor Emanuel and Cavour with a ruthless determination drove Garibaldi to retire to Caprera, the island he had bought off the coast of Sardinia. Abdication, exile, the sense that he had been a conqueror and was now a hermit, added to his aura, to a star quality that nobody else in Europe could match. In 1864 his visit to England was a triumph. In London he drew a crowd of half a million, more even than Kossuth had attracted. Lionized everywhere, he met William Gladstone, steadfast in his enthusiast for Italian unification, Lord Palmerston, Alexander Herzen and Mazzini, the poet Alfred Tennyson, Florence Nightingale, and the Prince of Wales. In Cornwall he stayed with his supporter Colonel Peard. A whole Garibaldi fashion was created, expressed in clothes, china, and songs and much else described by Lucy Riall. What seems the explanation, she goes on, is that people saw in him what they wanted to see, "a 'noble Roman,'[15] a working class radical, an English gentleman and a romantic Italian lover." He became engaged to Mrs. Emma Roberts. Ladies including duchesses wrote to him with scarcely veiled sexuality. Queen Victoria was glad to see him leave, however, Disraeli refused to meet him, and Karl Marx, always selective in the nationalisms he endorsed, mocked him as a donkey.

The reaction to Garibaldi shows the hold that causes acquire on the imagination. Did those hundreds of thousands of British men and women who mobbed him really care so profoundly about Italian unification? Were they so many Peards? What did they know about Massimo d'Azeglio, Bettino Ricasoli, or King Victor Emanuel jostling for power back in the country of Garibaldi's exploits? His success or failure does not really come into it. Realistically Garibaldi was responsible for quite a lot of death and much politicking, but the people crowding and cheering in the streets needed to ignore that because they saw in him hope for a better life, which of course he was in no position to provide for them. To that extent, they were their own dupes.

For liberals and radicals Garibaldi came to exemplify hope for a better life, although this was always tantalizingly out of reach, mirage-like. Weighing up Garibaldi long after the man was dead and could be judged objectively, G. M. Trevelyan, a conspicuously intelligent man, could write as though in absolute thrall to his emotions, in the process consolidating what is a romanticized historical picture. For him, Garibaldi had raised "the story of Italian freedom to a pinnacle of history far above common nationalist struggles [to make it] a part of the imperishable and international poetry of the European races." Garibaldi was "the synonym of simple heroism," and his was "the most romantic life that history records." He resembled "a perfect type of ancient Greek beauty, and lit up with that serene and simple regard of fortitude and faith which gave him power to lead the feeble multitudes of mortal men." Historians today perpetuate the memory of the man and the cause with only slightly diminished transcendence: "No other figure in the nineteenth century, save perhaps Napoleon, entered the realm of legend as swiftly as Giuseppe Garibaldi."[16] This particular encomium goes on to speak of "His expedition to Sicily in 1860, when, most wondrously of all, his thousand or so volunteers, the *Mille,* defeated the regular Neapolitan army and so made possible the creation of a united Italy. His humble origins, candour, modesty, courage, generosity and utter incorruptibility marked him out as a popular hero, a saint, a second Christ."

The American Civil War gave rise to another romanticized historical picture. A lobby in England defended the Confederate cause on the grounds that it was a last bastion of the good old agrarian life based on landed estates and now menaced everywhere by the industrial revolution and the unfeeling social relationships developing from it. An Irish landlord, Sir William Gregory, and half a dozen other members of Parliament campaigned for the recognition of the Confederacy. James Spencer, a prominent industrialist in Liverpool, was the Confederacy's financial agent in England, and Henry Hotze was its commercial agent and a leading propagandist at the same time.

Those who travelled to the United States in support of the Confederates were mostly military men, well connected, priding themselves on taking a stand for aristocratic or traditional values. Colonel Edward Bruce Hamley, a military strategist, and Colonel Garnet Wolseley (later the general commanding the expedition to avenge Gordon in the Sudan) observed the Confederates in action and published reports that identified whole-heartedly with them. George Alfred Lawrence, a popular novelist, hoped to join the Army of Northern Virginia as a staff officer, but was captured, held for eight months, and then deported. C. J. Cridland, the acting British consul in Richmond, Virginia, put his position at risk by playing host to British officers, among them Captain Fitzgerald Ross, an English cavalryman in the army of the Habsburgs (and therefore wearing a Hungarian Hussar uniform), Colonel Arthur Fremantle of the Coldstream Guards, and Colonel George Gordon. Captain Edward Wynne of the Grenadier Guards was arrested by the Northerners as a spy. Colonel George St. Leger Grenfell served with General Jeb Stuart as an inspector, and Lord Edward St. Mawr fought alongside General Longstreet in the Seven Days' Battle, as did Captain Francis Dawson. Charles Augustus Hobart-Hampden, son of the Duke of Buckingham, helped run the blockade imposed by the Federals, explaining in his autobiography *Sketches from My Life* how the enthusiasm of the Confederates had carried him and others away: "We could not believe that men who were fighting and enduring as these men could ever be beaten."

During the Crimean War, *The Times* correspondent William Howard Russell had been the first journalist to bring up-to-the-minute news to readers by means of the telegram, then a technological novelty. In March 1861, this famous figure reached New York and was to cover the Civil War for the next thirty months, always from the point of view of the South. His replacement, Frank Lawley, also a fine descriptive writer, was even more biased in favor of the Confederacy. A handsome and charming man, he admired the top civilian and military circles and took his place among them. The son of Lord Wenlock, he had enjoyed a brilliant start as a young man, becoming

Gladstone's private secretary. Caught in insider trading on the stock exchange, he was disgraced and obliged to change his career. W. Stanley Hoole, the author of *Lawley Covers the Confederacy,* portrays him in the field, "constantly with the Confederate fighting men, sharing their joys and sorrows, eating at their tables, sleeping in their tents, warming by their campfires, marching, foraging, singing, helping the wounded and comforting the dying." Lawley published about a hundred long despatches in *The Times,* steadily refusing to consider in public the possibility of Southern defeat. To Sir William Gregory in private, however, he admitted that he had misrepresented the fighting qualities of the Northerners.

The same aura of glamour and sacrifice attaches to winners who fought for a united Italy and losers who at that very same moment were fighting against a united America, a strange contrast that speaks volumes about the way those with the skills for it succeed in manipulating public opinion.

CHAPTER SEVEN

Pasha Inglesi

G. M. Young, the eminent historian of Victorian England, floated the thought that the best moment to be born English was in 1840. A period was opening when these fortunate Victorians had the world at their feet. Enlarging steadily and at relatively little cost, the Empire offered fame and fortune. Moreover, a man-of-war flying the White Ensign was likely to be on station in the nearest port, with a British consul conveniently on shore. Economic, military, and naval power induced in many the belief that they could do whatever they might set their minds on. Those who had the status and the means were able to give free rein to their predilections and prejudices in pretty well any country of their choice. As a rule, a private income underwrote the astonishing freedom of action enjoyed by so many varied and colourful British men and women, and with it, of course, went absolute confidence in their own identity.

Given these characteristics, foreigners for the most part were to be seen as heirs to a defective and indeed inferior identity that was in need of urgent reform to raise it up to British standards. Whether out of sentimentality, exoticism, or sheer contrariness, some quite differently felt that the identity of foreigners was valuable in itself and ought to be protected, even occasionally adopted. The more foreign custom differed from British, the greater the protection it required.

This was the soil in which many a cause could take root. Those with these attitudes were almost always a danger to themselves and those they purported to be saving.

The Ottoman Turks were foreigners *par excellence,* they did everything very differently, but they were close by, just on the far side of European borders right up against the empires of the Habsburgs and the Russian Tsars. Familiarity with the Turks certainly bred contempt. Ottoman subjects, at least the Christians among them, demanded rights, autonomy, independence for their nation, only to be met by massacre, as the Greeks had been. Travelers, diplomats, and politicians took the view that the Ottoman system of government had to be reformed radically, if not swept away. *The Turks in Europe* was the title of a polemic that appeared in 1853 by Bayle St. John, a fellow of a Cambridge college, and completely representative of informed opinion at that time: "It is absurd that the whole of Europe should be periodically kept in hot water . . . because a race of barbarians . . . now finds itself too weak for independent existence." He went on, "Statesmen have now given up all idea of even staying the progress of decay for a limited period."

David Urquhart might well have earned a place in the great gallery of British eccentrics even if he had not campaigned on behalf of the Ottomans. Born in 1805, he was the second son of the second wife of a Scottish laird. Inspired like other Philhellenes by a classical education, he had set off for Greece in 1827 and served on board ship with Frank Abney Hastings until wounded in battle by the Turks. The following year, he traveled through Greece and into Turkey, on the way reversing his emotional allegiances. When he had landed in Greece, he recorded in his two-volume book *The Spirit of the East,* he had been filled with hatred and aversion for the Turks, and "with the enthusiasm of youthful feeling, I became a partisan. But the Ottoman, who had aroused this animosity by the violence of triumph, dispelled it when he appeared in defeat and captivity—a personification of stoical firmness and of dignified resignation. The sympathy which is the tribute of misfortune, I now transferred to the vanquished."[1]

A Russian fleet had participated at Navarino, and Russia was threatening the integrity of the Ottoman Empire. What began as fellow-feeling for the underdog turned into the cause of defending the Ottomans. Well-connected young men could then associate in one capacity or another with the embassy, and Urquhart soon had a role as a confidential agent and then a secretary to the British ambassador in Istanbul. The Foreign Secretary, Lord Palmerston, sent him on a trade mission round the country in 1833 with samples of English merchandise that cost the Exchequer the huge sum of £1,200. The following year, he traveled to the settlements of Circassians—as Chechens were then generically described—north of the Black Sea, within the Russian empire. Muslims, the Circassians were complaining of ill-treatment at the hands of the Tsars. Shamil, their imam and military commander, was leading a prolonged and last-ditch fight for independence. The Foreign Office was persuaded to subsidize the occasional issues of Urquhart's publication, "The Portfolio." In one of its issues he spoke in his usual quixotic way of the noble Circassians, who needed defending because they "possessed the key to the happiness of mankind." He was to found a Circassian committee to promote their cause.[2]

Thanks to his social connections and in particular friendship with Sir Herbert Taylor, the private secretary of King William IV, one of his memoranda was read aloud to that monarch back in London. Karl Marx was also intrigued by Urquhart's carry-on. The two met as friends, and corresponded. In *The Eastern Question* Marx made the observation, "If Mr Urquhart were not a British subject, he would decidedly prefer being a Turk; if he was not a Presbyterian Calvinist, he would not belong to any other religion than Islam."[3] Geoffrey Nash, the author of a specialist study, points out that for Urquhart the difference between Protestantism and Islam rested on the Muslim declaration of faith and the Prophet's claim of finality, neither of which were insuperable barriers between the two religions.

Geoffrey Nash makes a great deal of Urquhart's determination to
"live like a Turk among the Turks,"[4] in particular stressing his adoption of Turkish dress as "cross-cultural." His position had given him
access to the Sultan Mahmud II and the Grand Vizier, Reshid Pasha,
and perhaps Urquhart had expectations of entering their service, as
an increasing number of Englishmen were to do. A letter in *The Times*
on 2 May 1837 mocked Urquhart's "affectation of Turkish customs
and his associations with the eunuchs of the Seraglio instead of such
of the better-informed Europeans whom he might select, his primitive preference of fingers for the purposes usually performed by
knives and forks, his assuming the designation of Daoud Bey and a
thousand other conceits he has adopted."[5] One quirk among others
was to walk barefoot. The ambassador, Charles Ponsonby, soon had
had enough of what he took to be Urquhart's play-acting as Daoud
Bey, and Palmerston recalled this impulsive and unmanageable secretary of his.

Preposterous as he was in many ways, deluded by self-impor-
tance, Urquhart nonetheless had pertinent things to say in *The Spirit
of the East*. Ottoman Turkey was a despotism, he conceded, but Turks
had such long practice in steering through the tyranny of one-man
rule that the society did function according to its own lights, and
even had its version of tolerance. If introduced, the rule of law would
seem harsh and inflexible to people accustomed to the old ways of
getting round officials by bargaining or buying them off. Urquhart
objected to the almost universal demands for reforming the
Ottoman Empire from top to bottom: "Wherever manners, customs, laws, institutions, are touched, evil is done, and danger created." The Turk, he conceded, was far below his European
counterpart in terms of capacity, but "above any of them in his
domestic virtues or his social integrity." A proto-Islamist, then, he
was one of the first to maintain that reform should mean a return to
"ancient rule" and authenticity rather than mimicry of European
models.

Palmerston carefully calculated that the weakening of Turkey was not in Britain's interest, necessarily carrying the risk of confrontation between the great powers over the division of the spoils of the collapsing empire. Back in London, Urquhart completely ignored the government's rather balanced policy to keep the peace in his zeal to get his own back on Palmerston. Russia was the enemy of his friend Turkey, and therefore his enemy too. His Russia was capable of unlimited perfidy. He popularized the fear that Russia intended to capture and hold Constantinople and the Dardanelles. In pamphlets and letters to newspapers, he accused Palmerston of failing to support Turkey fully because he was a paid agent of the Tsar's. In a letter to Lord Melbourne, the Prime Minister, he accused Palmerston of high treason. Elected to Parliament in 1847 and nominally a Conservative, he became a celebrity throughout Europe for his campaign against Russia, giving the impression that "he might have been the messiah of a religious revival."[6] The Chartist movement in his view was a Russian plot to incite an uprising designed to paralyze Britain as a preliminary to the conquest of Europe by Tsardom, and he wrote an angry letter of denunciation to the Home Secretary Lord Normanby. He went to Lebanon to protest against the Anglo-French proposals that weakened the Ottoman hold there. On behalf of his Circassian committee, he sent a detachment with rifles and six field-guns to the Black Sea to spend six months fighting for the cause. All in all, as Geoffrey Nash sums up, Urquhart was a man alienated from his own nation, and founder of "a school proclaiming a narrative of betrayal."[7]

A far more temperate personality, Sir Adolphus Slade nonetheless came to see the plight of the Ottomans in much the same perspective as Urquhart. After a career as a rear-admiral in the British navy, he became an advisor to the commander of the Ottoman navy. On the title page of his books he put in print his new name and rank of Mushaver Pasha under his original English name and rank. He made a point of noting how a fellow British admiral, Sir T. Malcolm, marked his warship's entry to the Bosphorus correctly by firing a nineteen-gun salute. He had no illusions about his adopted country. Once he had witnessed the beheading of a young man in the street, and "No sight ever made so painful an impression on my mind." The Turkish Empire was crumbling to pieces, and the stability of the old order was better than the insecurity and war he could foresee. Wrenching Greece away was "a mortal stroke to the Sultan, because it established a precedent for successful revolt, which will be acted on."[8] In old days, Turkey had governed itself in its own way and fought its own battles unaided, giving rise to national pride. The best of the Turks were "loyal without flattery, hospitable without ostentation, self-respectful without arrogance"[9] and they might have developed an Eastern civilization, adapting existing institutions to modern requirements. Now instead, "In servile admiration of every European fashion, Turkey abandoned much of what was suitable in its own system and borrowed much of the unsuitable from Europe." The imposition of reform was against the wishes of the majority and therefore not liberal at all but an act of pure despotism. A hundred and fifty years later, as Turkey struggles to adapt to the demands of the European Union, that paradox has still not been unraveled.

The Victorian ruling class took to the business of ordering the world as though by right. The range of a career like Laurence Oliphant's is nonetheless outstanding even by the standards of that age. To his generation, writes Anne Taylor in her careful biography of Oliphant, he was one of the most fascinating men, someone who had observed at close quarters many of the significant events of his time. The Oliphants were an ancient Scottish family from Condie in Perthshire. Born in 1829, the young Laurence never really settled anywhere. His father, Sir Anthony, had been first Attorney General of South Africa and then Chief Justice of Ceylon. Obsessed with religion, they were Irvingites, that is to say followers of Edward Irving, an eccentric clergyman who built his own church in London and preached that the Second Coming of Christ was imminent.

Nevertheless, their social position was impregnable. Queen Victoria enjoyed Laurence Oliphant's company and invited him to royal residences, and for a while he was a Liberal Member of Parliament of whom great things were expected.

Laurence Oliphant happened to be with his parents in Rome when the 1848 revolution broke out and he saw the Pope blessing volunteers off to fight the Austrians. It was his first experience of nationalism, says Anne Taylor, and this was to be the organizing principle he strove to advance for other people "with all the fervour at his command."[10] He went about it by having access as a social equal to ministers in London and ambassadors abroad. His first book, *The Russian Shores of the Black Sea,* published in 1853, went over some of the same ground as Urquhart.

Muslim resistance to Russia and allegiance to the Turkish Sultan in his role as Caliph impressed him too. Then as secretary to Lord Elgin on a mission to Canada, he found himself Superintendent of Indian Affairs, taking up the cause of the Chippewa. Next he went with a consignment of arms and a party of international mercenaries to Nicaragua, where William Walker, an American journalist, was trying to set himself up as dictator. Walker was executed and Oliphant got a book out of it, *Patriots and Filibusters.* Again on a mission with Lord Elgin, Oliphant went to China and was present at the bombardment of Canton. Further adventures in Japan followed.

In Italy in 1860, he took a train journey with Garibaldi at the point when the latter was deciding to go to Sicily. In a letter Oliphant wrote, "Why I should take such an intense interest in affairs that don't concern me I don't know, except that I cannot stand by and see a good cause ruined. . . . I have got him [Garibaldi] regularly in tow, but cannot din the only practical plan for the salvation of his country into his head."[11] In the course of a train journey they took together, Garibaldi offered to take him to Sicily and it was afterwards the regret of Oliphant's life that, owing to engagements at home, he had refused the chance of representing England among "the Thousand."[12]

When the Polish insurrection of 1863 broke out, Oliphant wrote, "I had by this time acquired a habit of fishing in troubled waters, I determined to go and see it."[13] Perhaps more revealingly he asked, "Instead of plunging into the centre of Africa to discover the sources of the Nile like Speke and Grant why not dive into the sources of revolutions?" To be in the forest listening to partisans singing the Polish national anthem moved him deeply. Anne Taylor says that the Foreign Secretary in fact had sent him to Poland, which would make of him some sort of secret agent. *The Times* commissioned him to cover the Franco-Prussian war of 1870.

With self-awareness, he had once written to his mother that he longed for a creed to which he could commit himself whole-heartedly: "It must invade with overwhelming force a man's whole nature, obliging him by its purity and the strength of its appeal to his convictions to recognise the truth."[14] His Irvingite religious upbringing seems to have led him to become a follower of Thomas Lake Harris, the founder of a community or Brotherhood at Brocton on the shores of Lake Erie. Whether or not Harris was a mystic in any genuine sense, he was certainly a crook, and increasingly deranged by sexuality. Association with this unsavory character did Oliphant great harm by destroying his credibility.

One last cause occupied the end of his life: the settlement of Jews in what was then the Ottoman province of Palestine. He put this proto-Zionism to Prime Minister Disraeli and Foreign Secretary Lord Salisbury, as well as members of the royal family. He did the same with Midhat Pasha, Sultan Abdul Hamid's former Grand Vizier, disgraced for showing too great an enthusiasm for reforming the Empire on lines demanded by the great powers, exiled and strangled on orders of the Sultan. In Constantinople, the ambassador, Sir Henry Layard, eventually arranged for Oliphant to meet the Sultan. Nothing came of it. In 1882, in what became known as the first aliyah, or immigration, Jews were already escaping to Palestine from persecution in Russia. Oliphant settled in a Druse village near Haifa in that same moment and lived there until his death, actively but improbably supporting the Jewish national revival.

The Crimean War had done nothing to settle the expansion of Russia or the internal confusion of the Ottoman Empire. War between these two uneven powers broke out in again in 1876, and the subsequent fighting was particularly brutal. The whole region was destabilized as the various ethnicities that had previously been subjected to Ottoman rule saw their chance of independence, and national movements mobilized to fight for it. In repeated atrocities, Muslim Turkish soldiers massacred Christian communities mostly consisting of defenseless peasants who almost all had no real understanding of the national sentiments with which they were being credited. Dorothy Anderson has described how for the British public there followed "two years' concentrated interest in all aspects of Turkey and her subject races, the Bulgarians, the Serbians, the Bosnians, the Montenegrins; it was a period of deep moral indignation, of bitter personal invective, of wild political theorising, and of generous giving. There was a great divide: people were Turkophile, 'home-Turks,' 'philo-Turks,' Russophobists, readers of the *Daily Telegraph* and the *Standard,* supporters of the Prime Minister and his government' policy; or they were Russophiles, Turcophobes, 'Muscovites,' the ardent believers in everything the *Daily News* printed about the unspeakable Turk, supporters of Gladstone's attacks against the barbarities of Turkish misrule."[15]

While campaigning in a general election, William Gladstone had denounced the Turks in word and print. In his pamphlet *Bulgarian Horrors* he wrote that the Turks "were, upon the whole, from the black day when they first entered Europe, the one great anti-human specimen of humanity. Wherever they went, a broad line of blood marked the track behind them." The galvanizing effect on public opinion was matched only when Winston Churchill spoke to the nation in the Second World War. Gladstone's moral onslaught inhibited Disraeli and Lord Salisbury for the Conservatives from putting up the political defense of Turkey, never mind take military measures. Dorothy Anderson singles out the distinguished historian Professor E. A. Freeman as so venomous in his condemnation of the Turks and Conservative policy that he had become "obsessional."

Viscountess Strangford set up the Bulgarian Peasant Relief Fund, and then the British Hospital and Ambulance Fund for the Sick and Wounded, therefore including Turks in need. She defended helping both sides by asking, "Is not humanity better than neutrality?"[16] Four relief bodies, namely Stafford House run by upper-class ladies, the National Aid Society, the Red Crescent, and the Turkish Compassionate Fund, between them sent 105 doctors into the field. Men and women from all walks of life rushed out to the Balkans. Dr. Humphrey Sandwich had lived in Serbia, and hurried there when Serbia declared war on Turkey. Lieutenant Philip Salusbury of the Light Infantry, aged twenty-one, went to Belgrade to join the Serbian army with the idea, "that having nothing particular to do, I might gain some experience of real warfare." Among others were Emma Pearson and Louisa McLaughlin, both nurses, two Scottish members of Parliament, and Colonel Robert McIver, a professional soldier now raising a cavalry troop for the Serbian army. Journalists benefited from the new technology of the telegraph. The *Daily News* had as many as seventeen correspondents including Edmund O'Donovan and the intrepid American J. A. MacGahan, covering from Constantinople, Bucharest, Adrianople, and Erzeroum, while the paper's star, Archibald Forbes, was with the Russians.

Edward Vizetelly appears to have taken up the Turkish cause out of sheer bravado. His autobiography, *The Reminiscences of a Bashi-Bazouk,* is an exercise in self-congratulation. Brother of the better-known Frank Vizetelly of the *Illustrated London News,* he had been a journalist, and seen some fighting in France and Algeria. In the autumn of 1876 when yet again the Russians and the Turks were fighting, he writes, "I was weary of Fleet Street and the Strand, and thirsting for activity and more adventure. I remembered, as a child, the Crimean War, with bread at a shilling the quartern loaf, and hated the Russians. I determined to travel eastward and enlist in the Sultan's service." When he landed in Constantinople he had "half a mind to become a Mohammedan, and say goodbye to Western Europe." In his boarding house were Hungarians, Poles, Frenchmen, Germans, Swiss, Italians, Carlists, Communists, and other Revolutionists, all seeking occupation and excitement, wishing to enrol in the Ottoman army and proceed to the front: "Owing to questions of religion and language, which were fatal obstacles, very little encouragement was given them by the Turks."[17] He had no doubt that he was doing the Turks a favour: "In those days the name of Englishman was respected throughout the length and breath of the Ottoman Empire."

On the way to the front, Vizetelly met a young Scotsman named Cowan, who had been travelling for some English firm in the Danubian States and was drawn by rumors of the war. At Trebizond on the Black Sea, he and Cowan joined up with Circassian irregulars, perceived as admirable for "their bravery, independence, and intense love of freedom." Soon Vizetelly was able to dress for the part he was playing, his head shaved, and wearing "a kaftan in pure home-spun wool, with breeches to match, tapering at the ends, which were tucked into my boots." He was also pleased to note a broad-bladed knife with a double edge, as well as a saber with a yataghan handle in silver-work from the Caucasus. The theatricality of his prose speaks for itself. "When the last of our men had ridden into Illidjah in the morning, and all were in the saddle, we formed into column four deep. Hassan and Youssouf Bey placed themselves at the head of the regiment, side by side; next came all the Deré Beys, then the standard-bearers, with the green and crimson banners taken from the mosque at Trebizond, and now unfurled for the first time; immediately behind the colours Cowan and myself, and following us the twelve hundred Circassian Bashi-Bazouks. In this order, we marched to Erzeroum."

In that city, Vizetelly met up with the British consul, James Zohrab, and a key figure in the unfolding of events. The consul, he noted with some satisfaction, "regarded me as little better than a cut-throat, and that if I was caught and hanged it would serve me right." Cowan, on the other hand, had little distinction, drab in his fez and tweed suit. Moving on, Vizetelly and the Circassians settled in tents at the extremity of the Turkish camp on the northern side of the Aladjah Dagh, near Kars. He found himself close to Sir Arnold Kemball, the British military attaché, his aide-de-camp Lieutenant Dougall of the Royal Navy, and Captain Norman, the correspondent of *The Times:* "These three gentlemen lived and messed together in a little camp of their own."

Vizetelly was where he wanted to be, at the center of drama. He could pay tribute to the brilliant defense of Kars by Sir Fenwick Williams, a senior British soldier in the Ottoman service. Somehow he lost contact with Cowan, and seems to have been reluctant to oppose the invading Russians when it came to that. Three of his Circassians then robbed an Armenian priest, shot him, and raped the women with him. They were hanged for these crimes, whereupon all the others, over a thousand in all, defected and went home. At Kars, besieged by the Russian army, some Turks tried to push Vizetelly to "duty in the casemates" which presumably would have involved him in fighting at close quarters. "That sort of occupation would not have suited me at all," he had the honesty to admit. Instead he spurred away on his horse, knocking down a sergeant and shouting "Pasha Inglesi!" intending to convey that he belonged to the escort of the English General Sir Fenwick Williams.

In Kars he again contrived to lose contact with his companion Cowan, who was ill in hospital and therefore should have been easy to track down. Vizetelly was breezy about him: "God Almighty had not blessed him with the right kind of bones and vital organs,"[18] and besides the poor chap was "troubled with a voracious appetite." Vizetelly left the city to return to Erzeroum where he spent three months, earning money by writing for a London newspaper. Involvement with the Ottoman cause had brought him a high degree of self-

promotion and show-off, and encouraged him to adopt local prejudices that by the time his memoir was published were about to erupt
in killing on a scale not yet experienced. The Turkish masses, he concluded from such contact as he had had with them, exhibited "a
quiet, heroic patience worthy of the Osmanli race" while in contrast
"The Armenian has all the vices of the Turk and not one of his qualities He is, moreover, cowardly, cringing, fawning, deceitful, prover-
bially dishonest, and the most shame-faced liar."[19] Qualifying for
some of these descriptive adjectives, Vizetelly had also left the unfortunate Cowan to die of dysentery.

"It would appear that there is a quality in some Englishmen that is
rarely possessed by men of other nations, which produces unique relations between themselves and the people of the East," so wrote
Aubrey Herbert in his autobiography *Ben Kendim* (Turkish for "myself
alone"), subtitled *A Record of Eastern Travel* and published posthumously
in 1924.[20] Framing that opinion, was he simply but perhaps unconsciously boasting that there were plenty of Englishmen like himself, at
the center of the world's stage with the license of the British Empire
to cast themselves into leading roles? Born in 1880, Herbert was the
younger son of the fourth Earl of Carnarvon, that is to say a member
of a conspicuously rich and aristocratic family. Educated at Eton and
Oxford, he soon made his mark on his generation. Poor eyesight and
maternal pressure stopped him going to fight in the Boer war. He had
a picturesque view of foreigners, seeing them in the colors of his
imagination, itself the product of power and privilege. Aesthetic judgments about how they looked, how they dressed, how they handled
themselves, flowed into political judgments. Writing his biography,
Margaret FitzHerbert, a grand-daughter of his, characterized him as a
throwback to his own grandfather, the third Earl of Carnarvon, quite
a model of eccentricity: "A keen observer of revolutions, he traveled
from one European disturbance to another. At Nice he harangued a
revolutionary mob in French. In Genoa he was nearly killed in a political brawl; in Spain he was captured by Catalan guerrillas; in Paris he

fought a duel."[21] Herbert's half-brother, the fifth Earl, financed the
excavations of Tutankhamun's tomb in Egypt.

Aubrey Herbert began his career as an honorary attaché in the
British embassy in Tokyo. There was no permanent attraction for an
Englishman in that country, he thought, unless he became a Japanese
scholar, and then outright Japanese. So he applied for the same sort
of position in the embassy in Constantinople. The Near East offered
"sufficient uncertainty to excite the imagination of any young man."
At the outset, he shared the conventional prejudice of most English
people, scandalized by the recurrent massacres of Christians in
Ottoman-ruled provinces: "Turkey seemed to me to be an Empire
whose foundations were rooted in iniquity."[22] He began to travel
through outlying parts of that empire, discovering new ethnicities to
admire. Cretans carried their weapons with pride and elegance; they
seemed the heroic descendants of the men who had fought the Turks
in Greece. In Macedonia he felt for the first time the fascination of
contact with the Balkans. In Salonika in 1904 he met a wild Albanian
highlander named Kiazim, described as Riza in *Ben Kendim*. The
Turkish authorities had exiled him for killing a man in a blood feud,
and he now became Herbert's guide, bodyguard, and servant.
Brought to England and to Pixton, the Herberts' large country
house, Kiazim donned national dress, a spotless fustanella with jew-
eled pistol and dagger in his scarlet sash.

Friendship with the Sultan's brother-in-law and other Western-
ized Turks was a first step in reversing Herbert's antagonism. In
Yemen he found himself on a long march with Turkish soldiers in a
landscape full of skeletons from recent fighting. Margaret FitzHerbert comments, "It was on this march that his love and admiration for
the Turkish race blossomed . . . his companions, far from their homeland, stolid and sturdy in their suffering, generous in their poverty,
and comradely to the stranger, won him to their cause, and he
became henceforth their champion and defender."

To friends and contemporaries, for instance Raymond Asquith, the son of Prime Minister Asquith, he appeared a misguided Turcophile and therefore by definition an enemy of the Greeks. Turcophile he might be, but at the same time, and perhaps involuntarily, he was making a personal contribution to the final stages of Ottoman disintegration. In 1907 he and his henchman Kiazim went to Albania. The expedition was not a success, but from then on Herbert took up single-mindedly the cause of Albanian nationalism. The impulse was fanciful, devoid of principle. Albanians, he thought, "have always been and are passionate lovers of their soil . . . they have a charm that is their own, and their land has an almost magical attraction."[23] The country might be rough and lawless but the people esteemed truth, courage, and fidelity. It was a strange apologia to say that "if men died a violent death by the wayside, there was no petty larceny." How this identification with Albania was to be squared with his pro-Turkish stance was never explained. The revolutionary events of 1908 and 1909 brought the downfall of the reigning Sultan Abdul Hamid and the installation of the Young Turks, irrevocably pushing the Ottoman Empire towards its disastrous end.

In 1911 Herbert was elected to Parliament as a Conservative. The following year he returned to Albania, then in full revolt against their Ottoman overlords. One night, he met an Albanian chieftain by the name of Issa Bey Bolletin (he spells the name Boletin), reputed to have 20,000 men at his command, "wild Albanian mountaineers, covered with weapons. They made a fine picture in the moonlight. . . . I found Issa Bolletin, a very tall, lithe, well-made Albanian, aquiline, with restless eyes and a handsome fierce face, in the Gheg dress." An uneducated man, Bolletin was "the Robin Hood of Albania." He asked if Herbert would do what he could to help the Albanian people. "I said that I would most gladly do all in my power, because I admired the Albanian people."[24] Shots then rang outside the house they were in, and the way the clansmen gathered round Bol-

letin confirmed Herbert's admiration of them. Excitement and conspiracy evidently suited his temperament.

Back in London, true to form in the launching of these foreign
causes, Herbert formed an Albanian Committee. The public had a
very limited knowledge of Albania, and the committee was not in a
position to do much about that. Besides Herbert, only one other of
its members, a Major Paget, had actually been to Albania. Its eventual
secretary, Edith Durham, was a Balkans specialist who had traveled
extensively in areas which others considered too dangerous to
explore. In a letter to his wife, Herbert described her and her dedication to the Albanian cause: "She cuts her hair short as a man, has a
cockney accent and a roving eye, is clever, aggressive and competitive
but she has really done a lot for these people."[25] In her polemics
Durham did not hesitate to come out with phrases like the "Serb ver-
min," which led the pro-Serb Rebecca West to write her off as
belonging to the class of Balkan travelers who come back with their
pet people, established in their hearts as "suffering and innocent,
eternally the massacree and never the massacrer." Edith Durham's
general view was that the Balkan wars then breaking out might
appear to be religious because Christians and Muslims were mas-
sacring one another, but fundamentally they were national in character, being so many revolts against Ottoman rule. Observing people
and places, she had an eye for the telling detail. Among her several
books is *The Burden of the Balkans,* published in 1905, with a section of
over a hundred pages vividly presenting Albanian history and society.
In another book, *High Albania* published in 1909, she acknowledged
that she was indeed something of a legend in that country: "It is an
awful responsibility—to be fallen in love with by a whole nation."[26]

Herbert made repeated speeches in the House of Commons in
favor of Albanian independence. Receiving a delegation of Albanians
in London, he took them to the House of Commons, and introduced
Issa Bolletin to Lloyd George, then Chancellor of the Exchequer. The
Albanians had no international representative or support except

Herbert and his Committee, and so when they wanted a king to rule the country after liberation another delegation sent to London in 1913 offered him the position. To his mother he wrote, "If I had fifty thousand a year, I think I should take Albania." To a romantic like him, "the appeal of thrones, chieftains, bandits, dangerous territory and fierce loyalties was almost irresistible. He could, however, see that the financial drawback was insurmountable. He was, quite simply, not rich enough to be a king."[27]

Because of his experience of Turkey and the Turks, Herbert was appointed Liaison Officer and Interpreter on the staff of the New Zealander General Godley at Gallipoli. His published diaries show how horrifying the fighting was, and the danger he was in of being killed at any moment. Humiliation followed when he was posted to Mesopotamia at a time when British forces under General Townshend were trapped by the Turks at Kut al-Amara with no possibility either of reinforcements or of breaking out. Herbert was one of those who had to negotiate the surrender. Reaching the Turkish camp, he recognized an officer and asked where they had last met, to be told, "At a dance at the British Embassy." His sympathies for the Turks were of course known widely and resented. Lord Bertie, the British ambassador in Paris, described him as a "dangerous pacifist Turcophile lunatic in khaki."[28] His own half-brother, Lord Carnarvon, rebuked him. "You must not only see through Turkish glasses. Remember they have *not* behaved well to England and that you are an Englishman first and as far as I know with no drop of Turkish blood."[29] An Oxford friend and contemporary, the novelist and politician John Buchan, took the opposite view and used him and his deeds as the model for Sandy Arbuthnot, the hero of his First World War thriller *Greenmantle,* a character who knows the ways and the languages of foreigners so well that he is able to pass himself off undetected among them. To Buchan, the real Aubrey Herbert was "a sort of survivor from crusader times."

Aubrey Herbert's premature death from blood poisoning in 1923 at the age of forty-three fixed an aura of romanticizing around him.

Had the Albanian fantasy paid off, he would in fact have found himself ruler of a country divided by religion, in the grip of tribal custom including the blood feud, and devoid of the resources necessary for a modern society. He was inviting disaster. Worse still, in the event of a long life he would have been swept away by Mussolini and Italian ambitions, as happened to Ahmed Zogu, the Albanian unfortunate enough to become King of the country.

CHAPTER EIGHT

"Those Poor Armenians"

U ntil the Middle Ages Armenia had been an independent
kingdom in the Caucasus, its borders expanding or
shrinking between the Black Sea and the Caspian Sea.
Inviting sympathy, the Armenians were numerically a small but
defensive people with a distinctive language, alphabet, and culture—
Byron had asked Armenian monks in Venice to teach him their language. Moreover they were a Christian minority amid surrounding
Muslims. After the fall of Byzantium, many became Ottoman subjects, and as such were organized into a millet, according to the system of the Ottoman empire that gave autonomy to ethnic and
religious minorities. In 1600, there were virtually no Armenians in
Smyrna, for example, but by 1650 several thousand had settled to
serve other Christians in the Street of the Franks there. So well did
the millet system work that Armenians were known in the empire as
"the faithful community." A number rose high in the Sultan's service.
They were, however, cut off from Armenians in that part of the original kingdom annexed by Russia, and from yet other compatriots in
Persia. A colorful figure, Joseph Emin, an Armenian and friend of
Burke and the great linguist Sir William Jones, published a book in
1792 recommending transplanting an English-style constitution to
Armenia

In "Minorities," one of the most eloquent essays in *The Chatham House Version,* Elie Kedourie has condemned the nationalism that spread from Europe to the Ottoman Empire and then beyond it as an alien imposition, an agent of change that could not be accommodated without distress, "A rash, a malady, an infection . . . eating up the fabric of settled society."[1] In the aftermath of Russian victory in the 1877 war with Turkey, and then the weakening of the Ottoman Empire through international treaties, a handful of Armenians launched what today would be considered a national liberation movement. During the 1880s Armenians within Ottoman Turkey and Russia began to form the Dashnaks and Hunchaks, political parties that were in the nature of secret societies. Influenced by Marxism and the Nihilist terrorism then dominating political life in Russia, these Armenians acted in the belief that violence must create conditions so unstable that the Great Powers would be obliged to intervene. The consequence, they imagined, would be independence for a revolutionary and socialist Armenia. Why the Turks or the Russians and then the Great Powers might be willing to grant the Armenians freedom to achieve these ends was left unexamined. In what they deemed was a progressive nationalist spirit, Dashnaks and Hunchaks were prepared to murder other Armenians who stood in their way or remained loyal to the Ottoman Empire, to attack the Turkish military or gendarmerie, to rob banks, and to force Armenian peasants to withhold their taxes.

Perceiving Armenian violence as a threat to the integrity of his empire, Sultan Abdul Hamid loosed Muslim soldiers, Kurds in particular, in reprisals. His sobriquet was "the Damned," but Professor Marriott, the author of what is still a definitive work, *The Eastern Question,* considered him "the cleverest Sultan Islam had known since the sixteenth century,"[2] driven to despotic means in self-defense. Sir Edwin Pears, whose journalistic career was spent in Constantinople, reported that to the Sultan "the very name of Armenia had become anathema."[3] The news reaching England during the 1890s was that innocent and defenseless Armenians, mostly villagers and all of them Christian, were now being massacred in their thousands by Muslim Turks, extending the hateful fate previously suffered by Greeks, Serbs, Bulgarians, and Montenegrins. Conservatives of the Disraeli type understood that the Armenians had to some extent brought disaster on themselves, but this was hardly an argument weighty enough to overcome the humanitarian instincts and religious solidarity of Gladstone and the Liberals.

In his book *The Burning Tigris,* Peter Balakian lists pressure groups including the International Association of the Friends of Armenia, the Scottish Armenian Association, the British Armenian Committee, the Anglo-Armenian Association, Friends of Armenia, and the Armenian United Association. Compared to the London Greek Committee of Philhellenist days, the variety and even competition of these bodies shows how greatly the public's involvement with foreign causes had developed. One activist was E. J. Dillon, a student of Oriental languages and the *Daily Telegraph* correspondent in St. Petersburg. Reporting on the Armenian massacres of 1894 and 1895, he had disguised himself as a Turk. Other activists were Prime Minister Gladstone, Lady Frederick Cavendish (whose husband had been murdered by Irish terrorists in Dublin), the Duke of Argyll (onetime Secretary of State for India), and James Bryce. Balakian singles out the latter for his outstanding contribution to the Armenian Question over a period of forty years.

Born in 1838 in Belfast, Bryce was the son of a teacher. At the precocious age of thirty-two he became Regius Professor of Civil Law at Oxford. His magnum opus, still read, was *The Holy Roman Empire.* An inveterate traveler, he visited Russia and Asia Minor on the eve of the 1877 hostilities, at one point climbing Mount Ararat. Conventionally, he held that the steady process of decay over the previous century had rendered the Turks "more and more powerless for everything except evil."[4] When Russia declared war on Turkey, Bryce and Stopford Brooke, a clergyman, organized a National Conference on the Eastern Question, going on to form the Eastern Question Association. Under its auspices they further organized some five hundred public meetings, enrolling into the anti-Ottoman and pro-Armenian cause the leading public intellectuals of the time: William Morris, Professor J. R. Green, Carlyle, Ruskin, Burne-Jones, and Canon H. P. Liddon. In 1886 Bryce was briefly Gladstone's Under Secretary of State for Foreign Affairs, a post he had badly wanted, and six years later he was again in the cabinet as Chancellor of the Duchy of Lancaster. Bryce's book *The American Commonwealth* is also still read, and Balakian suggests that his article in *Century Magazine* in November 1895 effected a timely and important hardening of American public opinion against Turkey. Bryce believed that Europe was morally responsible for the "sufferings of the subjects of Turkey."[5] He advocated the use of force against Turkey, and also urged the United States to send gunboats if American lives or property were threatened. Towards the end of his life he published *The Treatment of the Armenians in the Ottoman Empire, 1915–16,* a study of the atrocities resulting from the First World War whereby something in the order of a million Armenians were murdered and as many again driven out of the country. Fear of defeat drove the Turks to this genocidal cruelty but the Dashnaks and Hunchaks bear responsibility for terrorist tactics that could only transform Armenians in Turkish eyes from a faithful community into traitors.

Another public intellectual vociferously devoted to the Armenian cause was Canon Malcolm MacColl. Born in Glenfinnan in Inverness in 1831, he was the son of a tenant farmer, and his education in Scotland proved a hard struggle. Ordained, he plunged into ecclesiastical issues in the manner of many a Victorian clergyman. In 1863 he became chaplain to the British Embassy in St. Petersburg, but the appointment lasted only a year and did not make a Russophile of him. Out of the blue he had written to Gladstone, whose helpful response and especially his defense of Christianity seems to have decided MacColl to be a Liberal. In a letter to Gladstone in 1876 he

could call Disraeli a "clever charlatan" and wish that he were "a prisoner in the hands of the Bashi-Bazouks." He took the trouble to go to
Constantinople and other places in the Ottoman Empire, but this
only reinforced his prejudices. In 1895, when the massacres of Armenians were intensifying, he published a pamphlet, *England's Responsibility Towards Armenia.* Disraeli's government, he held, was "largely
responsible" for these massacres because it had not settled "a plan of
Coercion." The right policy was to depose the Sultan. A prime busybody, MacColl organized meetings; he pestered Gladstone and Lord
Salisbury, Disraeli's successor as Conservative leader. He could flatter
these decision-makers, and explain in letters to one or other of them
how his lobbying the newspapers and magazines was keeping them
"straight," and how he was slanting his meetings to have the maximum appeal by being "more Christian than political." Perhaps he
exhausted them. Gladstone at any rate wrote to him in December
1896 in apparent defeatism, "Armenia.—We are on our backs. We
have done what we could. The Great Avenger may yet show that He
has an account to settle with the Great Assassin and his works."[6]
Dying soon afterwards, Gladstone is supposed to have said in almost
his last intelligible words, "Those poor Armenians." For many intellectuals, the failure of Europe, and Britain in particular, to intervene
in Turkey, became a standing reproach. Henry James, for one, saw the
massacres as "a world-defining event," brought about by "hideous
cowardice and baseness" on the part of the English.

　　Oliver Baldwin seems to have come to the Armenian cause more
by chance than conviction. He took life rather hard. One of his psychological burdens, evidently, was the fact that his father was Stanley
Baldwin, the Conservative politician and eventually Prime Minister.
Eton College, he felt, had failed to teach him how to come to terms
with unwanted privilege: "I have never been more pleased to leave
anywhere, except prison, than I was to leave Eton, and the four years
I spent there were the most useless and unhappy years of my life up
till then."[7] There followed a similarly mistaken spell at Cambridge,

and then service in the First World War in the Irish Guards. He was hardly twenty when he was fighting in the trenches. He stresses how frightened he was, how he expected to be wounded, how others let him down, and he makes repeated references to his nervous system. Peace found him at a loose end, a rolling stone who haphazardly landed in Algeria. "I decided to live as an Arab, learn their language, and find out something of their philosophy."[8] Naively revealing his ignorance about the relationship between French settlers and Algerians, he thought that the beating of natives was unheard of, "and the result is a contented population."

A self-declared socialist, and probably inspired by the Bolshevik revolution, he impulsively decided to head for Russia. On the way, in Alexandria, he stayed in the same hotel as M. Khatissian, then the President of the Armenian Republic who was raising funds to pursue war against Turkey. "Almost before I realized it I had arranged with him to proceed to Armenia and train his troops for continuing the fight." The timing was disastrous. After a journey through Batum and Tiflis, Baldwin reached Erivan just at the moment when the Bolsheviks were about to drive out the Turks and stifle Armenia's brief period of post-war independence. He chose not to leave with the abortive British Military Mission, and was therefore at the mercy of a series of confused and bloody events, involving imprisonment by the Bolsheviks, liberation, fighting the Bolsheviks, and further imprisonment by the Turks for three months in Kars and then Erzerum. Mixing boastfulness with self-pity, he recorded in his autobiography *The Questing Beast* that he was made a Dashnak, "the only non-Armenian member of this world-famous and once dreaded organization that was founded for the liberation of Armenia from Turkish and Russian domination."[9] Arbitrary terror and death were all around him. "I might have escaped much had I disclosed the fact that my father was in the British Government, but at the time, as I had got myself into the mess, I felt capable of getting myself out."[10] And so he did. The Lausanne Conference was held in 1922 to decide the fate of Armenia among other small nations, and Baldwin, the honorary Dashnak, was on the delegation led by his acquaintance M. Khatissian, the one-time president. In the light of Bolshevik and Turkish military successes, however, there was no possibility that the Great Powers would try to revive an independent Armenia. In his disappointment with his country's expedient policy, Baldwin concluded that he had been a "silly little English patriot" ever to imagine that Britain might back the Armenian cause. In this respect he was the last in quite a line of Englishmen whose promotion of Armenian nationalism could only encourage that unfortunate people to nurture false hopes and so help to seal their fate.

CHAPTER NINE

"To Heal This Ancient Nation"

T he gradual expansion of the Jewish community in Britain from the seventeenth century onwards stimulated perplexed reactions. Who were these strangers, and what did their differences amount to? What might their ultimate identity be? In the absence of informed opinion on the subject, those who came in contact with Jews relied on biblical sources. Concerned with establishing their relationship to God, Puritan sectarians perceived themselves as the lost tribes of Israel. In this scheme of things, Jews had a role in the fulfillment of prophecies and other messianic visions of the time. Scientists as distinguished as Isaac Newton and Joseph Priestley advocated the restoration of Jews to their land as a sign of the millennium.

In an erudite book *The Lost Tribes of Israel,* Tudor Parfitt tells the story of individuals trying to come to terms with the presence of Jews. John Sadler, for example, a Member of Parliament and friend of Oliver Cromwell's, invented an Israelite genealogy for the British. The poet Christopher Smart believed that "the English are the seed of Abraham."[1] According to William Blake, Jerusalem "was, and is, the Emanation of the Giant Albion," built, as he put it in what has become virtually a national hymn, in England's green and pleasant land. His poem *A Song of Liberty* has an exhortation to which future kibbutzniks could have subscribed: "O Jew, leave counting gold! Return to thy oil and wine." An eminent disturber of the peace, Lord George Gordon set off the severe London riots of 1780 against Catholics, converted afterwards to Judaism, and sought to mobilize Jews as a world-force. Most far-fetched of all was Richard Brothers, a one-time lieutenant in the navy, who proclaimed himself the Prince of the Hebrews and so the nephew of God. In common with other scholars including the authoritative Mayir Vereté, Parfitt links the explosion of anti-rationalism to anxiety about the End of Days brought on by the French Revolution. No fewer than fifty books on the subject of the Jews' return to Palestine were published between 1796 and the end of the century.[2] This restoration of the Jews was held to be a necessary prelude to the Second Coming of the Messiah.

In September 1789 the National Assembly in Paris took it upon itself to define the place Jews were to occupy. A famous decree posited: "The Jews should be denied everything as a nation but granted everything as individuals." Historic events were to expose the flaws in this apparently well-intentioned formula: Fascists deny them individual rights, and anti-Zionists deny them national rights. In any case, ten short years after the National Assembly decree, Napoleon expressed its exact opposite. Campaigning in the Middle East in 1799 he invited all the Jews of Asia and Africa to come to take a place under his flags in order to re-establish the Jerusalem of old. He went on, "The moment has come to reclaim your political existence as a nation among the nations."

The proto-Zionism of the nineteenth century was a general European phenomenon. Schiller's play *The Robbers* has a Jewish character who calls on "those who do not eat pork" to move with him to Palestine. The poet Adam Mickiewicz organized a vigil in the Paris synagogue on the anniversary of the destruction of the Temple in Jerusalem. The Marquis de Lafayette had a committee whose intention was to form Jews into military units for purposes of emancipation. There was talk of the Hussars of Israel. In 1829, Henry Hart Milman, a Protestant dean, published *The History of the Jews,* a work of scholarship at last, but deemed so favorable to its subject that it had to be withdrawn. Macaulay wrote in the same spirit: "Let us not presume to say that there is no genius among the countrymen of Isaiah, no heroism among the descendants of the Maccabees." A verse in a hymn by Charles Lyte was closer to recruitment than worship, "O that the Lord's salvation/ Were out of Zion come,/ To heal this ancient nation,/ To lead His outcasts home!"

In 1840 Lord Shaftesbury began a correspondence with Lord Palmerston, who was Foreign Secretary as well as his stepfather-in-law. Shaftesbury anticipated that the Ottomans would soon lose the provinces of Greater Syria, and these should be assigned to someone else, namely "the ancient and rightful lords of the soil, the Jews!" In his diary he noted, "There is a country without a nation; and God now in his wisdom and mercy, directs us to a nation without a country." Shaftesbury has always be credited with this encapsulation, but actually he was borrowing it from Alexander Keith, an evangelical clergyman, who had spent five years in Jerusalem and must have known that he was embellishing the facts. Nonetheless Shaftesbury was "the first Gentile to succeed in marrying a biblical interest in the Jews and their ancient homeland with the colder exigencies of a national foreign policy."[3] As early as 1845, E. L. Mitford of the Ceylon Civil Service suggested that the "re-establishment of the Jewish nation in Palestine as a protected state under the guardianship of Great Britain [would] place the management of our steam communications entirely in our hands," and "place us in a commanding position" to overawe and repel enemies.[4] Staff officers, including the Chief of Staff Field Marshal Montgomery, could be found deploying that argument a century later, on the eve of Israel's independence.

The furor around George Eliot's positive depiction of Daniel Deronda, and the negative stereotypes of Dickins' Fagin or Trollope's Melmotte, seems evidence that the British might well vote to give Jews equal rights but nevertheless remained unsure quite what to make of them. Disraeli settled the issue. His unparalleled feat was to

glamorize the entire Jewish heritage. This novelty encouraged a significant number of influential British people to sympathize with
Jews, whether these chose to identify themselves as members of a
faith or supporters of a national movement, that is to say Zionism.
British Jews did not have to invent strategies of emigration or revolution to escape the kind of persecution current elsewhere in
Europe.

Disraeli's character was complex, usually described as mysterious. He was an *arriviste* in whom "pose and sincerity were inextrica-
bly interwoven" as his biographer Robert Blake puts it, a dandy who
acted the part to exaggeration, destined, it would seem, to be a mere
exhibitionist.[5] At the outset of his public life, in 1830, he had a plan
to volunteer for the Turkish army, then in the process of crushing the
Albanian revolt. Time spent in Constantinople and then Jerusalem
fired his imagination. To his delight at such a connection, he engaged
on these travels the Venetian Giovanni Falcieri who had been one of
Byron's servants. It was not just unexpected but extraordinary, quite
without parallel, that he should have been a Conservative, pro-
Ottoman, romantic novelist, a favorite of Queen Victoria, Prime
Minister, an outright imperialist, and be ennobled as Earl of Beacons-
field. In drawing-rooms he was ridiculed as the "Jew d'esprit." E. A.
Freeman, the obsessional anti-Ottoman historian and publicist,
called him a "loathsome Jew," and blamed the Queen for "going
ostentatiously to eat with Disraeli in his ghetto." *The Satirist,* to be
sure a gutter-press publication, asked, "Was there ever such an impu-
dent, insolent, Hebrew varlet as this fellow Disraeli?"[6] When Gladstone lost the 1874 election, his wife wrote to her son Herbert, "Is it
not disgusting after all Papa's labour and patriotism and years of work
to think of handing over his nest-egg to that Jew?"[7] Disraeli carried
off such vilification, and much more besides, by the force of his personality and the panache of his achievements. In his flamboyant wake,
Jews were able to acquire a settled identity, and so could integrate in
a way that was impossible in the France of Dreyfus or the Russia of

pogroms and Mendel Beilis. Sir John Skelton, a Scottish author who had known and liked Disraeli, wrote a sketch of him containing the perceptive aphorism, "England is the Israel of his imagination."[8]

The Israel that most Jews actually imagined was a distant and idealized entity intimately connected to their faith, therefore abstract. The nationalism that arose with the Romantic era, the very idea of the nation-state, was far removed from anything in the experience of the Jewish masses. More than millenarian fantasy, more than colorful images of restoration, Jewish nationalism necessitated a radical change of identity, and little or nothing suggested that this was at all probable. True, Theodore Herzl had founded the Zionist movement, but English Jews like Israel Zangwill who adhered to it were exceptional. Besides, all sorts of preconditions for the realization of Zionism could not be met. Nobody in Constantinople was prepared to cede a nation-state to the Jews. Jewish pioneers were few and far between, far too few to attract one or another of the European Great Powers to volunteer to become their protectors.

Quite unpredictably, the First World War created the circumstances that converted Zionism from a somewhat wishful thought-process into a practical proposition. Misjudging the balance of forces, the Turks threw their lot in with Germany, and so lost their empire. The victorious British and French occupied the Arab provinces of that empire, and a number of influential British figures had firm preconceptions about the rightful disposal of these provinces. Sir Mark Sykes was one such, an extremely rich Yorkshire landowner and a Conservative Member of Parliament. He had traveled extensively in the Ottoman Empire, studied Arabic at Cambridge under E. G. Browne, and been an honorary attaché in Constantinople in 1905 along with George Lloyd and Aubrey Herbert. In sprightly travel books, he came out with the sort of opinions that a man of his privileged background would hold at the time, for example: "it is not a good thing to know too much of orientals; if you do, perhaps you may wake up one morning and find you have become one."[9] He

appeared to be an expert on the East, says his biographer Roger
Adelson, but his was really the personal experience of an amateur.
Dearly espousing a cause, he supported the non-Turkish people who
had suffered from Ottoman misrule, whether Arabs, Armenians,
Kurds, or Zionists. In the war he was Lord Kitchener's agent for
Middle East affairs at the War Office, then political secretary to the
War Cabinet with special responsibility for Middle East affairs. With
François Georges-Picot, Sykes negotiated the 1917 treaty that bears
their joint names and allocated the conquered Arab provinces to
Britain and France. That November, Zionism received what might be
called its birth certificate. The Balfour Declaration, named after the
then Foreign Secretary, committed Britain to facilitating "the establishment in Palestine of a national home for the Jewish people."

Leonard Stein, the author of the most exhaustive analysis of the
whys and wherefores of the Balfour Declaration, could not really
explain the motives of the War Cabinet in promulgating it. Politics
and emotions were somehow mixed up. Perhaps Christian millenar-
ianism had finally come to flower. Perhaps Captain Warren in charge
of archaeology financed by the Palestine Exploration Fund, or books
like Charles Condor's *Tent Work in Palestine* and George Adam Smith's
immensely popular *Historical Geography of the Holy Land* had created
imaginative ties to the past and the life of Jesus. Perhaps Prime Minister Lloyd George's Non-Conformism in the Wales of his childhood
had played a part. Gentile Zionists were usually Conservative, however, a powerful and like-minded group including Winston Churchill,
Leo Amery, and Sir William Ormsby-Gore (who had both been colleagues of Mark Sykes in the War Cabinet Secretariat), Alfred Milner,
and Joseph Chamberlain. John Buchan might concoct sinister Jewish
villains in his fiction, but he was so ardently pro-Zionist that his name
was later inscribed in the Golden Book of the Jewish National Fund,
the agency financing development in what was to become Israel. Neither of them Jewish, T. E. Lawrence and Richard Meinertzhagen had
both become public figures for their leading roles as intelligence

officers operating against the Turks in Arabia. Both had been present when General Allenby entered Jerusalem in November 1917. Both were present at the Versailles Peace Conference, after which Meinertzhagen was the Chief Political Officer in Palestine, and then Middle East Military Advisor at the Colonial Office. Lawrence thought that Meinertzhagen was a man who "knew no half-measures," what with his "immensely powerful body and a savage brain." Meinertzhagen found Lawrence effeminate, even girlish. In spite of such differences in character, they became friends through a shared conviction that Zionism was the right solution for Palestine.

Men of that kind were evidently engaged in the high-handed imperialism in which they believed, promoting either Zionists or Arabs, and sometimes both together under British auspices and seeing no contradiction in doing so. Some have put forward a conspiracy theory that the world war was then stale-mated, the Great Powers were all gripped by the stereotype of Jews as secret rulers of the world, and Britain was simply first to get in its bid for their support.

National causes on behalf of minorities are likely to generate violence and most probably succeed in their aim only if a Great Power is engaged in support. Credit for linking Zionism to British foreign policy has to go to Chaim Weizmann. He arrived in England from his native Russia in 1904, to live in Manchester where he did research in the chemical industry. Having worked his way into the Establishment through "immense natural authority, dignity and strength,"[10] he moved to London at the outset of the war. Mark Sykes is reported to have announced the news of the Balfour Declaration to him with the words, "It's a boy!"—evidence of how Weizmann had come to be on the closest of terms with the power-brokers. Isaiah Berlin, the eminent political theorist who made a point of keeping in touch with current affairs, knew him quite well and described him as "clearly the greatest figure in the public life of the Jews since the death of Herzl, and was recognised as such by Zionists and non-Zionists, Jews and Gentiles."[11] Sir Charles Webster, one of the leading historians of cabinets and chancelleries, considered Weizmann's achievement the greatest of all feats of diplomacy he had known.

The London offices of the Jewish Agency and Zionist Federation were in Great Russell Street, near the British Museum, and Blanche Dugdale, always known as Baffy, a childish version of her maiden name of Balfour, worked there as a volunteer. Born in 1880, she was a Scottish aristocrat, daughter of Lady Frances Campbell, an energetic suffragette, and grand-daughter of the Duke of Argyll who had been in Gladstone's cabinet. Her father was one of the brothers of A. J. Balfour, who gave his name to the 1917 Declaration, and they were nephews of Prime Minister Lord Salisbury. In the First World War, Blanche Dugdale had served in Naval Intelligence. She supported the post-war League of Nations but the diaries that she kept from 1936 to 1947 display a commitment to Zionism of a different order, something absolute and consuming. N. A. Rose, the editor of these diaries, speaks variously of Zionism as a "sacred trust" for her, an obsession that "increased in intensity over the years," and a "combination of political conviction and moral indignation" usually sufficient to sweep away all opposition.

Her Zionism was in one way a tribute to Weizmann, whom she had known apparently since 1923. She regularly attended the Zionist Congress, and in 1937 at Zurich she heard Weizmann speak for two hours: "It was not a speech—it was an inspired utterance." Furthermore, "When one is with Chaim one feels the infinite nobility of soul—the vast intellect—and knows that here is one of God's greatest instruments."[12] Thanks to her social position, she had ready access to anyone she wanted, and also make the introduction of Weizmann seem a natural social occasion. She could invite herself to tea with Leo Amery in the House of Commons, and push him to intervene with Prime Minister Stanley Baldwin. Her diaries refer constantly to meeting friends in high places like Walter Elliot, Harold Nicolson, Lewis Namier, Josiah Wedgwood (a Socialist as well as a genuine Zionist, a rare combination), William Ormsby-Gore, and Victor

Cazalet. Several of these were in Parliament, and she was evidently enlisting their sympathy and help, passing on to those in the Zionist office whatever information she could extract.

At the same time, she was prone to outbursts of rapture. A sojourn in Palestine under the British Mandate prompted her to exclaim at the end of April 1936, "How one loves it all! And how sad to see so many English—officials and tourists—walk unseeingly amidst so many miracles!"[13] Then soon afterwards, in the first week of May, she speaks of "this dear country. The past two weeks have made me love it and its Jewish people, more passionately than ever." In Palestine again in 1938 she contrasts the indomitable spirit of the Jews and the cringing, vacillating blindness of British policy. In the course of a tour with Weizmann and his wife, Vera, she addressed nearly 4,000 people in a hall in Tel Aviv. Returning to Palestine a year later, she wrote, "What a wonderful experience to be as one with these people," and again, "what an utterly different world the British officials inhabit—and how much more at home I feel with the Jews."[14] These were the years of the Peel Commission which recommended partition, and of the prolonged Arab uprising to drive out the British and the Jews, yet there is no hint of danger in the diaries, only the note of exaltation. "I feel every hour that passes before negotiations for the Jewish State begin is an hour wasted." This was "the heroic age of Jewish history." Although she went to Palestine one more time after the war, the Holocaust and the side-lining of Weizmann by David Ben-Gurion were events that went against her spirit, and were too painful to be acknowledged. On her death-bed she was told that the State of Israel had been established, and the old and defeated Weizmann was to receive the consolation prize of becoming President. Clapping her hands, she said, "It will all come right now. You'll see."

During her visit to Palestine in 1938, Blanche Dugdale had met Orde Wingate, recording how lucky it was that his fanatical Zionism got the better of his sense of duty as an officer. She was right in this assessment of Wingate's priorities, and accordingly she repeated the glorifying praise she had earlier pinned on to Weizmann, that he was clearly one of the instruments in God's hand. Wingate seems to have had some such perception of himself. He felt, he sometimes said, that there was "a vision of glory" beckoning him. In his early thirties, according to his biographer Christopher Sykes, he would say that he wanted a cause to fight for, one that he could believe in heart and soul.[15] Ambition and divine destiny were one and the same. The Word of the Lord was as live to him as it had been to John Sadler or Richard Brothers in an earlier age. He came from a family of strict Evangelicals, the Plymouth Brethren. His grandfather, a lay missionary, had been out walking in Glasgow when it struck him that he did nothing for the Jews. So he learnt Hebrew, was ordained, and went on a mission to the Jews of Hungary. His son George had a similar religious illumination. In the next generation, his children, Orde, born in 1903, and his younger sister Sybil, so the latter recalled, were reared at home in Godalming on a diet of porridge, bread and dripping, and "the sincere milk of the Word."

Perhaps some inferiority complex gnawed at him. He resented being small, only five foot six, "a little rat-like fellow," as a contemporary at Charterhouse said of him. Out hunting, he rode as though to break his neck. Commissioned into the Royal Artillery, he got himself posted to Sudan, where his father's first cousin, Sir Reginald Wingate, had risen from being an intelligence officer at the battle of Omdurman to become a long-serving Governor-General. In the Sudan Defence Force, Orde Wingate was the only European at his lonely base in the desert, and was obliged to become proficient in Arabic. He seemed set to be one among the multitude of British officers serving routine imperial purposes in the Middle East. In September 1936 he arrived in Palestine as the Arab uprising was turning violent, endangering public order. Almost at once, he committed himself to the Jews, because, as he told Tony Symonds, a colleague in intelligence and a life-long friend, "Everyone's against the Jews, so

I'm for them."[16] To Wilfred Thesiger he said much the same: "When I was at school I was looked down on, and made to feel that I was a failure and not wanted in the world. When I came to Palestine I found a whole people who had been treated like that through scores of generations, and yet at the end of it they were undefeated, were a great power in the world, building their country anew. I felt I belonged to such people."[17]

If so, it was a case of all being under-dogs together. Symonds discovered that Wingate was passing raw military intelligence to the Jewish Agency, and is quoted saying, "I got on very well with him, but I must admit he was a fanatic." John Bierman and Colin Smith, authors of a recent study of Wingate, concede the fanaticism but are doubtful that he would have compromised himself in this reckless way with the Jewish Agency.

What is beyond dispute is that Wingate devised tactics to defeat the uprising. The Arabs were accustomed to stop fighting at the end of the day, and even disband until the following dawn. That was a cultural feature, and Wingate saw how to take military advantage of it, raising Special Night Squads to track Arab groups and ambush them at unexpected times in unexpected places. About 200 carefully selected men were trained in this type of guerrilla warfare, two-thirds of them Jews in the underground army or Haganah. Some of these became household names in the wars an independent Israel had to fight: Yigal Yadin, Yigal Allon, and Moshe Dayan among them. Wingate was undoubtedly harsh, and he and his men "countered terrorism with terror of their own," in the rebuke of Tom Segev, one of the more critical contemporary Israeli writers.[18] That too was a feature of Arab culture, in which victory and honor belong to whoever has superior power and the will to use it. Today Wingate would no doubt be accused of war crimes.

Wingate's first biographer, Leonard Mosley, describes a gathering of senior Haganah officers in Haifa in May 1939, at the moment when the British had published the White Paper limiting Jewish immigration, already a matter of life and death as a result of Hitler's policies. "The time has come to declare war on the English," Wingate is supposed to have said, his face pale and his eyes burning, going on to urge them to blow up the strategically vital Haifa oil refinery and even offering to lead the operation himself.[19] This would have been outright treason. Bierman and Smith concede that Wingate longed to command a Jewish army, and had an image of himself as the biblical Gideon, but this proposal to lead saboteurs is another story they find improbable.

Be that as it may, that same month of May 1939 General Sir Robert Haining, in command in Palestine and thoroughly opposed to Zionism, had Wingate transferred back to England. Just before the outbreak of war, the Chief of Staff, Sir Edmund Ironside, wrote to the Director of Military Operations that Wingate "got a bad mark for being too Jewish. He is a most remarkable soldier and leader of men. He infused glory into his Jewish squads."[20] Always absorbed in the conduct of war, Churchill approved of the way that the Special Night Squads had overpowered the Arab rebellion, and the original thinking that lay behind it. Wingate's wife Lorna was his equal in pro-Jewish fanaticism. After Wingate's return to London, Churchill duly invited them both to lunch. During the meal, another guest tried to change the conversation, whereupon, Lorna records, Churchill turned on her slowly, like the gun turret of a tank, saying, "Here is a man who has seen and done and been amid great actions, and when he is telling us about them you had better be quiet." After the successful campaign to drive the Italians out of Ethiopia, Wingate tried to commit suicide, apparently feeling victimized by superior officers and politicians unwilling to acknowledge his military feat, the sole success of the war to date. Wilfred Thesiger had been his second in command, visited him in hospital in Cairo, and held that there was something genuinely unbalanced about him. The suicide attempt did not deter Churchill, who pushed for Wingate's promotion after the first Chindit campaign: "I consider Wingate should command the army against the Japanese in Burma. He is a man of genius and audacity."[21] The only British general with a reputation to match Rommel's, Wingate always hoped to lead Jewish troops against the Germans in the Western Desert. Whenever possible, he was in contact with Weizmann or Haganah friends trying to mobilize such a unit. On one occasion on the way to India, his flying boat put down on the Sea of Galilee, and he then wrote to Lorna, "How lovely it would be if you and I were there now, working to defend Haaretz [the land, in Hebrew]. Let it happen, please God."[22] There can be little doubt that if he had survived the fatal air crash in Burma in March 1944, he would have resigned his commission in order to take part in Israel's war of independence in 1948.

A number of British Jews volunteered for the Haganah in that war, and so did a handful of British people who were not Jews, including a few who had deserted as their units were pulling out of Palestine, and may have taken their arms with them, or sold them. The evidence so far is purely anecdotal. Richard Meinertzhagen was seventy in 1948. Stereotypes of "the Jew, virile, brave, determined and intelligent: the Arab decadent, stupid, dishonest," dominated his outlook.[23] The violence of his character was well established; he had once shot a tribal chief in Kenya, and clever ruses of his had led to the death of many Ottoman soldiers in the First World War. In April 1948 in Cairo, he had thrown off two toughs attempting to rob him. Five days later, he arrived in Haifa just as Jews and Arabs were skirmishing there. A company of Coldstream Guards was present. His *Middle East Diary* describes how he borrowed a rifle and 200 rounds from one of the guardsmen, and made his way towards the firing. First he came across the Haganah. Then he shot and killed five Arabs, withdrawing only once the other armed Arabs had been accounted for and he had fired all his ammunition. The diary rejoices: "Altogether I had a glorious day. May Israel flourish!"[24] But details to do with the typing of the diary and its pagination in manuscript indicate that Meinertzhagen may have inserted loose sheets at some later date, indeed may have made up the whole incident to add to his credentials as a fire-eater. So this evidence too is anecdotal.

CHAPTER TEN

"Every Englishman's Idea of Nature's Gentleman"

C hristendom and the world of Islam had survived over centuries in mutual ignorance and suspicion, physically and intellectually separated by what in later times would have qualified as an Iron Curtain. European diplomats and a few intrepid travelers did leave reports of their adventures in faraway regions whose inhabitants were generalized and mostly feared by the public as Saracens, Moors, Turks, Mohammedans, and the like, with Arabs as such a largely unknown quantity. Edward Gibbon captured very well what an educated Englishman in his century would have thought about these people identified only remotely and at second hand: "The life of a wandering Arab is a life of danger and distress; and though sometimes, by rapine or exchange, he may appropriate the fruits of industry, a private citizen in Europe is in the possession of more solid and pleasing luxury than the proudest emir who marches in the field at the head of ten thousand horse."

Men from Europe who crossed the divide involuntarily were victims, captured at sea by pirates, sold to slavery, or offered for ransom, while European women might find themselves in a harem. Some crossed it voluntarily, however, usually to escape what would have been the grim fate of captivity, or in a few cases for other opportunistic reasons. Converting to Islam and adopting a Muslim name, they were called "renegades," the equivalent of defectors in a later and more ideological age. Their destinies intrigued, shocked, or frightened contemporaries. In the late sixteenth century, for instance, one Samson Rowlie became an influential eunuch known as Hasan Aga at the Sultan's court in Constantinople. In Algiers one of the official executioners was a butcher from Exeter who changed his name from Absalom into Abd es-Salaam. Benjamin Bishop had been consul in Egypt in 1606, only to become a Muslim and vanish from the scene. A dragoman in Constantinople was described as "a Turk, but a Cornishman born." A Scot called Campbell converted to Islam, joined the elite janissary force, and became an Ottoman general under the name of Ingliz Mustapha.

The British government took the lead in suppressing the piracy and slavery that had ruined many lives and restricted trade. In the Mediterranean, a fleet under Lord Exmouth bombarded Algiers in 1816, and the local Dey then freed the slaves he had been holding and took no more. Three years later, a naval and military expedition crushed the Qawasim pirates who had been a menace to shipping in the waters of the Gulf, as far as the Indian Ocean. However violent, these actions were undoubtedly progressive, humanitarian according to the current idiom, but they also served to swing the balance of power in favor of Europeans. Those with a taste for danger, the physique to withstand hardship, and a gift for languages began to explore what had hitherto been inaccessible lands, and very remarkable individuals they were too. Some were soldiers, usually officers serving in India; others were men of private means driven by curiosity to learn whatever Muslims had to teach. Out of the experiences of such pioneers there developed in due course what many British believed was a privileged relationship with Muslims, especially Arabs once they began to emerge in their own right from the subject populations of the Ottoman Empire.

One of the earliest to choose freely to live in a Muslim country was E. W. Lane. Born in Hereford in 1801, the son of a clergyman, Lane was determined to go to Egypt. Jason Thompson, his very thorough biographer, cannot pinpoint quite what his motive was to study this particular society and its culture. Writing in recollection about first setting foot in Egypt, Lane gave little away: "I was about to throw myself entirely among strangers; to adopt their language, their customs and their dress; and, in associating almost exclusively with the natives, to prosecute the study of their literature."[1] In Cairo, a renegade took him in hand. This was one William Thomson, a Scot, who had run away to join the army, been sent to Egypt, where he was captured in an action against the soldiers of Muhammad Ali, and sold into slavery. To save his life, he converted to Islam, and became Osman Effendi, which helped him in his employment as dragoman, or interpreter, at the British Consulate. "There was an incongruity to his impeccable Turkish attire and equally perfect Scottish accent."[2] Less dramatically, Lane acquired a new identity as Mansour Effendi, and though he never converted to Islam he "always began each day's work by saying the bismillah," as a good Muslim should.[3] Lane and his circle of friends, including his fellow scholar Sir John Gardner Wilkinson, known as Ismail Effendi, played the part of passing as locals by dressing only as Egyptians. Lane empathized with the life he observed around him; his *Manners and Customs of the Modern Egyptians* was published in 1836, has been in print ever since, and has a claim to be the best book ever written by an Englishman about another society. His *Arabic-English Lexicon* is another scholarly landmark of permanent value.

Until about 1830, according to Alexander Kinglake, the author of *Eothen*, a Middle East travel book that educated Victorians rightly cherished above all others, no one would dare go to Damascus dressed as a European, as that city was notorious for its fanaticism. Sir Henry Layard, the archaeologist who excavated Nineveh and later became ambassador in Constantinople, left Baghdad for Persia in June 1840, having grown a beard and dressed as a Persian. He came to have a special affinity for the Bakhtiari tribesmen and records how a Persian provincial governor burst out, "You Englishmen are always meddling in matters which do not concern you, and interfering in the affairs of other countries."[4]

To venture into Bokhara under the rule of an Emir notorious for having infidels put to death, the great traveler Armin Vambéry disguised himself as a dervish, achieved his objective, and lived to tell the tale. Major Charles Stewart, an army officer, and Brigadier Sir Percy Sykes, the Consul General in Mashhad, both wrote books describing how they had traveled in Persian dress. E. G. Browne's famous book *A Year Amongst the Persians* has a frontispiece photograph of him in Persian dress with worry beads dangling from one hand. For many years an authoritative correspondent for *The Times* in Morocco, Walter Harris used to travel in the 1880s in that country in native dress. This was quite customary up to the eve of the First World War. One of the most capable of intelligence officers, E. B. Soane, explained on the opening page of the exemplary book he published in 1912, *To Mesopotamia and Kurdistan in Disguise*, that he was susceptible to the "magnetism" of the Middle East. He had learnt Persian and Kurdish well enough to pass as a man from Shiraz; he had not converted to Islam but had learnt to pray as a Shia and to "dispute the Qur'an with the best of them." By the mere fact of wearing a fez, he says, he was isolated from Europeans, thus understanding better how native people felt looked down upon. From there, it was a short step for him to be disparaging England to the headman of a mule caravan going to Kirkuk, "it is a land of little hills and little valleys, of no seclusion, of no peace and no rest."[5] To another local he said, "people of my race are given to wandering over the face of the earth with no other reason than to see it and the people it supports."[6] Which was true, but not the whole truth, concealing the fact that Soane had been acquiring knowledge that fitted him to become Political Officer when the British invaded Mesopotamia in 1914.

The gratification that comes through role-playing of this kind stands out in the case of Richard Burton, a most complicated character, a man whose achievements and writings Victorian England recognized as exceptional, but was never quite sure whether praise or condemnation was in order. The son of a colonel of uncertain moods, Burton was born in 1 8 2 1 and brought up largely in France. Consequently he and his brother, Burton believed, "never thoroughly understood English society, nor did society understand us." He went further, "England is the only country where I never feel at home."[7] His explorations, the changes in his career, his incarnations and disguises as he assumed one personality after another, all suggest a rather desperate search for somewhere in which to feel at home.

Undoubtedly he was brilliantly intelligent and also immensely strong physically. The fierceness of his manner and his appearance warned people not to trifle with him. By the time he reached Trinity College, Oxford, he had acquired the nickname of Ruffian Dick, and a reputation for wildness and violence. Reputed to be one of the best swordsmen in Europe, he saw military service in India and the Crimea. In India he pursued his gift for languages. In her study of Burton, Fawn M. Brodie rates him "one of the three or four great linguists of his time,"[8] mastering in the end twenty-nine languages and more than forty dialects. In India, ostensibly as an intelligence officer, he went underground, pretending to be Mirza Abdullah from Bushire, his face stained with henna and wearing long false hair and a beard.

Mecca and Medina, the holy cities of Arabia, are closed to all except Muslims, and any infidel caught there in Burton's day, or indeed afterwards, could be certain that he would be put to death. Over the centuries, one or two European Christians had in fact succeeded in penetrating these forbidden cities, but Burton could be assured that the exploit was singular and would make him famous. Having resigned his commission in the army, he sailed in April 1 8 5 3 to Egypt to prepare for the journey across the desert. Now he had stained his skin with walnut juice, and shaved his head. The role of Mirza Abdullah coming from a presumed Persian background identified him as a Shia, however, and this would have involved confrontation and possible exposure in Wahhabi Arabia. Disguised instead as a Pathan from India, he set off, explaining that he was "thoroughly tired of 'progress' and of 'civilisation;' curious to see with my eyes what others are content to 'hear with ears,' namely, Moslem inner life in a really Mohammedan country; and longing, if truth be told, to set foot on that mysterious spot which no tourist has yet described."[9] The disguise held. Burton survived robbers, Bedouin, illness, and the infection of his foot from the poisonous prickle of a sea urchin. Reacting at last to the sight of the Kaaba, the huge stone in the Great Mosque of Mecca, he wrote that of all the worshippers who were weeping or pressing against it, none felt a deeper emotion than he did. "It was as if the poetical legends of the Arab spoke truth, and that the waving wings of angels, not the sweet breeze of morning, were agitating and swelling the black covering of the shrine. But, to confess humbling truth, theirs was the high feeling of religious enthusiasm, mine was the ecstasy of gratified pride."

Personal Narrative of a Pilgrimage to El-Medinah and Meccah was published in 1855, establishing Burton's reputation. More than anyone else at the time, he shaped public attitudes towards Arabs. His placing of the words "progress" and "civilisation" in inverted comments was to appeal to many subsequent Englishmen who imagined Arabs to be uncontaminated by such developments, free spirits in their vast deserts while British ladies and gentlemen in their conventional drawing-rooms were bound by artificial manners and polite constraints of all sorts. Burton detected a quality innate to Arabs that he called *kayf,* and this meant in his style of poeticism, "the savouring of animal existence; the passive enjoyment of mere sense; the pleasant languor, the dreamy tranquillity, the airy castle-building, which in Asia stand in lieu of the vigorous, intensive, passionate life of Europe. It is the result of a lively, impressible, excitable nature, and exquisite sensibility of nerve,—a faculty for voluptuousness unknown in northern regions." Such generalized contrasting of Arab spirituality with European crassness and decadence was a derivative of the myth of the Noble Savage, and as such destined to have a long literary run in spite of, or perhaps because of, the virtually total detachment from reality.

This journey of Burton's was certainly epic, but at least some of the incidents of violence and attempted murder that he described in its course appear to have been invented for the purpose of making Arabs more wild and mysterious than they were, and himself harder and more heroic. In short, he had discovered that the Arab world was a perfect backdrop against which to play out the various parts that took his fancy. Lines in his poem *Kasidah* encapsulate his derring-do view of himself: "He noblest lives and noblest dies/ Who makes and keeps his self-made laws." He staged a characteristically theatrical moment upon his return to Cairo from Mecca. Shepherd's Hotel was already the center of British social life and he could not resist entering it in Arab dress. His burnous brushed against one of the officers who snapped angrily that if this Arab had the impudence to do it again, he would get a kicking. Whereupon Burton said, "Well, damn it Hawkins, that's a nice way to welcome a fellow after two years' absence." "By God, it's Ruffian Dick," cried Hawkins, as he and his brother officers crowded round Burton in amazement.

In the pioneering study *Heart-Beguiling Araby*, Kathryn Tidrick gives academic approval to the proposition that Burton and other travelers at that date were headstrong personalities acting out their own dramas of identity and making use of Arabs as a handy means of self-expression. Their experiences laid the foundation for a truism that "It was in the nature of Englishmen to understand Arabs, and it was in the nature of Arabs to be understandable to Englishmen."[10] The essential vagueness of this idea, she continues, rendered it almost indestructible, with the additional dimension that it offered the English the possibility of dominance with a good conscience. Wilfrid Scawen Blunt exemplifies how this delusion and its inherent condescension impeded the emergence of an equal relationship. With him begins Arabism, the cultivation of an outlook that was to turn doctrinaire, especially among Foreign Office officials, whereby Arabs are not active agents in their own lives but passive sufferers of other people, above all the British. This central proposition of Arabism means that Arabs are granted a moral and spiritual superiority, and everyone else has only to acknowledge it and help to bring it out. This of course absolves Arabs of anything retrograde or destructive in the way they conduct themselves, infantilizing them and making reform far more difficult than it might otherwise have been.

In a life lasting from 1840 to 1922, Blunt swung about in unstable personal relationships and even more unstable political attitudes. In his mature years, the one constant element in his character was hatred of England and its empire. He was free to enjoy inherited wealth, but others should not have expectations of that kind: "In England I find nothing noble. We are too rich and strong and prosperous to have any cause left us worth dying for." Depicting Arabs as nothing but victims, he would make it his cause to rescue them first from Ottoman imperialism, and then the British imperialism gradually replacing it. So with a good conscience he was able to dominate Arabs and exploit them as prime instruments in the anti-British cause that really mattered to him

Born in Petworth, one of England's grandest country houses, Blunt seemed destined for an allotted place in the governing class, for he knew or was related to everyone who was anyone, and all doors were open to him. In his own country house, Crabbet in Sussex, he had fifteen indoor servants, one of them a totemic little African boy. The Crabbet estate of four thousand acre made him independently rich. A handsome man, he was to be widely resented as a serial seducer of the wives of his friends. He was also to attract attention as a minor poet in the sub-Tennysonian mode then fashionable. Like so many other men from a background as fortunate as his, he started his career as an honorary attaché in British embassies. In Athens, he met Sir Richard Church and George Finlay, and was influenced by these surviving Philhellenes. Soon he imagined himself as a Byronic hero, and lived up to this self-flattery by marrying Byron's granddaughter, Lady Anne King-Noel. Dressed in eastern clothes, the two of them made several adventurous journeys in the Arabian provinces of the Ottoman Empire, reaching remote oases. What he admired among the Bedouin, he wrote in his memoirs, was their nonchalance, their freedom, "They had solved the riddle of life by refusing to consider it"—this misconception of Bedouin life, even more fanciful than Burton's, was destined to linger. A long-suffering woman, a thoughtful writer, also a well-known breeder of Arabian horses, Lady Anne early understood that her husband was opposed temperamentally to everything his own country did and stood for.

In 1879 Blunt visited India, staying naturally with Lord Lytton, a friend who was also the Viceroy. When he left India, he was later to write, his faith in the British Empire and its ways in the East had been "shaken to its foundations." The Empire was the "great engine of evil" for the rest of the world. European civilization was anyhow doomed. The future lay in the regeneration of Islam with England's help, and he was the "rising prophet" of this. Published in 1882, *The Future of Islam* put together a number of his magazine articles arguing that the Arabs should be freed from Ottoman rule, and an Arab caliphate established. Some years after publication, he was to boast, "I committed myself without reserve to the Cause of Islam as essentially the 'Cause of Good.'" In this book, he asserts with a straight face that "Cairo has now declared itself as the home of progressive thought in Islam." Al-Azhar, the repository of Sunni tradition, had "liberal ulema." Nomads in Arabia were "a peculiarly noble race." There was a progressive party in Mecca, and the transfer there of the seat of spiritual power from Constantinople would be "easy and natural." Needless to say, this transference to Islam and the Arabs of British political organization and terms had no correspondence with reality, indeed was nonsense.

Vanity, an exaggerated sense of his own importance as an English aristocrat, fired the abuse of privilege that marked the rest of his life. Opportunity to show himself off came in 1882. Ruling Egypt, the

Khedive Tewfiq was involved in an intrigue with a careerist soldier, Ahmed Arabi Pasha, who was making a bid for power. On the assumption that Arabi was a proto-nationalist, Blunt drafted a program in Arabi's name, and published it in *The Times.* Blunt proposed to mediate between the Egyptians contending for power. He used his social position to call on Prime Minister Gladstone in Downing Street, and wrote an angry letter to *The Times* attacking him. In the event, the British invaded Egypt and backed the Khedive. Warning Arabi where British troops would land, Blunt was responsible for encouraging him to fight a campaign he could not conceivably win. After a short battle Arabi was captured and put on trial. Blunt paid for A. M. Broadly, an expensive Queen's Counsel, to come from London to defend Arabi, who was then sentenced to exile. Nobody criticized the subsequent British occupation of Egypt more harshly or more regularly than Blunt, but nobody had done more to ensure that it would take place.

Leaving Crabbet, he liked to winter at Sheikh Obeid, a property he had bought on the outskirts of Cairo. Campaigning there against the British presence, he did what he could to encourage the Arab nationalism and Islamic fervor just beginning to be a political factor. He paid for issues of a magazine put out by one particularly dubious Arab journalist building a career on the supposed failings of British policy. At the time of the Sudan crisis that led to the death of General Gordon, Blunt expressed the hope that the whole British expeditionary force had been wiped out. What were British soldiers doing in the Sudan? They were "a mongrel scum of thieves from Whitechapel and Seven Dials, commanded by young fellows . . . without beliefs, without traditions, without other principle . . . than just to get their promotion and have a little fun."[11] The Sudanese meanwhile were men with the memory of a thousand years of freedom, "worshipping God and serving him in arms like the heroes of the ancient world they are." Returning from London to Crabbet and hearing the news that Khartoum had fallen to the Mahdi and Gordon was dead, "I could not help singing all the way down in the train."[12] Irrational emotion and invective came easily to him. Returning by ship to India in 1883, he made a point of openly reading the Qur'an and felt like declaring jihad against the English passengers, mostly tea-planters. At one point he took up the cause of Irish Home Rule. The trial of two Irish nationalists prompted this outburst: "I cursed my country with its red coats and black coats and its absurd truculent ministers of an infamous law." When he pulled down a handbill in an Irish country town where two men had just been killed in a riot, the police intervened. A scuffle followed, and he was sentenced to two months in prison, but was acquitted on appeal. He liked to boast that he was the first Englishman to have taken the Celtic Irish side.

In his copious diaries, Blunt describes how he was in the habit of calling on Lord Cromer, who under the title of British Agent was effectively the Viceroy of Egypt from 1883 to 1907. They met as English gentlemen, social equals. Moreover, as an attaché in Madrid, Blunt had once engaged someone to procure Cromer a "respectable mistress,"[13] and this woman had given Cromer a child, for whom he always paid. Commissioned as a young man into the Royal Artillery, Cromer had been in America to observe the Civil War. Cromer proved one of the most capable administrators in the entire history of the Empire, and under his rule Egypt consolidated and prospered as never before or indeed since. It must have been galling for him to entertain the louche Blunt and have to listen to his advice on how to treat Egyptians when he was well aware that Blunt was simultaneously recruiting Egyptian nationalists and pressing them to demonstrate and if possible revolt. In the curious political dueling between these two men, Cromer won a round when without obtaining permission Blunt visited some of the nationalists then in prison. For this, Blunt was banned from Egypt for three years. In 1906, however, a party of British officers was out shooting pigeons in the village of Denshawi. The villagers objected that the birds were being reared for domestic purposes. A fracas followed. A British officer died from a heart attack as he ran for help. Misinterpreting this incident as nationalist protest, the authorities panicked. Four of the villagers were hanged, others were flogged and imprisoned. Cromer happened to be away in England at the time and could not be held responsible for what had occurred, but Blunt rejoiced that Denshawi would "smash" him. In an immediate onslaught, he wrote a pamphlet titled *Atrocities of Justice under British Rule in Egypt* and had it translated into Arabic and published in a Cairo newspaper. The following year, he published a much longer work titled *Secret History of the English Occupation of Egypt*, a compendium of the supposed conspiracies and bad faith of the British, and the "abomination" of their rule. Egyptians and other Arabs and Muslims were quick to appreciate that if an Englishman of such standing could depict his country in this hateful way, they could do so too.

In old age, wandering about Crabbet in Bedouin dress and holding court with other poets, Blunt became more and more irascible. The Boers were making "a splendid fight for their freedom," "driving the first nail into the coffin of the British Empire." He advised Gokhale, leader of the India Reform movement, to put a couple of bombs in his pocket when he called on the India Office. The coming collapse of the British Empire meant that Indian self-government must be brought forward. In one diary entry he gloats that British troops were being nicely "punished" by Indian rebels. In addition, his predictions were more and more bizarre: "There is but one chance for Islam, and that is Germany's friendship." To Winston Churchill on a visit to Crabbet he advised an alliance with Turkey against Italy and Russia. The geo-strategy was preposterous: "Italy could easily be dealt with by the Fleet, while Turkey would willingly help to turn the Russians out of Persia."[14] Lady Anne had had enough, and left him. Turning his idiom back on him, his daughter Judith had the last word: "He was completely at the mercy of Oriental deceit and Irish blarney and believed every woeful tale of oppression by the British Government, however fantastic. A born agitator, he became an ideal 'bomb thrower' for every schemer who dared not throw his own explosives, and his house soon became famous as a hot-bed of conspiracy for the scum of every nation."

By the twentieth century, travel had developed so that it became easy for others to buy a house in an Arab country and live there as Blunt had done in Sheikh Obeid. An artist who traded on her upper-class connections, Claire Sheridan was one such. Settling into Biskra, in Algeria, she found "the Arabs all seemed so tall, handsome, and elegant." Her ambition, she explained, "was to live in an Arab house, in an Arab way, and have peace."[15] Lady Evelyn Cobbold, daughter of an earl, went further. As a child, she recollected, she spent the winter in a Moorish villa outside Algiers, where her parents were in search of the sun. Grown-up, she surrendered to Arabist sentimentality. "The heart of an Arab has no room for anything if not for love, pure, true and constant."[16] Changing her name to Zainab, she converted to Islam and in 1933 was apparently the first Englishwoman to perform the pilgrimage to Mecca and Medina. A photograph in her book about this experience shows her fully veiled. Thanks to her status, she was provided with a car, special permission and a guide, but saw no irony in praising Islam for its purported equality. "Here among the perfumes he loves, sits an Arab cross-legged reading the Koran, gently swaying to the rhythm of the beautiful verses as he intones them in a slow melodious voice. Turbaned sheikhs, veiled women, children dressed in all the colours of the rainbow pass by; no beggars spoil the picture and the cry for 'backsheesh' is unknown."[17] In spite of this unusually misleading idyll of the Muslim scene, rather comically Lady Evelyn informs readers how she clung to her tube of Flit against mosquitoes.

Contact with Islam placed a block on the powers of observation and reason even of intelligent people. Marmaduke Pickthall, for instance, the son of a clergyman, wandered for some months in 1895 in Ottoman Palestine, turning up in Jerusalem "in semi-native garb and with a love for Arabs which, I was made to understand, was hardly decent." Like so many, he had been "bowled over by the romance of the East."[18] Converting to Islam he was known as Muhammad, throwing off the European and plunging into the native way of living, as he put it, because "These were happy people." Between 1903 and 1921 he published nine novels with Islamic themes and settings, rarified beyond recognition. In the First World War, he was threatened with arrest for his partisan defense of the Ottomans.

The expansion of the British Empire also brought ever-increasing numbers of District Commissioners, judges, civil servants, diplomats, members of the armed forces, and often their families into contact with Arabs. A huge literature shows how some of these people made a cause of helping Arabs to modernize with the objective that in the end they would meet on equal terms a society as different as the British, while others held quite as passionately that modernization would only ruin the qualities that made Arabs so distinctive. Among Arabists, then, practical considerations vied with sentimentality, but there was room for many nuances between these opposing extremes.

Harold Ingrams was a Political Officer much admired between the world wars for negotiating calmly and patiently over a thousand peace treaties between Arabian tribes who had been at war immemorially. A decent man, a dutiful colonial official, he was more hardheaded than sentimental, yet, "I do not think my affection for the Southern Arabs, whether in Zanzibar, al-Yemen or the Hadhramaut, has ever been superseded." Here he is evoking Zanzibar:

> Down the long creek on the far horizon the sun sunk lower to the sea in a blaze of gold, while fantastic cloudbanks, heavily fringed with dull red, hung suspended above it. In them I saw tall houses—ceaselessly plodding camel caravans. All the scene was tinged with glory: mud and mangroves became like fairy gardens filled with trees of gold and jewels. The sea beyond seemed turned to blood. The nearer sand formed to ripples by the falling tide, gleamed opalescent. . . . I looked back at the town where the minaret of the Bedwi mosque was silhouetted against the darkening sky.

At the top a white-robed figure stood, his hands cupped to his mouth: "A—llahu Akbar, A—llahu Akbar." His voice proclaimed the eternal truth.

The elements in such a passage reveal a man enthralled by aesthetic properties peculiar to Arabs. The strangeness, the colors, the physical setting, the evidence of the faith, do more than generate purple prose—he may have been the local representative of the British King and Emperor with all sorts of plenary powers, but nonetheless he is putting himself in an inferior position: he is paying homage. Many of the tribes he pacified lived in a state of savagery, he could concede, but he came up with the ingenious apology that this was "of course not so shocking as the savagery of American gangsterism or of revolution in Russia or Spain, because it is more innocent."

Started in Cairo in 1916, the Arab Bureau was unique in British officialdom at the time, an early example of a think tank, given the task of planning policy in the Middle East during the world war and for future peacetime. Its chief was Colonel Gilbert Clayton, an old colonial hand. Those under his orders were men familiar with the desert as travelers or archaeologists, including T. E. Lawrence, St. John Philby, Sir Ronald Storrs, Kinahan Cornwallis, and George Lloyd, future High Commissioner in Egypt. Gertrude Bell, the only woman in the Bureau and a regular contributor to the *Arab Bulletin,* its publication, thought her colleagues were a "brilliant constellation." All of them had language skills and most had literary gifts as well.

Among themselves, the staff of the Arab Bureau could never quite decide where the balance lay between the practical and the sentimental approach to the Arabs. Resented for its disputes and quarrels by higher authority, the Arab Bureau was dissolved in 1920, but by then its foremost members were already well advanced in establishing as an article of faith the orthodox Arabist version of the relationship between the British and the post-Ottoman Arabs: this relationship had gone wrong, and the British were to blame, they had deceived the Arabs and let them down. The British public had no way of knowing whether this version of remote and largely unverifiable events was true or not, but they were willing to trust specialists apparently passing judgment on issues in which they had been personally involved. The lasting legacy of the Arab Bureau was the sense that British policy in the Middle East had been a failure, maybe even a crime. The Arabs had indeed been victimized and the British ought to accept guilt and do penance. Innumerable books and the media take this line, pro-Arab lobbies continue to promote it, and for decades now schools and universities have taught it as orthodoxy.

When the Ottoman Empire threw in its lot with Germany and the Central Powers the fate of the entire Middle East was suddenly open. Anticipating that the Ottoman Empire might well lose the war and at long last collapse, Sherif Hussein of Mecca and Abdul Aziz Ibn Saud and other tribal chiefs in Arabia prepared to extend their reach and replace the Turks. As the old order disintegrated, territory was at stake and tribal warfare was bound to become more general than usual. On the solid old grounds that my enemy's enemy is my friend, the tribal chiefs turned to the British. In effect, they were inviting the British to fight their battles for them, or at least to provide finance, in the virtual certainty that British intervention spelled victory. The only question was what the British would demand in return.

The Sherif Hussein-MacMahon Correspondence laid out the terms of the deal between the parties, and it has been minutely examined over the years, every nuance analyzed. High Commissioner in Egypt and a somewhat colorless personality, Sir Henry MacMahon was stating intentions for a future about which neither he nor the British government could be sure. His proposals were not legal documents. Perhaps Sir Ronald Storrs, acting as go-between, did not speak Arabic as well as he thought. Perhaps British phrasing was not as explicit as it might have been. Perhaps proposals promulgated in conditions of war are likely to be no longer valid in the altered conditions of peace. After grave setbacks, at any rate, British forces eventually drove the Ottomans out of their Arab provinces, and Sherifian tribesmen joined them if and when the spirit moved them, and they had received the inducement of gold sovereigns dispatched in crates from Whitehall.

Sherif Hussein now claimed to take his place as King of the Arabs. Personal ambition motivated his bid for power and glory, but this was illusory since the force to back it was absent. The even more ambitious Ibn Saud declared war on him in the customary tribal manner, and he had the power to conquer his domain and drive him into exile. Clever diplomacy in the first place had enabled Sherif Hussein to inveigle the British into backing him, and it was yet more of that same diplomacy on his part now to assert that he had lost his position not through any miscalculation of his own but because the British had reneged on their part of the bargain agreed through MacMahon. If he could establish that the British really had betrayed him and taken for themselves the power that was his due, he might manage to make them reverse their policy and help him fight his battles once again. Although overplaying his hand with fellow Arabs, he utilized this approach to run rings round British politicians and diplomats. T. E. Lawrence then persuaded the public that this supposed betrayal was the true account of what had happened. As in the case of Wilfrid Scawen Blunt, if an Englishman famous for the part he had played in the events in question was leveling a serious charge of perfidy against his own people, Arabs had every reason to believe the worst. And so they did, and still do.

Lawrence had been born in 1888, the illegitimate son of an Irish baronet, and his drama of identity was as personal as it was painful. Generally read as reportage, his famous *Seven Pillars of Wisdom* is ostensibly about the thrills and spills of the desert campaign with the Sherifian tribesmen but actually is a pseudo-autobiography, written with the false modesty that is a form of boasting. As one critic puts it, this is a work "seething with rancour and resentment, full of advocacy and

rhetoric,"[19] and impregnated with that demonic quality manifest in his
career. Certainly a clever man and a writer with narrative skills, he
developed a self-deprecating and highly misleading approach to the
world, which enabled him time and again to back into the limelight.
Cultivating influential figures and writing confessional letters to them,
he made sure to maintain alternatives to his pose as a social hermit.
Twice he was to conceal himself under assumed names, a course of
action bound to be discovered and add to the oracular aura in which
he cloaked himself. He can be found saying things and the opposite, as
though determined not to be pinned down. A man by the name of
John Bruce provided evidence that between 1922 and 1935 he used to
birch Lawrence though otherwise never touching him. Masochism
seems to explain every aspect of Lawrence's life. At the very center of
Seven Pillars is the episode when he claims that the Turkish governor of
Deraa forcefully sodomized him. "Unclean! Unclean!" wails
Lawrence, "decent men don't talk about such things." Nonetheless
here he was doing so, in a letter to the wife of Bernard Shaw, for
whom everything about sex was objectionable. Richard Aldington,
who as late as 1955 was the first biographer to examine Lawrence
critically, pointed out that he "could very seldom resist making small
episodes into a startling tale, and would even invent them."[20] Documents suggest that at the time of this alleged rape Lawrence could not
have been in Deraa. It may be that the sadistic Turkish governor was a
creature fantasized from tormented psychological depths.

"You rightly guessed that the Arab appealed to my imagination,"
Lawrence was writing to a friend, Vyvyan Richards, in July 1918,
going on to say that he could understand their point of view enough
to look at himself and other foreigners from their direction. Another
friend, G. J. Kidston of the Foreign Office, asked him what his
motives had been in "the Arab affair," and in November 1919
Lawrence answered, revealing the extraordinarily inflated picture he
had of himself. First came the personal: "I liked a particular Arab very
much, and I thought that freedom for the race would be an accept-

able present."This particular Arab was one Dahum, a youth of fourteen or fifteen whom Lawrence had met as an archaeologist in his pre-war career. He brought him to his home in Oxford and was to dedicate *Seven Pillars* to him in what amounts to a cryptic declaration of love. Only a fantasist could entertain the notion that someone as junior as he was could make a present of freedom to the Arab race. Second came patriotism, and he embellished this with the doubtful claim that Arab help reduced British losses by thousands.Third, intellectual curiosity: "I wanted to feel what it was like to be the mainspring of a national movement, and to have some millions of people expressing themselves through me." But he was one among several British intelligence officers in the field, a subordinate, and the mainspring of nothing at all. In no conceivable manner could millions of Arabs express themselves through him, and besides at that time only scores or at a pinch a few hundred were nationalists. The fourth motive he gives is "Ambition," the drive to create "an Arab Dominion in the Empire." At that same time in the autumn of 1919, he was writing to Lord Curzon, the Foreign Secretary, "My own ambition is that the Arabs should be our first brown dominion, and not our last brown colony." How did "dominion" square with "freedom for the race" and a nationalist movement for millions?

Faisal was one of the sons of Sherif Hussein, with responsibility for Arab participation in the campaign against the Ottomans. Clayton of the Arab Bureau judged, "The value of Lawrence in the position he has made for himself with Faisal is enormous." In a much quoted sentence in *Seven Pillars,* Lawrence gushed, "I felt at first glance that this was the man I had come to Arabia to seek—the leader who would bring the Arab Revolt to full glory. Faisal looked very tall and pillar-like, very slender, in his long white silk robes and his brown head-cloth bound with a brilliant scarlet and gold cloth. His eyelids were dropped; and his black beard and colourless face were like a mask against the strange, still watchfulness of his body. His hands were crossed in front of him on his dagger."

In the style of Harold Ingrams and so many Englishmen and women coming into contact with Arabs, this response of Lawrence's is primarily aesthetic, based on appearance, on dress and style. In real or practical terms, he had come to Arabia to fulfill the orders of his military superiors, and it was none of his business to seek a leader. Nevertheless he was as star-struck with Faisal as he had been once with the youth Dahum, and he kept up the high level of aesthetic appreciation. As operations were getting under way towards the end of 1916, Faisal addressed his tribesmen before an attack, and Lawrence reported how they "rushed over one another with joy to kiss his headrope." A fortnight later, in mid-January 1917, he was informing his mother how he admired Faisal, who "is about 31, tall, slight, lively, well-educated. He is charming towards me, and we get on perfectly together. He has a tremendous reputation in the Arab world as a leader of men, and a diplomat. His strong point is handling tribes: he has the manner that gets on perfectly with tribesmen, and they all love him."

By the middle of June 1917 the fantasist in him was writing to Clayton, "I've decided to go off alone to Damascus [where the main Turkish garrison was], hoping to get killed on the way: for all [our] sakes try and clear up this show before it goes further. We are calling them to fight for us on a lie, and I can't stand it." This referred to the Sykes-Picot Agreement, whereby after the war Britain and France were to set up administrations in some Ottoman provinces. Sherif Hussein had been consulted about the changing conditions but did not inform Faisal. Once the Agreement became known, Lawrence had chosen to interpret it as contrary to what had been specified by Sir Henry MacMahon. Britain, in Lawrence's view, was supporting the Arab Revolt to extend its own Empire and not for the sake of Arab independence. In fact, he had always been an imperialist, in particular anxious that Palestine should be in the British sphere, not the French. But then, and for the rest of his life, he thought that it was a disgrace, the abiding source of guilt and shame, that Britain might have acted in what it perceived as its own interest. Like Wilfred Scawen Blunt, he came to scorn his fellow countrymen; even the sight of them was unappealing. A British raiding party in the desert consisted of "healthy-looking tommies, like stiff-bodied schoolboys in their shirts and shorts—they were a broad-faced, low-browed people, blunt-featured beside the decadent Arabs, whose fine-curved shapes had been sharpened by generations of breeding to a radiance ages older than those primitive, blotched, honest Englishmen."

Years later, this Arabist apologia was still at the level of innuendo and self-promotion. Arabs, Lawrence declared, "saw in me a free agent of the British Government, and demanded from me an endorsement of its written promises. So I had to join the conspiracy and, for what my word was worth, assured the men of their reward . . . instead of being proud of what we did together, I was continually and bitterly ashamed. It was evident from the beginning that if we won the war these promises would be dead paper, and had I been an honest advisor of the Arabs I would have advised them to go home and not risk their lives fighting for such stuff." There was no conspiracy. Holding the rank of captain, he was not in a position to assure or advise anyone of anything, never mind adjudicating post-war Arab demands. But if he felt that British policy was duplicitous, he had only to resign his commission. Instead he stayed to campaign for another year. The Australian Light Horse finally captured Damascus and then rode through the city in pursuit of the enemy. In their wake Sherifian tribesmen entered the city and massacred captured Turks by the hundred, some of them already prisoners, others wounded and in hospital. Lawrence stood by as this war crime unfolded. Revolvers in hand, other British officers had to restore discipline. So eager to blame his superiors for dishonorable conduct, he was guilty of it himself and should have been court-martialed.

As Faisal's deputy he attended the Paris Peace Conference in 1919, drawing special attention to himself by appearing in full Arab dress among the world's leading statesmen. This pose signified that allegiance was no longer due to his own country, but in the words of one historian, "confirmed his standing as a champion of the Arab cause."[21] He hoped, he said, not merely to be able to defeat the Turks in the battlefield "but my own country and its allies in the council-chamber." Faisal did not wait, but in March 1920 claimed the spoils of war by declaring himself King of Syria. The French soon deposed him, and the British in 1921 invented a monarchy for him in Iraq as a consolation prize. Lawrence liked to maintain that this was the great achievement of his life. Faisal was a Sunni, and the Shia majority in what was becoming the state of Iraq therefore warned the British that they could not accept a Sunni king parachuted over them in this way. In his writings, for instance in the *Arab Bulletin,* Lawrence refers in passing to this sectarian divide in Islam but otherwise—most notably in *Seven Pillars*—he passes over in mysterious silence this crucial factor determining the fate of that country. Six thousand British soldiers lost their lives dealing with the Shia revolt, and a reluctant British Government was obliged to spend tens of millions of pounds to restore order. That was the outcome to which Lawrence had mightily contributed, and a genuine reason for him to feel guilt and shame.

Sir Arnold Wilson, acting as High Commissioner in the new Iraq, had warned his superiors about the danger of the Shia revolt. He blamed the Arab Bureau, "captured at a very early date by partisans of a policy which sought to impose King Hussein and his family upon the whole of Arabia."[22] Speaking out like that, he was soon fired. Gertrude Bell was prominent among partisans of Sherif Hussein and his family doing the damage that Wilson rightly feared. In part because she was a woman with political responsibility at a time when this was almost unheard of, and in part because she was the epitome of Arabism, she has been admired and held up as a model for emulation ever since. Born in 1868, she was the daughter of Sir Hugh Bell, one of the richest industrialists in England, and so always enjoying a large private income. She was the first woman at Oxford to obtain a First in Modern History. Eagerness to learn is her most attractive trait. In her early thirties, she began to travel, to study Persian and Arabic, and to take an interest in archaeology. All her life she wrote letters home to her mother and father. This extended correspondence has a remarkable girlish tone. Sentimentality invariably infused her undoubted intelligence. She vaunted the "Intimacy and friendship" with the Arabs which she thought made her "useful," without the least intimation that these intimate friends were highly skilled in deceptions and intrigues in pursuit of their very different ends.

Once the British were in the course of driving the Ottomans out of their Mesopotamian provinces, she was appointed head of the local branch of the Arab Bureau, and then Oriental Secretary under Sir Percy Cox, an experienced colonial official and eventual High Commissioner in Iraq. "Sir Percy gives me lots of thrilling things to do," she enthused, "Bagdad is a mass of roses and congratulations." The people were so "outgoing," genuinely delighted to be free of the Turks and glad to have the British. There was, however, a future to plan, a regime to organize: "I feel at times rather like the Creator in the middle of the week." This self-intoxication soon collided with the varied and complex demands of the population. The towns wanted an Arab Emir but could not fix upon the individual; Arab nationalists held demonstrations; full-blown jihad loomed; the tribes did not want to form part of a unified state; the British were facing the collapse of society. By the end of 1920, nevertheless, her spirits had revived. "Oh, if we can pull this thing off; rope together the young hotheads and the Shiah obscurantists, and enthusiasts—polished old statesmen—and scholars—if we can make them work together and find their own salvation for themselves, what a fine thing it would be. I see visions and dream dreams."[23]

Faisal was the object of these visions and dreams of hers. A referendum was rigged to install him on the throne of Iraq. The coronation was in August 1921. Influential Iraqis made plain that they well understood the workings of power, swearing allegiance to Faisal "because you are acceptable to the British Government." The irredeemably sentimental Gertrude Bell thought this was "a tremendous moment," and Faisal was "the finest living representative of his race." He was "a man of high principles and high ideals." He had "hitched his wagon to the stars—I feel as if I and all of us were playing the most magical tunes on their heart strings."

In fact, Faisal had quite other intentions. Never mind how the Arab Bureau, T. E. Lawrence, and Gertrude Bell had picked him out and projected him into kingship to which he had no right, he intended to reward them by getting rid of the British and assuming absolute power in their stead. This was only natural in the Arab order and the tribal politics to which he was accustomed. As his anti-British intrigues became plainer and more damaging, Gertrude Bell sought an interview with him. The letter she wrote afterwards to her parents is a classic rendering of the mirage befuddling the Arabist mindset, and it bears quoting at some length.

> I began by asking him whether he believed in my personal sincerity and devotion to him. He said he could not doubt it because he knew what I had done for him last year. I said in that case I could speak with perfect freedom and that I was extremely unhappy. I had formed a beautiful and gracious snow image to which I had given allegiance and I saw it melting before my eyes. Before every noble outline had been obliterated, I preferred to go, in spite of my love for the Arab nation and my sense of responsibility for its future. I did not think I could bear to see the evaporation of the dream which had guided me day by day.

At intervals during this meeting Faisal kissed her hand, and in the end she attempted to kiss his hand, a little exchange encapsulating the embarrassment of conducting politics in this manner. She was eased into a more suitable position as head of the archaeological museum of Baghdad. In July 1926 she was found dead with an empty bottle of pills beside her, but it is not known if she had killed herself by accident or by design. In any case, inability like hers to separate sentimentality from responsibility was to become the hall-mark of Arabism, spreading from her to infect wide swathes of the British administration in the disastrous closing years of the Empire, and enduring into the present. The difficulties of constructing a nation-state and constitutional government out of the different ethnicities and sects of Iraq have remained constant. Those who marched in European capitals to demonstrate against war with Saddam Hussein were Gertrude Bell's heirs, even if they had no idea who she might have been.

During Gertrude Bell's time in Iraq, Ibn Saud was deploying his Ikhwan, or Brotherhood, not only to destroy Sherif Hussein and to threaten his sons Faisal and Abdullah, but also to conquer tribal territories within reach. War was the select means of expanding his own kingdom in Arabia. The Ikhwan's Wahhabi and extremist version of Sunni Islam spread murder and destruction far and wide, including into Iraq. Unconsciously condescending, as easily deceived by Ibn Saud as she had been by Faisal, Gertrude Bell thought this exploitative warmonger was one of the most striking personalities she had ever encountered, with immense dignity and self-possession. "He asked innumerable questions and made intelligent comments. He's a big man." The Arab Bureau representative posted to Ibn Saud was Harry St. John Philby. As tenuous as Iraq, Saudi Arabia might well have fallen apart after its inception. Philby helped Ibn Saud to find openings and make a success of the country he had put on the map at the expense of neighbors. The key components of Arabism motivated the cantankerous and wholly unscrupulous Philby: flattery of Arabs and open contempt and hatred for his own country.

Philby came from a modest background. Born in 1885, he obtained scholarships to Westminster School and Trinity, Cambridge, ostensibly moving up the social ladder. Beginning his career as a District Officer in India, he was soon in trouble for dubious judgments in the law courts and for striking an Indian. His promotion was stopped, and when he was sent with British and Indian troops to Iraq in 1915, the authorities must have been glad to be rid of him. He was another gifted linguist, however, and Sir Percy Cox picked him out as

his personal assistant and Revenue Commissioner. In 1917 he was
sent on a mission to take British Government money to Ibn Saud.
Already receiving a stipend, Ibn Saud was further demanding arms
and a permanent subsidy, in effect successfully blackmailing the
British into co-operation exactly like his rival Sherif Hussein. Elizabeth Monroe, prone to apologetics in her biography of Philby, says
that what he liked best about this mission was that he was in sole control and out of reach of all communication. He felt comfortable in
Arab dress and grew the obligatory beard which he stained with
henna. Out of the £30,000 he was carrying, he seems to have handed
over £10,000, and what happened to the remainder is not clear.[24] Ibn
Saud, at any rate, became at once a friend "beyond all price." Arabist
fantasy was already on display: "The Arab is a democrat, and the
greatest and most powerful Arab ruler of the present day is proof of
it. Ibn Saud is no more than *primus inter pares;* his strength lies in the
fact that he has for twenty years accurately interpreted the aspira-
tions and will of his people." About to be mercilessly crushed by their
former leader and now absolute dynastic ruler, the Ikhwan might
have been surprised to learn from Philby that this was democracy.

On his return to Iraq, Philby fell out with Faisal and was caught stealing (or, as he put it, "purloining") papers from the files of Sir Percy Cox
and Gertrude Bell. Another posting was found for him in Amman, as
Chief Representative to Emir Abdullah, brother of Faisal and newly
installed in the same imperial manner as ruler of what was then Transjordan. Without authority, Philby began to pay himself a salary and expenses
out of the British grant to Abdullah. Whitehall accused him of "serious
irregularities," and he resigned before he was dismissed. Whitehall tried
to make Philby present an account, but in the end gave up the effort.
Seeking his fortunes in Saudi Arabia, he could rely on the favors of Ibn
Saud, starting an import-export business, obtaining lucrative concessions
and paid retainers to be a go-between with companies prospecting for
oil. Ibn Saud provided him with a number of houses in different towns
and also a concubine, and permitted him to explore the desert. Convert-

ing to Islam and calling himself Abdullah, he wrote an article with the title "Why I Turned Wahhabi," published in the *Egyptian Gazette*. The high standard of Arabian public morality, he thought, was "definitely superior" to the European ethical code based on Christianity. But some of those around Ibn Saud joked that Philby should not be Abdullah, meaning slave of God, but Abd al Qirsh, slave of halfpennies.[25]

Very few Englishmen were then in Saudi Arabia, but one of them was Reader Bullard, the British consul in Jiddah. There was in Philby, Bullard reported to the Foreign Office, "a simple dualism in which the powers of darkness are represented by H.M.G. [His Majesty's Government.]"[26] The Dutch consul, Colonel Daniel van der Meulen, himself an Orientalist of note, had read and respected the reports Philby had published about his desert explorations. On acquaintance with him, he too recorded his dismay that Philby put his knowledge of Saudi Arabia to such ill purposes, seeming "to go out of his way to oppose everything British and indeed, wherever Arab interests were concerned, openly scorned everything Western."[27] In January 1938 the British embassy in Cairo suspected that he was in the pay of Italy, as he was publishing articles that amounted to propaganda on behalf of Mussolini. In London the following year, he lectured about his desert explorations to the Royal Central Asian Society, and claimed that the British in Aden had wanted to shoot him. There were cries of "Rubbish!" and "Nonsense!" from the audience. Philby took things much further by joining the fascist and pro-German British People's Party, and standing as its candidate in a parliamentary by-election in the summer of 1939. He told electors, "An honourable peace could be assured by agreement with Germany. Germany wants it." He lost his deposit.

Back in Arabia in the early months of the war, he had "the queer consolation of knowing that another King and Country not only need me but want me desperately." Hugh Stonehewer-Bird, the British minister in Jiddah, reported that Philby was going around saying that the Allies should not have embarked on an unnecessary war, one that they could not win. To the outraged French minister, Philby said that Hitler was "*un homme très fin* [a most sophisticated man]," and a mystic comparable to Christ and Muhammad. In the face of Germany's initial onslaught, the government under Churchill could not tolerate defeatism, never mind treason. In the summer of 1940, Philby left Saudi Arabia on a round-about journey to the United States, "for the purposes of conducting anti-British propaganda," as Stonehewer-Bird informed the Foreign Office. He was "giving aid and comfort to the King's enemies." Stopping at Bombay, he was on British soil; the authorities took the opportunity to arrest him, and imprison him in England. When the radio announced yet more British shipping losses, he used to cheer. After the war, he settled down to the business of making money in Saudi Arabia, dying in 1960 on his way back from a congress of Orientalists in the Soviet Union. Not since Wilfrid Scawen Blunt had there been a more egregious example of the destructive impulses and perversities of Arabism.

The books Philby devoted to Arabia and the desert are hard to read, so heavy and labored is his prose. The same cannot be said about Wilfred Thesiger. His *Arabian Sands* is magnificent, the literary tour de force of someone able to turn his experience into fable. The son of a diplomat, educated at Eton and Oxford, in certain ways he was conventional. Reaching the rank of brigadier, he had served with distinction in the campaign in Ethiopia as second-in-command to Wingate, and in the Long Range Desert Patrol sabotaging in Libya far behind the German lines. Identifying with the Bedouin was for him not the expression of hatred for England. Like others before him, however, he was using the Bedouin as a stage on which to act out the drama of his exceptional and masterful character. "I wanted colour and savagery, hardship and adventure," he confessed, and he found all this in the Empty Quarter on long and arduous treks riding camels with his Bedouin companions. To them, he was Umbarak. "While I was with the Arabs I wished only to live as they lived." He wore a loin-cloth, he says, a long shirt, and a head-cloth with the ends

twisted round his head "in the Bait Kathir fashion." His British passport photograph showed him in full Arab dress. In England, he
longed with "an ache that was almost physical" to be back in Arabia.

"All that is best in the Arabs has come to them from the desert," is
a sentence that Thesiger put into print more than once, and surely it
came from the heart. This is an expression of pure romance. Arab
architecture, music, religion, literature, science, the glories of the
Ummayids and Abbasids, in fact came from the city. Like so many
Arabists, Thesiger admires the Bedouin for the freedom they are supposed to be enjoying, a freedom moreover that city folk, Europeans
above all, have long lost. Quite the opposite: the rigid codes of tribal
custom and fealty to the sheikhs, of arranged marriage and of shame
and honor, enforce patterns of behavior a good deal stricter than in
even highly regulated urban societies. No individual dare disobey for
fear of ostracism from the collective. The Bedouin life that Thesiger
experienced was a harsh repetitive round of feuding, murder, tribal
raiding, the rustling of animals, and all at the mercy of infant mortal-
ity, chronic physical ills such as tuberculosis, eye and skin diseases,
with little or no prospect of medicine or education. In his inner self,
Thesiger needed to believe that such hardships and primitive violence were truer to human nature than any form of civilization.
Change could only be for the worse.

Presenting the Bedouin as the Noblest Savages of them all, he
raised what seems destined to be the final monument to Arabist
sentimentality.

Arabism has sub-sets, and one of them centers on sexuality. Islam
lays down an unequal relationship between men and women,
who are prevented from socializing as a result. No doubt a good deal
of fantasy has conditioned Western impressions of the private lives of
Arabs. Nonetheless there is plenty of evidence that Western men and
women in Arab countries for one reason or another have felt free to
take advantage of what they perceive as the frustrations or the grati-

fications implicit in the segregation of the sexes there. Westerners are free to behave according to their taste, impervious to the social censure that applies to Arabs who break the codes. For many Westerners of either sex, the opportunity to conduct affairs abroad, unobserved, and usually as a monetary transaction without emotional attachment, has led to a widespread view of Arabs as sexual instruments worthy of special praise and flattery.

Discreet enough to abstain from personal confession but suggestive all the same, the artist Claire Sheridan in Algeria, for instance, generalized that Arabs "have two supreme qualifications: In spite of their lethargy they can always make love (I never heard of an impotent Arab), and even the most physically degenerate has strength to hold a horse." Wilfred Thesiger lived for long periods exclusively among Arab males, and states that homosexuality is very rare among the Bedouin though "common among most Arabs, specially in the towns," thus confirming his view of the moral superiority of the Bedouin. Testifying to the contrary is Robin Maugham, the son of a Lord Chancellor and the nephew of the novelist Somerset Maugham. He allowed his young Bedouin guide to seduce him: "Instinctively, he had known that I was attracted to him." Usually not quite so frank, many a memoir with a Middle East background nevertheless conveys approval of the sexual indulgence of whatever kind apparently available in Arab society.

Another powerful sub-set of Arabism is anti-Semitism. In common with many of his class, Wilfrid Scawen Blunt believed that Jews were engaged in conspiracies to further their selfish ends at the expense of everyone else. In his diaries, he scattered disparaging references to "Hebrews" and accused Disraeli, the Rothschilds, and Prime Minister Rosebery (whose wife was a Rothschild) of acting against the national interest. Lord Cromer's family name was Baring, and Blunt wrongly assumed this made him another Jew to be damned.

The Balfour Declaration in November 1917 acknowledged Jewish nationalism, which was something Blunt and his likes could never accept. The old Ottoman discrimination was dying. However carefully qualified, the concept of a home in Palestine placed Jews there on an equal footing with Muslims. British official circles lost no time interpreting this as a traditional selfish conspiracy on the part of Jews, but in a new guise, this time directed against Arabs. Writing to her mother in January 1919 Gertrude Bell spoke for many in a position of influence: "I hate Mr Balfour's Zionist pronouncement. It's my belief that it can't be carried out; the country is wholly unsuited to what the Jews have in view; it is a poor land, incapable of great development and with a solid two-thirds of its population Mohammedan Arabs who look on Jews with contempt . . . it's a wholly artificial scheme divorced from all relation to facts and I wish it the ill-success it deserves and will get, I fancy." Arab contempt for Jews was in the natural order of things, then, and deference was due to it.

In the early days of the Palestine Mandate, the British rigged the election of Haj Amin al-Husseini to be the Mufti of Jerusalem, de facto leader of the Arab population. Haj Amin's traditional tribal outlook unfitted him for his responsibilities. To him, Zionist Jews were indeed contemptible and he could imagine no possible relationship with them except a trial of strength. This catastrophic misjudgment was to culminate in his exile, and the adoption by Palestinian society of an ideology derived from fascism which was bound to perpetuate ruin.

An extensive literature debates the extent to which Whitehall and Mandate officials took one side or the other in the crucial years between the world wars. Individuals and pressure groups lobbied for one cause or the other. St. John Philby was one who kept his options open. He had excused himself from the charge of misappropriating public funds on the grounds that he could not work with the High Commissioner, Sir Herbert Samuel, "being a Zionist Jew." In a letter to the *Manchester Guardian,* he expressed the opinion that Haj Amin, already committed to armed rebellion, was "a good enough fellow if properly handled."[28] In London, Miss Farquharson and Miss Broadhurst, a militant pair of former suffragettes, took up the cause of Palestine, and whenever the Arabs could obtain no satisfaction, they would appeal to these ladies with a telegram ending, "Help!"[29] Another former suffragette turned strident anti-Zionist was Dr. Maude Royden Shaw. Frances Newton had been a missionary before settling in Haifa. "The Arabs looked on me as one of themselves," she proclaimed in her book *Fifty Years in Palestine.* "They trusted in me, drew me into their councils."[30] In a Palestinian paper she published a manifesto with the provocative title *J'Accuse:* "The British Government [has] allowed itself to become a tool in the hands of the Jews." In her view, Haj Amin was "much maligned,"[31] and when he organized and launched the Arab Revolt in 1936 she set up the Palestine Information Centre on his behalf. Among its members were several prominent Arabist publicists, among them Mrs. Steuart Erskine, J. M. Jefferies, and Colonel S. F. Newcombe. Frances Newton and others were deported in 1939, and not allowed back into Palestine until victory in the war was in sight.

Freya Stark, well-known for her Middle East travels and writings, went to extremes that an S.S. officer could have endorsed: "I really can't see that there is any kind of way of dealing with the Zionist question except by a massacre now and then . . . the world has chosen to massacre them at intervals, and whose fault is that?"[32] A stock feature of Arabism is to conflate Judaism and Zionism, and she was among the earliest to do so. In 1943, when Nazi extermination camps were engaged in just such a massacre, the Foreign Office sent her to the United States for a tour of seven months, in order to campaign against Zionism.

As a civil servant in Palestine, Aubrey Lees had been Deputy Governor of the Jaffa District. He was recalled home because "he had been engaging in anti-Semite and pro-Arab activities."[33] In England, like Philby, he joined the British People's Party. A Home Office report states that he made "no secret of his great admiration for the Nazi regime," and criticized the British government for "its failure to get rid of the Jewish menace." Arnold Toynbee was shrewd enough to cloak much the same views in pseudo-academic discourse. Born in 1889, he had dodged military service in the First World War, instead becoming a member of the Political Intelligence Department of the Foreign Office. In that capacity, he opposed the Balfour Declaration. Sitting next to him at dinner in January 1918, Virginia Woolf recorded approvingly how "Arnold outdid me in anti-nationalism, anti-patriotism, and anti-militarism." As director of Chatham House, a think-tank whose association with the Foreign Office provided cachet and influence, he gave these sentiments of guilt and defeat a wide circulation through meetings and publications. During trips to Germany, he became friendly with Alfred Rosenberg, the Nazi ideologue. In February 1936 he had a long interview with Hitler, returning "convinced of his sincerity in desiring peace in Europe." S.S. General Walter Schellenberg, in charge of planning for Britain in the event of an invasion, described Toynbee as "personally obliging." Judaism and Jews, Toynbee liked to maintain, were historic fossils. In a notorious lecture at McGill University in 1961, he said, "the Jewish treatment of Arabs in 1947 is comparable to the Nazi murder of six million Jews"—had this vicious smear been true, it would have made nonsense of the prior smear of fossilization. At the start of the 1973 war in the Middle East, Syria mounted a surprise invasion of Israel, whereupon Toynbee communicated to the Syrian Minister of Defense: "my heartfelt wishes for an Arab victory." In which case, Arab treatment of Jews would have been truly comparable to Nazi mass-murder.

Armed and financed by Britain, the Arab Legion was raised in Transjordan as a force to protect the Emir Abdullah. The officers were British, the rank-and-file Bedouin. Its pre-war commander, Colonel F. E. Peake, known as Peake Pasha, summed up common prejudices when he complained in 1938 in a letter to a friend that "we poor British taxpayers" were producing the money so that "the Jews may filch Palestine from the Arabs . . . to carry out a promise which Jews (notorious liars) say was made to them 5,000 years

ago."[34] Peake's second in command and the Legion's subsequent commander was John Glubb, who as Glubb Pasha was to become a public
figure. The son of a major-general in the Royal Engineers, he himself
had served in the First World War and then in 1920 in the Iraq Desert
Camel Corps, pacifying tribesmen and repelling the Ikhwan as they
raided across the Saudi Arabian border. Duty obliged him to kill a
good many of them and discipline the remainder, but the irony of it
escaped him when in one of his books he came to the standard Arabist conclusion: "The Bedouin was every Englishman's idea of
nature's gentleman."

Small in stature, a certain prissiness of manner was accentuated
by the receding chin that earned Glubb the Arab appellation Abu
Hunaik, Father of the Little Jaw. After five years, he resigned his commission in the British army to "devote my life to the Arabs. My decision was largely emotional. I loved them." What it means to love in
this unspecific and abstract way he did not explain. Baldly, "The people dwelling east of the Jordan were my people." He gave his word of
honor to the Emir Abdullah that he was a Transjordanian, and could
describe himself as "an old family retainer." Yet Major R. C. Broadhurst, an officer of the Arab Legion, had observed Glubb at close
quarters for a number of years. He told Peake Pasha that as far as he
knew Glubb had never entered an Arab's house or had a genuine conversation with an Arab, remaining "absolutely ignorant and indeed
careless of the mood, humour and indeed character of the cultivated
Arab."[35] This suggests that what Glubb really loved about the Arabs
was the stark and warlike setting they provided in which he might be
seen cutting a fine figure.

Prejudice warped Glubb's political and military judgment. In his
books he subscribed to the sort of sinister fictions common to anti-
Semites: "The Jews were too clever for the Arab leaders;" he had a
"distrust of Jewish motives;" "Jewish aggressiveness" was ever-pre-
sent; it would be an error to suppose that the introduction of Jewish
capital would be helpful to the Arabs of Transjordan; the Jews possess

"an enormous power over world publicity;" he thought Israel was "imitating the methods of Hitler and Stalin." The Public Record Office has filed "A Note on the Situation in Jordan" that he wrote at the beginning of July 1952. "It would seem probable that the Israeli army (or indeed perhaps the public) experience a psychological urge to shoot, burn, blow up and destroy by violence, and to work their free and uncontrolled will on persons of some other race, as a psychological compensation for the years during which they endured such treatment at the hands of others."[36] As from May 1948 Chaim Weizmann was President of the newly declared state of Israel. Writing to him that June, Isaiah Berlin feared that there might be "a minor massacre" carried out by Glubb and the nearly forty British officers of the Legion.[37] Throwing the Legion into battle in Jerusalem and the West Bank, Glubb virtually destroyed it as a fighting force, while also contributing to the extension of Palestinian division and collapse into the indefinite future.

Several dozen Britons did in fact fight in Palestinian ranks. The Haganah, now the embryo Israeli army, intercepted a letter from an Arab stating, "What surprises me is the British volunteers in the Arab army. Nablus is full of them. . . . Why do you think they chose to serve in the Arab army? Was it because of hatred of the Jews?"[38] Another intercepted letter was from a British policeman, Gregory Kimston, serving in Jenin on the West Bank. He informed the British vice-consul in Damascus of a group of British deserters in Arab ranks, who were receiving forty Palestinian pounds per month, with full board, free beer, and two packs of cigarettes a day. In Jerusalem Eddie Brown and Peter Madison, both deserters, drove a British army truck and a police car to the entrance of the *Palestine Post,* and detonated them, killing one man and injuring more than twenty. In another incident, six British deserters shot a suspicious Jewish guard and exploded three stolen trucks in front of two hotels in Tel Aviv, killing 58 people, and wounding 32.[39]

Old-style Arabism could not survive beyond the end of the British Empire. In the era of their independence and power, Arab nationalists made sure to repudiate as by-products of Western imperialism everything to do with Arabism and Arabists. Surprised and shocked, British ruling circles have since sought to curry Arab approval by backing away from Israel, uncertainly at first, then faster in response to militant Islamism. The Foreign Office and Chatham House, the media with the BBC and the *Guardian* newspaper in the lead, academia, trade unions, members of both houses of Parliament, pressure groups like the Palestine Solidarity Committee and Viva Palestina and the Council of Anglo-Arab Understanding, flatter Arabs and Muslims by finding ways to turn public opinion against Israel. Exactly as the Haj Amins and Gertrude Bells, the Freya Starks and Glubb Pashas would have wished, its anti-Semitic sub-set is the one vital legacy of Arabism.

CHAPTER ELEVEN

Germany Calling

T he Germany that well-disposed but long-forgotten travel writers such as Samuel Laing or William Howell evoked in the first half of the nineteenth century was a patchwork of kingdoms, grand duchies, margraves, and what have you. They and others painted for British readers a scene of provincial courts, pretty old towns and villages, music, first-rate universities, altogether picturesque and peaceful, even where Prussia was concerned. "Noble, patient, deep, pious and solid Germany," Thomas Carlyle rhapsodized in a letter to *The Times,* taking that country's side in the 1870 war with France. But by the end of that century, the country's constituent elements had united, and its armies had relegated on the battlefield the Habsburg Empire to second place as a German-speaking power, and captured Alsace and Lorraine from France. The stereotype of a picturesque and peaceful country could not survive the impact of a German nationalism that elided into militarism. Kaiser Wilhelm II aspired to expand his empire in the Middle East and Africa. In 1896, the Kaiser's telegram of congratulation to Paul Kruger, President of the Transvaal Republic campaigning for self-rule, made it plain that there was a new balance of forces and Germany was set to replace France as Britain's most challenging rival.

People all over the world could see the successes obtained by militant nationalism in Europe and hope to imitate it for themselves. In the face of this development, many British men and women in the Empire sympathized with local nationalists and did what they could to support them, if need be sacrificing primary loyalties and principles. Mohandas Gandhi, for instance, in his autobiography gives examples of English people who helped him around that time to undermine the British position in India. He mentions, indeed almost sanctifies, a Miss Manning of the National Indian Association; Mr. Ellerthorpe who apologized for being unable to invite Gandhi into his club; Mr. Saunders in Calcutta who placed his newspaper and office at Gandhi's disposal; Miss Schlesin who "knew neither night nor day in toiling for the cause" of Indian independence; two Englishmen from Johannesburg who came to him when the Boer War broke out were as good as members of his family, and adopted the Indian style. In India in 1926, a critical Aldous Huxley found Gandhi attended by Madeleine Slade, a young English woman, "who sits there worshipping [him] like a dog—handing him his spectacles, adjusting his loin cloth, giving him his food when it is brought and so on. He just treats her as though she weren't there."[1] Replicated wherever the British ruled, the behavior of such individuals was replacing self-confidence with guilt and abasement, destroying piecemeal the psychological foundations upon which the Empire had hitherto rested.

The Boers were determined to fight for their land, their race, and their religion, and to oppose them appeared to many in Britain to be imperialist bullying of a worthy minority. The issue was not simple, for an independent republic in Boer hands was certain to lead to oppression of the blacks and ultimately apartheid, as Kipling prophesied at the time and as eventually proved the case. Nonetheless, identification with those who had taken up arms against England was on a scale not seen since the War of American Independence. Hardened opponents of colonialism, the radical wing of the Liberal Party and especially foremost members like Lloyd George and John Morley, were so pro-Boer that they "invited misrepresentation as a party of separatists, defeatists, and even traitors." [2] Pamphlets and leaflets hammered at the same pro-Boer themes: "the war was inexcusable in its origins and immoral in its prosecution; it was inspired by alien capitalists; the British Government was hypocritical and unwilling to negotiate a just settlement; and the British public had been hood-winked and its soul corrupted." [3] Lord Salisbury, the Conservative prime minister at the time, was driven to complain: "England is, I believe the only country in which, during a great war, eminent men write and speak publicly as if they belonged to the enemy."

The combination of fabrication, self-reproach, and hot-air illusion was destined to set a pattern repeated easily and often. That veteran enthusiast of foreign causes, Lord Bryce, had visited South Africa in 1895, and "saw in the Boers a spirit of independence reminiscent of the Italian struggle against the French and Austrian empires." [4] Radical members of Parliament, academics like Gilbert Murray and the philosopher Herbert Spencer, journalists including W. T. Stead, styled as "physician to the nation's moral health," rapidly took the step of organizing a pressure group comprising the Transvaal Committee, the South African Conciliation Committee, and the Stop the War Committee (How many committees have subsequently appropriated that title in how many wars?). Henry Campbell-Bannerman, the future Liberal Prime Minister, wrote to Bryce in 1899 that the war was "a scandalous plot of money-seekers using the British Government as a cats-paw." Covering the war for the *Manchester Guardian,* J. A. Hobson, a Marxist and implacable critic of Britain and its Empire, spelled out that the money-seekers and alien capitalists responsible for war were all in a Jewish conspiracy to do down the "simple-mannered, plain living Boer farmers." In the view of the *Clarion,* a Labour weekly, "parvenu Hebrew diamond-thieves" controlled the press. [5] "The Boers are, man for man our superiors in dignity, devotion and capacity," Beatrice Webb noted in her diary in January 1900. Irish nationalists so identified with the Boers that they wanted to bomb British troop ships. Kruger was given the freedom of the city of Dublin. A couple of hundred volunteers from abroad fought with the Boers, about half of them forming an Irish Brigade under the command of a Major John MacBride. At Mafeking, a British trooper called Hay defected to the enemy, but perhaps surprisingly there was no pro-Boer British Legion.

The evolution of H. N. Brailsford as a scatter-gun public intellectual of his day is particularly instructive. Born in 1873, he came from a Methodist background, and his biographer holds that this accounts for "his moral fervour, his capacity for indignation, the certainty of his convictions." He loved the world, this assessment continues, "because he had no one else to love."[6] Commitment to a cause meant release from this absorption in himself. In April 1897 he volunteered to join another Philhellenic Legion in a renewal of fighting between Greeks and Turks. He saw himself defending liberty against despotism. In a Turkish attack, four of the sixteen British Legionaries were wounded, including Captain Birch, their commander. Within weeks, a disillusioned Brailsford was back in England lamenting that "the forces of Oriental barbarism" had turned out to be not as he had imagined: "I had not known I was firing at simple peasants." As a journalist, he had assignments in Crete and Thessaly and his experiences there angered him against the Greeks for whom he had just been fighting.

In the Boer War, he charged, the fault lay in the British government's "policy of adventure and provocation." England was similarly to blame for the plight of the Balkan populations. With other activists including Bryce and Noel Buxton, he formed the Balkan Committee with the purpose of liberating Macedonia from Turkish rule. Another body, the Macedonian Relief Committee, sent him out there as its agent. He became a member of the executive of the Society of Friends of Russian Freedom, and obtained British passports for three terrorists, one of whom blew himself up in the Hotel Bristol in St. Petersburg. In addition, he sat on committees concerned with Persia, Angolan slavery, Russian prisons, and the future of Albania. The wheel again came full circle in 1908 when the Young Turks seized power, and he could praise those against whom he had fought in the field and in political campaigns.

Emily Hobhouse had just this moral fervor, capacity for indignation, and certainty of conviction. She and other members of her prominent family suffered from a sense of guilt because their fortune came from the slave trade, and this obliged them to make amends. Her father was a forbidding Archdeacon, whom she looked after until his death in 1895, by which time she was thirty-four. Immediately she set off for America with the intention of being a missionary, Disappointed, breaking off an engagement to an unsuitable and dishonest man, she returned to England, to throw herself into the pro-Boer cause. She took advantage of her social position to pester politicians. At the end of 1900 she went to South Africa: "Deeply I had felt the call. Passionately I resented the injustice of English policy. Wholeheartedly I offered myself for relief to the distressed."[7] The evidence confirmed her emotions. Her dispatches in *The Times* broke the news of the diseases and malnutrition causing thousands of Boer deaths in prison camps. In the later half of 1901 she addressed forty meetings in England, becoming a household name. To the Boers, she claimed, the very word British meant "unjust, dishonest, grasping and oppressive."[8] The authorities, notably Lord Kitchener in charge of running the war, had had enough of someone they deemed a traitor. When she arrived back in South Africa, she was lifted bodily off one ship and on to another, to be deported.

Life without a cause was nothing to her, in the words of her admiring biographer John Hall. Gandhi was to comment, "Hers was a name to conjure with among the Boers. And she made my way smooth among them by throwing the whole weight of her influence with the Indian cause." Soon after the outbreak of the First World War she spent five months in Amsterdam as secretary to the International Committee of Women for Permanent Peace. Then in 1916, through the German embassy in Berne, she arranged to go to Germany. The

Foreign Office had seized her passport, but she traveled on German papers and was accompanied by a German official at all times. She inspected the camp for British internees at Ruhleben. In Berlin she was taken to Gottlieb von Jagow, Secretary of State in the Foreign Ministry. The message she could transmit to London was that Germany was willing to negotiate peace under the right conditions. She agreed to keep communications with Jagow open. One of her letters to him was intercepted in which she mentioned an imminent British offensive. Basil Thomson, head of the Criminal Investigation Department, interrogated her about this letter on July 1, 1916, the very day when the Battle of the Somme opened. He advised arresting her for trafficking with the enemy, but the powers that be decided otherwise. Had this secret correspondence been made public, John Hall writes, "the call for her to be charged with treason would have been deafening."[9] The day before Emily Hobhouse's interrogation, Sir Roger Casement had been sentenced to death for treason.

Casement's is a very odd case. Born a Protestant in Ireland in 1864, he was secretly baptized Catholic at the age of four. By the time he was twelve, both his parents had died, and he was a ward in Chancery in the care of his uncle in the Irish countryside. A clerk for a shipping firm, he made three trips to West Africa, and in 1884 went to work there for the Association Internationale du Congo, set up by the famous explorer H. M. Stanley as part and parcel of the callous exploitation of that country on behalf of the Belgian King Leopold. From 1892 to 1913, he was a member of the British Consular Service in various postings in South America and Africa, outwardly a successful official rewarded with a knighthood. After another stint in the Congo as a Consul, in 1901 he had submitted to Lord Lansdowne, the Foreign Secretary, a memorandum about the atrocities resulting from King Leopold's greed and which he had witnessed first-hand. It is alleged that Lansdowne's indifference to this memorandum alienated Casement. The intelligence service also obtained his so-called Black Diaries, in which he recorded his many homosexual encounters, or perhaps hectic fantasies. The campaign of Home Rule for Ireland triggered in him a violent hatred for England, of which there had been no previous indication. In an article which certainly was based on hectic fantasy he wrote in February 1914, "The true alliance to aim at for all who love peace is the friendly union of Germany, America and Ireland."[10]

Casement and his new nationalist colleagues therefore planned to obtain arms in America for shipping to Germany, for use in Ireland. In America when war was declared, he and other Irishmen negotiated with the German ambassador and the military attaché in Washington. Casement was to report to Berlin as the representative of Irish Home Rule. The ship he sailed on put in at the Norwegian port of Christiana. Casement had picked up a Norwegian sailor, who went to the British Embassy, betraying the betrayer by giving away Casement's identity and purpose, for which he was paid 25 kroner with a promise of £5,000 for information leading to Casement's capture. Reaching Germany, however, Casement tried to recruit an Irish Brigade from the 4,000 Irish prisoners of war held in a camp at Limburg. He was jeered, so much so that he became depressed and ill. Just three Irish renegades joined him, and they were "worse than useless."[11] Timed to coincide with the Irish nationalist Easter Rising of 1916, Casement sailed for Ireland with arms and ammunition. Wisely the Germans refused to send any troops. The British were waiting, and lost no time hanging him.

Houston Stewart Chamberlain spent the First World War in Germany, and might well have been hanged for treason if he had ever returned to England. His writings, especially the two volumes of his *Foundations of the Nineteenth Century,* are an early statement of the major themes of Nazi ideology. Rather in the manner of Arabists with the Bedouin, he imagined that Germans had a better way of life than other more materialistic peoples; they were simpler and nobler, idealistic and artistic. Only Germany could protect the "life-giving centre of western Europe." Aryan supremacy was the answer to "tartarised Russians," the "mongrels of Oceania and South America," the "millions of blacks," all of whom were "arming for the war of races in which there will be no quarter." Leading Nazis were to venerate him as a prophet whom they could present as certifying intellectually their *völkisch* myths at home and the racism with which they justified conquests abroad.

In an account of this unusually splenetic individual, Geoffrey Field attributes Chamberlain's generalized hatred of England to "strong elements of guilt and self-doubt, a sense of failure."[12] Born in 1855 into a wealthy and aristocratic family, he was one year old when his mother died; his father was an admiral whom he hardly knew; and a formidable grandmother brought him up in the town of Versailles. Sickly, he was nicknamed P.L.O. by his brother, standing for Poor Little One. Bullied at school, he felt "completely foreign and uncomfortable" in Britain and "shrieked with joy" when at last "the soil of the Continent" was underfoot. To a tutor in Germany, he said, "I would give my left arm to have been born a German."[13] Not surprisingly, he supported the Boers and Irish nationalists.

Settling in Bayreuth, he absorbed the music of Wagner and the accompanying anti-Semitism in which that town specialized. By 1895 he had become the foremost popularizer of the cult of Wagner. Glorying in Wagner's racist prejudice, he concurred that the Jew was "the destroyer of civilisation," and as Field puts it " the symbol of all that he loathed." One of his nightmares was that Jews had kidnapped him so that he disappeared without trace, and in another they abducted him to be crucified. Eventually he sealed his status in Bayreuth by marrying Wagner's daughter Eva and living in Wahnfried, the house that was already a shrine to the composer's memory and his anti-Semitism. Kaiser Wilhelm was eager to take up and correspond with someone whose *Deutschtum* was as aggressive and definitive as his own: "Their elaborate, wordy letters, full of mutual admiration and half-baked ideas [conveyed] the perplexing thought world of mythical and racist conservatism . . . that strange paranoid world of collapsed empires, Bolshevik terror, Jewish and Freemason conspiracies, and secret hope for a new crusade against the forces of racial decayed materialism."[14]

The likes of Paine, John Oswald, Byron, and Wilfrid Scawen Blunt had hoped in the past that Britain would lose whatever war it had been engaged in. Chamberlain, too. Once the First World War had been declared, he became a full-time agitator and publicist, demanding massive attacks on London and unrestricted submarine warfare to enforce the country's submission; in 1916, he became a naturalized German citizen. Somewhere between 750,000 and a million copies of his essays were sold in the war. Here in his view was a fight to the death between Teuton and Jew. England's victory, he told his brother, would be "terrible for the whole world, a catastrophe."

There was nothing in Nazi ideology to which the Kaiser could not have subscribed. The mind-set was continuous. In Bayreuth for a Party rally, on 30 September 1923 Adolf Hitler made sure to meet Chamberlain. They discovered at once that they were kindred spirits. Hitler, Chamberlain raved in a letter to him, was one of those "rare beautiful beings," moreover he was no "mere phrasemonger," and he went on, "You have immense achievements ahead of you, but for all your strength of will I do not regard you as a violent man." The editor of the Nazi Party newspaper wrote to Eva Chamberlain that Hitler had been childishly pleased by the letter.

Within a few weeks Chamberlain was proved wrong about his new hero refraining from violence, because Hitler staged the Beer Hall putsch in Munich, for which he was given a light prison sentence. For Chamberlain, this was a momentary set-back, reflecting the triumph of the Jews and the Jesuits, indeed a curious combination. Chamberlain was the first person of national and even international reputation to align himself with the Nazi movement, and the inner circle never forgot it. Alfred Rosenberg praised him as "the pioneer and founder of a German future." After reading Chamberlain's *Rasse und Nation,* Heinrich Himmler jotted in his diary, "Terrible

Jews."[15] For Josef Goebbels, Bayreuth was the height of German culture, and he wept when he found Chamberlain dying there. In 1927,
his voice trembling with emotion, Hitler spoke at his votary's
funeral. SA men in uniforms with swastika arm-bands escorted the
hearse.

Winifred Williams was also at the heart of Bayreuth. Born in England in 1897, she had lost both parents by the time she was two. Karl
Klindworth, a piano teacher, and his wife adopted this orphan and
brought her up in Germany. Just eighteen, in 1915 she married
Siegfried, Richard Wagner's son, widely thought to be homosexual.
He was willing to coast on his father's reputation and rather unsuccessfully to write music of his own, leaving to Winifred the organization of Wahnfried. She and Chamberlain, her brother-in-law by
marriage, never spoke English to one another. The end of the First
World War brought complete identification with her adopted nation:
"it's sickening—what have the Germans come to.—No sense of honour! No sense of shame! Terrible—that we've sunk so low."

In Wahnfried, "Anti-Semitism was a constant feature of everyday
life." "Nagods" was Winifred Wagner's private term for Jews. When
Hitler first came to breakfast there, she felt "full of awe." To a friend
she wrote that his power was "rooted in the moral strength and
purity of the man" and that the Beer Hall putsch opened up her "passionate commitment" to him and his ideas. "If we became completely
free of Nagods here, we would practically have achieved the impossible without even trying," she wrote to another close friend. Her anti-
Semitism turned a tour in the United States to publicize Bayreuth
into a fiasco. At Hitler's request, in January 1926 she joined the Nazi
Party with the number 29,249.

After Siegfried's death in 1930, she ran the opera, making atten-
dance at Bayreuth a highlight of the Nazi calendar. Hitler and
Goebbels were loyal patrons and financial sponsors. A week after
annexing Austria, Hitler came to Bayreuth: "I had him here completely
to myself from 2 till 6, completely relaxed . . . because with me he can

touch on the quite private things that went very deep with him." No English person, she liked to boast, knew Hitler better than she did. She and Hitler did not meet during the war, but in February 1942 he put the main point about her to his cronies: "after all, Frau Wagner did bring Bayreuth together with National Socialism—that is her great historical contribution." A year later, in February 1943, she drove to Prague to pick out for her son Wolfgang furniture and other posses-sions stolen and sold off from Jewish properties. As late as October 1944 she was declaring, "the Führer still stands before us, his example and his flawless personality a beacon . . . his stature has grown ever more heroic." Faced with a post-war tribunal, she remembered her origins. British nationality might now be helpful. Tracing a half-sister Maude, the daughter of her father's first marriage, she introduced her-self as " 'little' sister Winnie." At the end of her life, nonetheless, she confided in another old Party faithful that she was always dreaming of Hitler, and "he always appears in his former undiminished greatness."[16]

Hitler's Nazism was directed to the greater glory of Germany; Mussolini's Fascism to the greater glory of Italy. The central national-ist character of these movements excluded all possibility of universal appeal. Other features, therefore, had to motivate other nationals; for instance, the personal charisma of Hitler or Mussolini; the offen-sive against revolutionaries or capitalists, both terms usually short-hand for Jews, in spite of the mutual contradiction; the sense that these political systems stood for order and social discipline, or that only a rival totalitarianism could be an effective bulwark against Communism. For some, here was modernity in arms, while for oth-ers here was a revival of some supposedly heroic past.

Founder and leader of the British Union of Fascists (BUF) in 1932, Sir Oswald Mosley tried to recruit a mass following by appeal-ing to all these themes simultaneously. Then still only thirty-six, he had been both a Conservative and a Labour Member of Parliament, but felt that neither party recognized his talents. With Hitler and Mussolini as his models, he adopted the title of Leader, affected a bombastic style of speaking, showed himself off in jackboots, dressed his followers in black uniforms, and mustered them in military formations. Nazism, he further believed, owed its popularity on the streets to anti-Semitism, and he chose to activate it in Britain. Jews were attacked orally at one rally after another and physically in street battles of mounting violence. Mosley's declared intention was to emulate the Nuremberg Laws of 1935, to deprive Jews of citizenship and eventually deport them to Uganda.

Apologists have attempted to dress Mosley up as a Prime Minister *manqué,* a cross between Keynes and Nietzsche, a "Faustian riddle," a Lucifer, and so on. In fact, Mosley was too vain, too imperceptive, to be able to resolve the contradiction of trying to form a national mass movement copied from a foreign ideology, especially since that ideology was an increasingly clear danger to Britain. He chose to draw closer to Hitler and in April 1935 in Munich the two duly spent an hour together, with a lunch to follow. "Mosley boasted that Hitler liked him."[17] The public came to hear that in 1936 Mosley had married the openly Nazi Diana Mitford in Berlin, with Hitler and Goebbels present at the ceremony. Guy Liddell, deputy head of MI5, has recorded that the BUF had a secret military organization known as the Fellowship of the Services run by one F. G Geary. "The organisation was anti-Communist in 1936, is now anti-Jewish . . . is also pro-Nazi and each member is armed."[18] Had the Germans invaded, Mosley would have had the opportunity to play a Quisling role. As a precaution, Mosley was detained under emergency legislation from May 1940 to late 1943. About eight hundred of his followers were rounded up at the same moment, and the fact that they were nonentities proved what little headway Mosley had made. Years later, the public further learned that he had been in the pay first of Mussolini, then of Hitler. Though he always denied it, and played the patriotic card, Mosley had been the agent of foreign powers.

In the eight years of the BUF's existence those who joined as well as those who then left it numbered altogether no more than a quarter of a million. Few of them were in a position to bring the Party any experience of much value, with the exception of Major General J.F.C. Fuller, a student of military strategy. Typifying Party intellectuals (such as they were), Henry Williamson the novelist thought Hitler "a very wise and steadfast and truth-perceiving father of his people."[19] Olive Hawks was the BUF candidate in parliamentary elections in 1937, becoming Chief Women's Organiser in 1940. Interned during the war, she wrote a novel that Williamson revised but which has sunk without trace. Mosley's foreign policy advisor was Robert Gordon-Canning, a soldier who earlier had served on the staff of Abdel Krim in the Rif wars in Spanish Morocco. In classic Arabist style, he discovered in Fascism "a certain barbaric splendour" and "a warrior spirit opposed to that of the nightclub."[20]

A Home Office report quoted by Stephen Dorril found that membership of the BUF represented all social and economic classes and occupational groups, singling out domestic servants, shopkeepers and—strangely—middle-class cinema owners: "They were unpoliticized and had not voted for the major parties but supported a 'hero' in an 'heroic' age."[21] John Warburton was one such. He and his brother Ned were the sons of a blacksmith. At the end of 1933 they attended a Mosleyite meeting in Manchester. Ned lost an eye when Communists threw potatoes with razor blades stuck in them. John Warburton was taken with Mosley at first sight: "He was striding along, and to me he seemed a god." The brothers participated in the 1936 Battle of Cable Street, an episode that has entered London lore as the moment when the local Jewish population fought off a rally led by Mosley. John Warburton, a would-be storm-trooper, instead became the official BUF photographer.[22]

Sylvia Plath was reaching for psychological insight into the human propensity for violence when she wrote, "Every woman adores a Fascist / The boot in the face, the brute / Brute heart of a brute like you." The more violence there was, the greater the likelihood of chosen enemies getting their comeuppance, the greater grew the lure of a

Fascist movement. Trevor Grundy's rather disconsolate *Memoirs of a Fascist Childhood* bears this out. He was the son of a London taxi-driver who took knuckle-dusters to Mosley's rallies and had learnt to say *Sieg Heil*. His mother, he thought, became a Fascist partly for her husband's sake and partly to have revenge on her parents for their alleged mistreatment of her. In the house, they used to salute a prominently displayed photograph of Mosley. The father was interned along with Mosley, and the mother would say that after Hitler won the war, both these men would be released and, "Then the Jews would be for it."[23]

Five years in prison was the sentence usually handed out to anyone openly promoting Nazism in the war. Olive Baker, a thirty-nine-year-old nurse and BUF member, received this sentence for distributing postcards advertising German radio propaganda. In her cell she slashed her wrists and wrote "Hail Mosley" and "*Heil* Hitler" in blood on the wall. Another BUF member, Elsie Orrin, got five years for telling soldiers in a pub that Hitler was a better man and leader than Churchill.[24] Well into the war and in much the same spirit, one Norman Piggott of Englefield Green in Surrey threatened a policeman, "Your time's pretty short now. When Hitler has finished with Russia he'll soon put you where you belong, and the sooner the better."[25]

At the opposite end of the social scale were people who outwardly might shudder at the vulgarity of BUF brawling but sympathized with Hitler and in his defense devised astonishing misrepresentations of reality. Out of prejudice and self-interest they were willing to ignore or whitewash the rising brutality. Hitler had been in power for less than a year when the Prince of Wales, briefly King Edward VIII and then the Duke of Windsor after his abdication, was confiding his fondness for Nazism to Count Mensdorff, the former Austrian ambassador: "Of course, it is the only thing to do, we will have to come to it, as we are in great danger from the Communists here, too."[26] In his wartime table talk with his cronies Hitler several times regretted the abdication of the Duke of Windsor on the grounds that under different circumstances he could have been the head of a friendly English state. Ribbentrop called the Duke "a kind of English national socialist." Former Prime Minister Lloyd George had two audiences with Hitler and judged him to be "the George Washington of Germany."[27] Hitler, he thought, "likes to withdraw from the world for spiritual refreshment . . . he has no vices, or indulgences or ambitions."[28] Lord Lothian had been Lloyd George's private secretary and had cabinet experience. He came out of his audience with Hitler convinced that he had met a man of peace, "a visionary rather than a gangster," and "one of the creative figures of this generation."[29]

An old colonial hand, Sir Arnold Wilson had served in India, and then as Civil Commissioner in Baghdad at the end of the First World War. Fired on account of his unwelcome warning that British policy would lead to a Shia uprising, he entered politics and was elected a Conservative Member of Parliament in 1933. He began visiting Germany regularly, attended Nuremberg rallies, and met Hitler. He read Houston Stewart Chamberlain with approval. There was much in Nazism, he believed, "to inspire the hope and confidence of the youth of the world." Few others argued so consistently that Nazism had ideals and qualities that would serve Britain.

In a House of Commons debate in May 1935 he said there was "almost no country among the Great Powers with which we were less likely to go to war than Germany. . . . Hitler is absolutely sincere in his present denunciation of bombing."[30] At the outbreak of war, he realized how foolishly and even tragically he had allowed himself to be deceived. In spite of his age, he joined the air force, served in a bomber, and lost his life when it was shot down.

Others lacked the slightest covering of integrity. In the House of Commons Sir Thomas Moore, another Conservative M.P., made frequent speeches in favor of Hitler. "If I may judge from my personal knowledge of Herr Hitler," he wrote after his audience, "peace and justice are the keywords of his policy." When he spoke like that at a white-tie dinner, the writer Robert Byron memorably inquired if he was in German pay. Lord Londonderry, also a sometime cabinet minister, had a lengthy conversation with Hitler and in a speech soon afterwards described him as "a kindly man with a receding chin and an impressive face," which may be the silliest sentence ever uttered about Hitler. "Widely seen as the foremost apologists for Hitler's regime," Lord and Lady Londonderry made a point of having Ribbentrop, Hitler's ambassador to Britain at the time, as a guest in their splendid country house in Northern Ireland, with pictures of the week-end in the local press.[31] They were disappointed when for political reasons their good friend Goering could not accept their invitation. The Duke of Buccleuch wrote to Lord Halifax, the Foreign Secretary, to explain that he was taking a pair of Sevres vases to Hitler as a fiftieth birthday present, suggesting that the Royal Family might make a similar gesture. Whoever saw fit to complain, the Duke observed, had to be a Jew. After the outbreak of war the Duke of Westminster, another notable anti-Semite, was still supporting Hitler and tried to form a peace party until Churchill himself wrote to advise him that their pre-war friendship would not stand in the way of his arrest.

The Anglo-German Fellowship, the Link, the Right Club under Captain Archibald Ramsay, yet another Conservative M.P., were bodies that brought together Nazi apologists, whether politicians, peers, retired members of the armed forces, or journalists and businessmen, The historian Arthur Bryant's "Union and Reconstruction" organization was both an anti-war lobbying group and a propagator of Nationalist Socialist economic ideas. In these milieus the Chamberlain government's policy of appeasement seems like a premonition of Vichyite collaboration. In the event of invasion and occupation, an English Pétain would have been required, and there has been speculation that Lloyd George, Lord Halifax, or Sir Samuel Hoare could have fulfilled that role, with Mosley perhaps as an English Laval.

As once people had flocked to admire Napoleon's France, so now they toured Germany in admiration. Nazi organizations were adept at spotting and exploiting every sign of British enthusiasm. Sir Henry Channon, invariably known as Chips, was one among the thousands who attended the 1936 Olympic games in Berlin. "The English pour in," he observed in his diary. Because he was a Conservative Member of Parliament, he was provided with an ADC who had the title of Baron, and a grand car with a Storm Trooper as chauffeur. The Germans, he realized, were out to show the world "the grandeur, the permanency and respectability of the new regime." Worrying whether his wife should wear a tiara as well as her rubies, Channon was something of a special case, a snob in the midst of what he took to be high life. Moral and political considerations did not enter into it, and so could not spoil his excitement at a glimpse of Hitler in the stadium, the pharaonic luxury of the parties given by Goering, Ribbentrop, and Goebbels, and the presence of many royal and aristocratic guests.[32]

Maurice Willoughby, a Sandhurst cadet before being commissioned into the Highland Light Infantry, stayed with a family where two of the sons had joined the S.S. "I felt they were building a new heaven and a new earth, compared to which everything in England appeared stale and apathetic . . . and I left as an enthusiastic admirer of [the Nazi Party] and its Führer. . . . Nor was I alone in such sentiments about Germany. I never met anyone in England who had been there at the time who had not returned with similar opinions."[33] Many young women were like Rachel Fenwick, who confided in her friend Mary Wesley, the bohemian novelist, that she visited labor camps and attended Hitler Youth rallies because of the "very good-looking young men."[34] Unity Mitford, a sister of Diana Mosley, was living in Germany in the throes of a childish crush on Hitler, and she introduced to him a friend, Michael Burn, the son of an official in the Royal Household. Burn told an apparently attentive Hitler that he, Hitler, was very popular with young English people, and he recorded, "It has been so wonderful to see what Hitler has brought this country back to and taught to look forward to. . . . I heard him make a speech yesterday which I don't think I shall ever forget." Several years were to pass before he realized that he had been duped.[35] Sydney Larkin, the treasurer of Coventry City, had a swastika in his office, attended Nuremburg rallies, and took his fifteen-year-old son Philip, the future poet, on holiday in Nazi Germany. Well-known as a conductor of Wagner, Sir Reginald Goodall became "a keen apologist for Hitler" in Germany and Austria during the Thirties and to the end of his life. To him, Hitler was the protector of German culture, and the Holocaust was "a BBC Jewish plot," a concoction Wagner himself might have come up with.[36]

In the face of Hitler's foreign policy coups, all sorts of unexpected people came to accommodate Nazism. In 1938, Clive Bell, art critic and Bloomsbury stalwart, could write a pamphlet *War Mongers,* to say, "A Nazi Europe would be, to my mind, heaven on earth compared with Europe at war." That same year, in the wake of the Munich Conference, Gertrude Stein put her genius for obscuring what otherwise was perfectly clear into trying to get intellectuals to sign a petition that Hitler should receive the Nobel Peace Prize. When the racing driver Dick Seaman won the German Grand Prix in 1938, he gave the Hitler salute. "Hitler stands no nonsense," he wrote to his family, "He won't have any slackers about." Soon afterwards, he was killed in another Grand Prix, whereupon Hitler sent a wreath to his funeral. "I must say Nazism has some fine qualities," the popular author H. V. Morton was writing as late as 1941. He believed that Hitler had sound ideas about Jews and Bolsheviks: "I am appalled to discover how many of Hitler's theories appeal to me," a formula revealing that in fact Morton was highly satisfied with his prejudices.

In the last days of August 1939, a number of Nazi sympathizers slipped out of England into Germany in order to be on what they saw as the right side in the war that was now unavoidable. Several hundred British men and women were to spend the war of their own free will in Germany, employed in one or another Nazi organization. William Joyce and his wife Margaret were certainly the most prominent of these, singled out for devotion to Nazism, as well as for quarrelsome behavior usually fuelled by alcohol. Broadcasting to England from Berlin, Joyce took pleasure in describing himself as "a daily perpetrator of High Treason." Known as Lord Haw-Haw on account of his idiosyncratic nasal twang, he became something of a public bogey as he successfully spread demoralization. According to Peter Martland, a specialist in intelligence matters, six million people were regular listeners to *Germany Calling* as he called his program, and eighteen million, or half the population, listened occasionally. His references to daily life in wartime England implied that German spies were keeping him informed, but in fact he was making sly use of press reports from Britain or neutral countries. The authorities were rattled. At his post-war trial which condemned him to be hanged, though, the prosecution had to glide over the troubling fact that he may have owed no loyalty to the Crown, and was British only because he insisted vehemently on it. Initially Irish, he had been naturalized German in September 1940 with the alias of Wilhelm Froelich.

Seemingly Joyce was born in Brooklyn in 1906, the child of Michael Joyce, a builder, originally Irish but American by naturalization or by marriage to Queenie, a doctor's daughter. The family returned to Ireland, where Joyce was educated by the Jesuits. As a teenager he is said to have hung around the barracks of the paramilitary Black and Tans, the loyalists who matched the nationalists in savagery during the Troubles culminating in Irish independence. In the eyes of the observant Rebecca West who covered his eventual trial, he was "a tiny little creature" whose body looked "flimsy and coarse" though his voice reverberated with the desire for power.[37] One biographer has emphasized how Joyce grew up in a world of feud and betrayal and political hatred. In 1923, the family escaped by settling in London, to run a shop in Dulwich. The following year, when he was still only eighteen, Joyce acted as steward at a Conservative meeting in Lambeth when someone stormed the platform and slashed his face with a cut-throat razor, to leave a disfiguring scar from ear to mouth. His attacker, he always maintained, was a "Jewish Communist." In 1927 Joyce graduated with a first-class honors degree in English from London University. All his life he tended to quote from the English poets. This weirdly disoriented and frustrated man had a fantasy that he might be Viceroy of India, but when the Civil Service and the Foreign Office rejected him, he plumped for Nazism. Mosley recognized his capabilities, appointing him Deputy Leader of the BUF and Director of Propaganda. Two of a kind in their ambitions, they soon fell out. Joyce and John Macnab, a BUF colleague, formed a splinter group, "true believers in Adolf Hitler's Third Reich."[38] In a report dated March 1939, Maxwell Knight of MI5 with responsibility for internal security, stated that Joyce was "a complete pro-Nazi fanatic, who will go to any lengths to further what he considers to be Nazi aims in this country."[39] A somewhat equivocal figure himself, Maxwell Knight had been a double agent in the BUF; he is suspected of tipping Joyce off that he would be arrested if he did not make a run for it to Germany.

Probably two or three weeks after his arrival in Germany, Joyce was auditioned and then employed in the so-called Funkhaus, a 1920s building in the fashionable Charlottenburg district of Berlin.[40] Concordia was supposed to be a radio station broadcasting underground from England in English, with Joyce as its chief commentator. His assistant was Leonard Brown, a former teacher "who spoke well and also wrote polished scripts and commentaries."[41] Other make-believe emissions included the New British Broadcasting Station, Workers' Challenge to rally socialists against capitalism, a Christian Peace Movement, Radio Caledonia for Scottish nationalists, and Radio Metropole for Welsh nationalists. At least a hundred British Nazis, many of them from the BUF, some prisoners and turncoats, a few the human flotsam of war, wrote scripts or broadcasts indiscriminately for one or other of these nominal stations. They were reasonably well paid.

Goebbels was ultimately responsible for all propaganda, white or black, and he was soon satisfied that Joyce, his star, was "brilliant." What could Goebbels have made of Margaret Bothamley, who had a picture of the King and Queen on her desk in the office and was convinced she had had an affair with Hitler? Norman Baillie-Stewart had sold military secrets to the Germans before the war and was the last man imprisoned for treason in the Tower of London. He displayed his distrust of Joyce with the greeting, "I suppose you've come to take away our jobs." The atmosphere in the office was set by the likes of Pearl Joyce Vardon, of whom a German colleague said that she "simply hated all things English and loved all things German."[42] Although also a BUF member disgusted with Britain, Susan Hilton was there only because of a series of unlucky incidents, starting with being torpedoed. She worked for several stations including one aimed at Ireland, but in the end the Gestapo arrested this rather lost woman as a spy.[43] Walter Purdy, another BUF member and a naval engineer taken prisoner at Narvik, wrote scripts with titles like "The Air Racket" and "Jewish Profiteering in War." (Eventually the Gestapo arrested him for black-marketing, and he was lucky to escape the death sentence, first at the hands of the Germans, later at the hands of the British.) Margaret Joyce also soon began broadcasting a weekly talk to influence British women.

Twilight over England, Joyce's one book, was commissioned by the German Foreign Office, written in three weeks and published in English in mid-September 1940 by Cesare Santoro, a Brazilian Nazi. 100,000 copies were printed, and there were several foreign language editions. Joyce was paid 10,000 reichsmarks, which Terry Charman, the editor of the Imperial War Museum facsimile, values at approximately £500, a sum almost twice his yearly salary from Concordia. Surpassing even Houston Stewart Chamberlain, the book is the crudest expression of anti-Semitism in the language, an amalgam of conspiracy theory and hatred, as though written by and for an anglicized Julius Streicher. His defense was always that he had believed in what he was doing and saying. At the end of his life, he felt he had nothing to reproach himself with, but had been let down by those with whom he had thrown in his lot: "National Socialism is a fine cause, but most of the Germans, not all, are bloody fools."

John Amery was once described by Hitler as "by far the best propagandist to England that we have"—which only goes to show the limitations of Hitler's understanding either of Amery or England. True, Amery ought to have had social cachet. Born in 1912, he was the son of Leo Amery, a Privy Counsellor and a well-known friend and admirer of Churchill who in 1940 had made him Secretary of State for India. There was something sensational in having a British cabinet minister's son broadcasting from Berlin the standard Nazi line about the war serving Communists and Jews, not British interests. In 1943 he published his book, *England Faces Europe,* as short as it is vacuous, the work of "a semi-educated waster,"[44] rehearsing what his minders in the German Foreign Office wanted.

In his way, William Joyce had been sincere, but John Amery was merely unbalanced. Sacking him from Harrow school, one tutor had grasped what was to prove Amery's lifelong indifference to the consequences of his actions: "In the whole of my experience as a schoolmaster, I found him, without doubt, the most difficult boy I ever had to manage. He was certainly abnormal in that he seemed unable in those days to distinguish right from wrong. He seemed to think he could be a law unto himself and that every rule and regulation that bound others did not apply to him." Delinquency evolved into crime. His wife, "known to London police as a common prostitute," considered him a sexual pervert.[45] Throughout 1935 he visited Berlin, ostensibly for some film project. Time and again his father had to bail him out for writing false checks, stealing diamonds, and finally bankruptcy.

Inexplicably he was in Vichy France during the first part of the war, and in 1942 he broke anonymity by writing a letter to a newspaper in

Grenoble to protest against British bombing of French cities. German agents were quick on to him, offering him the good life in expensive hotels in Paris and Berlin. In return, they had a plan. In the world-view spread by Hitler, the Western Allies and the Soviet Union formed a coalition so unnatural that it was bound to fall apart. As recently as the winter of 1939, the British government had revealed an anti-Soviet disposition by allowing 225 British volunteers to fight for the Finns as they resisted the invading Red Army. A similar body of British volunteers fighting the Red Army on the Eastern front would expose the ambiguity of the British-Soviet relationship. Without demur, Amery accepted the task of recruiting for this purpose the Legion of Saint George, later to be called the British Free Corps. The Germans seem not to have grasped the petty crooked character of the man with whom they were working, or perhaps they did not care. In Berlin, Amery's mistress, Jeanine Barde, died in an alcoholic stupor. She, Amery, and his minder seem to have been drunk much of the time. Back in France, they went to an internment camp for foreigners at Saint-Denis in the outskirts of Paris. A small group of Britons were assembled and Amery lied to them that the Legion was already 1,500 strong, and that three bombers and their crews had also defected. He was jeered and cold-shouldered. The only one to join up for the Legion was Kenneth Berry, a boy of sixteen who had left school early and gone to sea in a ship that had been sunk. This episode sealed Amery's treason. Captured in Italy at the end of the war, he was handed to the English and tried at the Old Bailey. Influential people, including his father, failed to obtain a reprieve and he was hanged in December 1945.

When Amery took on his assignment, something in the order of 100,000 British prisoners were held. In order to recruit the Legionaries that Amery had not been able to do, Gestapo officers and Germans who spoke English were ordered to scour the camps and dig out BUF members or avowed anti-Communists. Previously the property of the State Railways, four wooden huts within a barbed-wire compound were to be the Legion's base at Genshagen, a few miles from Berlin. Classic renegades, Legionaries wore German uniforms with British shoulder-flashes, accepting that they were auxiliaries in the S.S. "We, the true soldiers of Britain," so they affirmed, "wish to swear allegiance to the Führer and the German Reich. We volunteer to fight side by side with the Germans to beat the enemies of Europe. For this purpose we, the undersigned, make application for a corps to be called the British Free Corps."

The camp commandant was Vivian Stranders, a man already in his mid-sixties. The son of a professor in the Guildhall School of Music, Stranders had been a Captain in the Royal Air Force in the First World War. Starting an aviation business in Germany, he used his contacts to pass on secrets about French developments, was caught and imprisoned in France. Settling in the Rhineland, he joined the Nazi Party in 1933, became a naturalized German and editor of a Nazi journal. At Genshagen he was an S.S Sturmbannführer, the only known Englishman to have held this rank.[46]

John Brown, a Quartermaster Sergeant in the Royal Artillery, agreed to carry out the daily running of the camp. Known as Busty or Teddy, he was a committed BUF member, though Oxford-educated. After the war he claimed to have been defying the Germans by trading on the black market for the benefit of camp inmates, and also sending coded messages in letters. The authorities chose to put a positive gloss on his dubious activities, and even decorated him. Other BUF members given responsibility in the camp were Sergeant Frank McLardy, Sergeant Arthur Chapple, Corporal Gordon Bowler, and Corporal Francis Maton. Thomas Cooper was the son of an English photographer and a German mother. Just before the war, he and his mother had returned to Germany. In due course he enrolled in the Waffen SS, serving in the Leibstandarte, Hitler's bodyguard, and the Totenkopf Division. Whether truthfully or not, he boasted that he had murdered Jews, specifically telling Francis Maton how in the Warsaw ghetto he and some Ukrainians had thrown Jews out of the window. He was one of the only two Englishmen to have been awarded the Iron Cross—the other being Eddie Chapman, the equivocal figure who spent the war alternating between England and Germany, a con man of the highest class, capable of persuading willing paymasters in British intelligence and the Abwehr simultaneously that he was their loyal agent.[47]

Yeomen of Valhalla and *The Frustrated Axis* are privately printed publications that give a description of Genshagen and the Legionaries with what appears to be an insider's knowledge. The author, however, obscures his narrative with prose so clotted that it is difficult to follow, and by the use of pseudonyms, for instance giving Brown the name Owen, and Cooper the name Butcher, while preposterously calling himself Marquis de Slade. Most Legionaries earned his scorn as opportunists hoping to escape prison camp, have better food, or meet women in Berlin. In the final months of the war, the Legionaries marched out of Genshagen to other barracks where a photograph of the Duke of Windsor adorned a wall. There were never more than about thirty of them at any one time, with about twenty more who had come and gone. Unfitted for action, they never saw a shot fired in anger, but simply drifted away in the final chaos, inventing alibis in the manner of John Brown and hoping to pass unnoticed. According to this unidentified author, the Home Secretary told the House of Commons that 125 men and women owing allegiance to the Crown were suspected of wartime aid to the enemy. One of them was Benson Freeman, a one-time airman, memorable for categorizing those who had been with him as "the finest collection of poor-type Englishmen one could hope to meet." Given a ten-year sentence, he told his lawyer, "this just shows how rotten this democracy is. The Germans would have had the honesty to shoot me."

CHAPTER TWELVE

There Are Many
Wicked Men in the World

Communism in Britain involved a transfer of loyalties to a foreign power on a scale never previously experienced, far exceeding identification with the American and French Revolutions or with Nazism, and reaching deep enough to raise questions about national identity.

The Bolshevik coup changed perceptions overnight. Czarist Russia, for so long the symbol of odious and retrograde despotism, blossomed into the progressive Soviet Union. The imperfect world, Communists proclaimed, was to be made perfect. To unexpected numbers of people this undertaking seemed so noble, so epic, that they hurried to support it. Once before, the whole social range from aristocrats like the Duke of Dorset, then ambassador in Paris, Lord Stanhope and the company in White's hotel, Wordsworth and his fellow poets, down to tradesmen and laborers, had greeted the French Revolution as the dawn of a new age. As unquestioningly, their twentieth-century equivalents overlooked the obvious contradictions immediately thrown up in practice in the Soviet Union: hate was laying the foundation of the brotherhood of man, and war was the indispensable component of peace. Communism was supposed to be a science, but instead it institutionalized arbitrary terror. It is doubtful whether those seduced by the new Soviet identity much understood the workings of dialectical materialism, weighed exactly what Marx owed to Hegel, or paused to visualize the bloodshed certain to mark the end of the class war and the initiation of the dictatorship of the proletariat. They wanted so urgently to believe the good news they were ceaselessly hearing about the Soviet Union that they constructed an imaginary universe in which reality was what they said it was and facts had no bearing on it. Lenin and then Stalin were widely idolized as though they were progressives in the line of Kossuth or Garibaldi, and Stalin even came to be familiarized as Uncle Joe, a figment very far removed from the suspicious conspirator in the Kremlin regularly condemning millions to Gulag, slavery, and death.

Arthur Ransome, later the author of the popular "Swallows and Amazons" books for children, was a newspaper correspondent in Petrograd and apparently also a British secret service agent. Like the celebrated John Reed and other first-hand observers of the events of 1917, he helped to put in place the general perception that the Bolshevik Revolution was a positive milestone for mankind: "These men who have made the Soviet government in Russia, if they must fail, they will none the less have written a page in history more daring than any other which I can remember in the history of humanity."[1] The correspondent of the *Manchester Guardian,* M. Philips Price, had forebears who had supported the American and the French Revolutions, and his turn had arrived, he thought, to be a radical. There was no mistaking the meaning of the Red Terror, he could write, but that could not staunch his admiration for the Bolsheviks. Lenin was a "towering figure." The two met, and he left feeling that Lenin "must have been not only a humble but a happy man." Back in England, he sold his share of an estate inherited in Gloucestershire, and entered Parliament where he promoted the Soviet Union. In a speech there as late as 1946 with the Red Army occupying half of Europe he was as confused as ever by his fantasies: "I do not believe that Russia has territorial intentions."

Bertrand Russell reached Moscow in June 1920 with a British delegation whose purpose was to evaluate the recent revolution.

Bolshevism, in his preconception, deserved "the gratitude and admiration of all the progressive part of mankind." Born into one of the most aristocratic families in England and himself a hereditary earl, mathematician, philosopher, and First World War pacifist, he was a public intellectual with unique prestige. He and Lenin spent an hour together, speaking in English: "His strength comes, I imagine, from his honesty, courage and unwavering faith—religious faith in the Marxian gospel, which takes the place of the Christian martyr's hopes of Paradise." This equation of Communism and religion has been repeated so often by so many that it has become a truism. It would have made a difference if a moral arbiter of his standing had gone public with the shock he expressed privately in a letter to Lady Ottoline Morrell, a duke's daughter at the center of society (and with whom he had an amorous fling). He had gone to Moscow hoping to find the Promised Land, he told her, but "Bolshevism is a close tyrannical bureaucracy, with a spy system more elaborate and terrible than the Tsar's, and an aristocracy as insolent and unfeeling, composed of Americanized Jews. No vestige of liberty remains, in thought or speech or action." In spite of this, he went on, "I think it is the right government for Russia at this moment." So even someone of the highest intelligence could concoct absurd anti-Semitic figments, lightly condemn millions to persecution and misery, and lie about his real opinion.

Acceptance at face value of whatever the Soviet regime might be saying or doing came to be known as fellow-traveling. The phenomenon is mysterious, not to say inexplicable, seeming to waft in with the spirit of the times. One of the earliest and most eagerly deluded fellow-travelers was H. G. Wells. He had come up the hard way; his mother had been in domestic service in a country house. His immense literary output comprised history and fiction, including books of futuristic science that were instant classics. He had earned wide respect. Before the First World War, he had met Maxim Gorky in the United States, and in 1920 he went to Moscow to stay with

Gorky, by then a Bolshevik propagandist with no moral objection to occupying a Moscow mansion complete with the servants and the silver of the former owners. Destitute people came to show Wells the rags they were wearing, but he was not impressed. His preconceptions shuttered out the evidence in front of him. The educational work of the Bolsheviks was astonishingly good, he thought, and he failed to wonder why children predominantly came up with his name when questioned about English writers.

In the course of the fortnight he spent in Russia, he met Lenin. Lenin did not think highly of him, informing Trotsky that Wells was a "petit bourgeois." Around this interview Wells constructed a book, *Russia in the Shadows,* a prototype of the many similar apologias to come from star-struck British visitors. Lenin had been steadily engaged in exterminating those he considered class enemies, but to Wells he was "The Dreamer in the Kremlin." Communism could be, after all, "enormously creative." The Communist Party was "morally higher than anything that has yet come against it." Shooting everybody was "clumsy and bloody but effective." Social hatred had inspired Red Terror, "but if it was fanatical it was honest." In 1934, a few weeks before the murder of Kirov, Wells had another interview with Stalin, who almost certainly was then planning the elimination of this potential rival. He and Stalin had agreed, Wells elaborated in a long article in the *New Statesman,* that there were many wicked men in the world. Stalin's smooth sentence, "I do not believe in the goodness of the bourgeoisie," was as good as a death certificate for anyone he singled out. Finally in later writings Wells took to reversing the truth like any lowly Party hack. Stalin had been "driven to self-defensive cruelty," he was "honest and benevolent . . . self-righteously impatient of criticism or opposition." Wells had never met a man "more candid, fair, and honest." Stalin "owes his position to the fact that no one is afraid of him and everybody trusts him."

To Lenin and then Stalin, the British Communist Party was primarily a tool for subverting a rival world power. Moscow selected leaders for the British arm of world Communism with care. Born in 1890 into a poverty-stricken Lancashire family, Harry Pollitt relied on the hardships of his background to strike "the authentic note of class hatred."[2] In his speeches and writings, this hatred is vaunted as admirable. In 1921, on the first of what he later said were at least fifty visits to Moscow, he had met Lenin, and for the rest of his life was under the spell of that moment. Elected the Party's General Secretary in 1929, he served twenty-six years in the post. Rough as he was, eager for violence to be a systematic political process, he astounded listeners once when he blurted out his slave-like obeisance to the cause, as well as awareness of its summary ways. Victor Gollancz once heard him say, "If I'd be summoned to Moscow, and knew for certain that I'd be shot in the back of the neck the moment I landed, I shouldn't have hesitated."[3] Between 1926 and 1937, he and something like 150 British Communists were trained at the International Lenin School in courses that lasted either for nine months or two years. Other key figures were recruited by the NKVD (the secret police) or Soviet Military Intelligence for clandestine operations in Britain. Douglas Springhall was one such. He is said to have been an officer in the Red Army. In 1943 he was arrested and sent to prison for passing Air Ministry secrets. Another Party official, Percy Glading, was also sent to prison for espionage at Woolwich Arsenal. Details of Eric Verney's career are still secret, but he appears to have been the only Englishman appointed to the central apparat of the secret police in Moscow. Evidence of treason still comes to light. The diaries of Guy Liddell of MI5 have been recently published. In September 1943 he was commenting, "Penetration of the services by the Communist Party is becoming rather serious." He was dealing with the cases of Oliver Green, Ray Milne (a woman), and Captain Ormond Uren, all of them British and voluntary agents of the Soviet Union.

Party finance was another clandestine issue. "Money," writes a historian, "was to form a central part of the relationship" between the Comintern (the body controlling Communist Parties abroad) and the British Party in the early years of the two organizations.[4] The subsidy in the eighteen months after August 1920 alone was the immense sum of £55,000. Moscow paid for the Party newspaper, *The Daily Worker,* whose sales peaked at 120,000 copies at the start of the Cold War, though this had halved by 1956. After Communism collapsed, Reuben Falber, once the Party's assistant general secretary, confessed that from 1957 to 1979 he had regularly been picking up suitcases of cash from the Soviet Embassy, in some years receiving more than £100,000.

Figures vary, but in the years from 1935 to 1939, the period of Stalin's Great Terror, membership in the British Communist Party rose from 6,500 to 17,750, but even in the war never exceeded 60,000.[5] Many, perhaps most, of these were working men and women, coal-miners from Wales, ship-builders on the Clyde or Tyneside. The tale reached them that in the Soviet Union the capitalists had been expropriated and the proletariat had taken over the means of production, laying hands on the wealth and power hitherto wrongfully denied to those who really deserved it. Every Party leader promised these same rewards. After the disappointment of the General Strike of 1926, for example, Willie Gallacher, a Scottish Communist Member of Parliament, had predicted, "The day will soon come when the oppressed and exploited working class will soon form a workers' republic in Britain." To his audience, that too was good news.

Harm to the nation came not so much from the Party and its activities as from sympathy for the Soviet Union in the society at large. Here was a nation-wide treason of the clerks. The sense that Communism was inevitable and desirable spread through the classes whose continued existence—and even whose lives—was threatened by it. Moral and intellectual collapse of the kind had not been seen in centuries, perhaps since the time of the Children's Crusade or the messianic sects of the Middle Ages evoked in Norman Cohn's *The*

Pursuit of the Millennium. All sorts of unexpected people internalized the politics and culture of Soviet Communism and its corresponding rejection of democracy and capitalism. To them, everything Soviet was right and beyond praise, everything British was decrepit and unjust. Mayakovsky was the best poet of the day, and Eisenstein was the best film-maker—Samuel Beckett, of all people, wrote to ask for his help in obtaining a place in the Moscow State School of Cinematography. The British Empire was a more criminal enterprise than Stalin's concentration camps, if they truly existed. The British had no cause for pride, but much to feel guilty about. These emotional hysterics were enough to shift British perceptions of themselves, erode the self-confidence that came with their history, and ultimately prepare them for future socialist governments whose collective values were a bloodless variation of Communism.

The literary and artistic world became the echo chamber of Soviet and fellow-traveling propaganda. The Left Book Club set the style. Starting in 1936, this was the brain-child of the publisher Victor Gollancz, someone "enthusiastically welcomed in progressive circles." His view was that "Our very salvation depends on the education of the masses."[6] By April 1939, the Left Book Club had become a powerful tool of indoctrination with 57,000 members in 1,200 groups nation-wide. In its first ten years the Club sold six million books. Besides Gollancz, the selectors of subjects and authors were John Strachey and Professor Harold Laski, both classic fellow-travelers. They chose like-minded writers. The Marxist H. N. Brailsford, for instance, took the standard line that the British in India were mere imperialists. Hewlett Johnson, Dean of Canterbury, delighted to be known as the Red Dean, wrote about the Soviet Union with a grotesque innocence as though it were heaven on earth. His studies led him to conclude that "the programme put into practice in Russia [was] profoundly Christian." At the height of the Terror, he published a pamphlet asking what was making the Soviet Union so successful. (Gollancz one day heard Harry Pollitt say of Johnson, "that bloody red arse of a dean.") G.D.H. Cole, an eminent Oxford Professor, wrote eight Left Club books. "Better be ruled by Stalin," in Cole's morbid opinion, "than by a pack of half-hearted and half-witted social democrats . . . who still believe in the 'independence' of their separate obsolete states." [7] Margaret Cole, his wife, saw the Soviet Union as "the negation of the immoralities of industrial capitalism and the system of private profit."

Published weekly, the *New Statesman* magazine had mastered the art of persuading thoughtful and well-intentioned readers that a Soviet future must be better than the capitalist present. Its editor Kingsley Martin began writing a regular column in 1931, and continued for thirty years. The son of a clergyman, he had been a conscientious objector in the First World War. England aroused disgust in him; he could see no way of stopping Fascism in the country; there would shortly be street fighting. As one commentator expressed it, he "was convinced that Stalin's Russia had the virtues England had lost. It had youth and youthful ideas, with easy divorce and experiments in prison reform."[8] In Spain, Orwell had witnessed the Communists attacking and killing other left-wing groups, and was himself lucky to escape. Self-appointed commissar that he was, Kingsley Martin refused to publish Orwell's account of this experience (Gollancz was similarly to refuse to publish Orwell's *Animal Farm*). In a restaurant one day with Malcolm Muggeridge, Orwell could see Kingsley Martin at an adjoining table, and asked to change places as the sight of so corrupt a face would spoil his luncheon. Kingsley, "by this time, would tell lies, or suppress the truth, if the cause were grave enough. . . . He constantly explained that 'Communism means lying and cheating in peace time . . . because they are fighting a war *all the time*'" in the words of C. H. Rolph, a colleague on the magazine and his biographer.[9]

The poet most in tune with the spirit of the Thirties was W. H. Auden, and he brought to Communism the popular sentimental guff with which Wordsworth had once smothered the French Revolution.

His promotion of "necessary murder," Orwell rubbed in, could only have been written by someone who would be elsewhere when the trigger was pulled. (Later Auden too was ashamed of his naivety and tried to atone by rewriting compromised poems.) Auden's friend Edward Upward, a novelist with maximum pretensions, thought that a writer had to take the side of the workers, otherwise he could not write a good book. He could not say where this side might be, or how to take it: "Ideology seemed to shrivel his natural gifts, leaving him an earnest, doctrinaire, and unimaginative stylist."[10] Marxist orthodoxy also stultified fictional characters in the novels of Cecil Day-Lewis. In the ruck of fellow-traveling poets, moreover, he stood out for the triteness of his poems. Lines like, "We came because our open eyes/ could see no other way" were natural to him. *Letters of Red* was an anthology to which he contributed a poem, "On the Twentieth Anniversary of Soviet Power," saluting Lenin as a hero "loved by the people," groveling as though he were a member of the Union of Soviet Writers under compulsion. To Stephen Spender, a Communist more out of herd instinct than anything else, he wrote, "the essence of Communism for us is that one goes over to the working class." This period cliché conveys not only the patronization of social inferiors but also a sense of repositioning for the sake of maintaining privilege.[11]

The letters of Michael Tippett, the composer, reveal a mind too incoherent to be capable of rational thought. A pacifist, he also assures his correspondents in 1936 that he is a reader of Marx and will take action as a revolutionary in the coming war, organizing illegal literature and preparing to shoot those who led the country into its mess. But "My one hope is that the British Empire will go under and Hitler win, rather than the reverse and the whole business begin over again. I hate the Empire as I hate nothing else. It is the key pin of world capitalism and it's our job to bring it to the ground. Actually a defeat of England means the freedom of India."[12] Dylan Thomas, not a man for the barricades, held that "the darkness of England" would never be lit, and there was only one thing for his generation to look forward to: "It is the Revolution."[13] E. J. Hobsbawm, himself a life-long promoter of Soviet apologias, gives an example of the extreme and almost insane lengths to which people could go when they mistook their abstraction of Communism for reality. In a wartime air raid, a woman described as comrade Freddie was trapped under falling beams, and expecting to die she called out, "Long live the Party, long live Stalin." From which Hobsbawm draws a conclusion that is unsuitably comic, "The Party was what our life was about."

Like a kind of plague or infection, Communism multiplied by means of social contact. Cambridge Communists included Joyce Wallace Whyte who was to marry Sir Cuthbert Ackroyd, later Lord Mayor of London; and Kathleen Raine who married Charles Madge, a poet remembered for the line, "Lenin, would you were living at this hour"; and of course Kim Philby, Guy Burgess, and Donald Maclean whose betrayal was to shake the country. When the American critic Alfred Kazin attended a meeting in the university, he discovered that the local Party secretary handing out leaflets was the younger son of a duke. The sister of Michael Ramsay, Archbishop of Canterbury, was a Communist. Oxford made Communists of Iris Murdoch, Kingsley Amis, and Denis Healey, the future Labour Chancellor of the Exchequer. Andrew Glyn, a member of a well-known banking family, was only one among many college fellows forcing their academic disciplines into a preconceived Marxist schema. Reggie Smith attended Marxist classes in Birmingham, and once when he was explaining how much better things were organized in Moscow than in London, his wife, the novelist Olivia Manning, replied that he knew only four words of Russian and one of them was *Pravda*. Paul Ignotus, a political refugee from Hungary, provides an unforgettable portrait of a true believer, a lodger in the same house in Southwark as him: "the black sheep of his family, except that it was a family where black sheep were unimaginable, because of their high liberalism . . . he was a Communist, very pure and simple. He had fought in the International Brigade. He was *anti-bourgeois,* body and soul. He ran about naked in the house because 'why not?'; he had no prejudices. He liked meat and vegetables for breakfast, always dressed shabbily, and had a boyish face."[14] During the French Revolution, Lord Stanhope had removed the coronet on the iron gates of his stately house, and now Sir Charles Trevelyan, head of a family celebrated for intellect and exclusivity, had a hammer and sickle painted on one of the pillars at the entrance gates at Wallington, his house in Northumberland with its estate of 13,000 acres. This baronet wrote to Stalin in January 1939 that all British workers, liberals, and anti-fascists "need to be made to understand [how? Gulags?] that you owe your ascendancy to the confidence of a free and democratic people, constantly renewed."

What happened within the Garman family—as recounted by Cressida Connolly in her book *The Rare and the Beautiful*—is completely representative of the cultural havoc and disintegration afflicting previously settled layers of society. Walter Garman was a magistrate, a churchwarden, and a member of the local Conservative Party. He rode to hounds. He and his wife lived in a fine old house in the Midlands, with ten servants and a governess for the children. Grown up, the girls became bohemian. A son, Douglas, went up to Cambridge to read English literature. There he made friends with Ernest Wishart, the well-off son of Sir Sidney Wishart, owner of an estate in Sussex. The two young men became Communists. Ernest Wishart subsidized a little magazine with a Communist editor, Edgell Rickword; published Douglas Garman's single book of poems with the wonderfully symbolic title *The Jaded Hero*; and founded Lawrence and Wishart, the one and only openly Communist publishing house. Douglas Garman and his wife Jeanne spent six months in Leningrad where he taught English. Then he moved to Paris, where he lived with the American heiress Peggy Guggenheim. To advocate compulsory collective equality while enjoying someone else's almost unlimited private fortune was the very acme of double standards. He studied Marx in a shed he had constructed at the end of the garden while she stayed in bed wearing fur gloves and reading Proust. Later still, he married Paddy Ayriss, a Communist he had met in Leningrad. As an educational officer for the Party in the 1940s, he lectured at trade union branches and literary institutes. He tried to write a novel and a polemic with a title beyond parody, "The Necessity of Revolution." Neither work was publishable. At the end of his life, a sense of inadequacy led to clinical depression.

Thousands like Douglas Garman flocked to the Soviet Union to work or to teach or simply to admire, thinking themselves holding a visa to Utopia. Intourist was the official Soviet agency in charge of arranging programs for these political pilgrims, as Paul Hollander has aptly called them. Obligatory escorts provided by Intourist were an indispensable part of the apparatus of control. Things could still go wrong, of course; inquisitive people might stray or see something they were not supposed to see. Evelyn Sharp, sister of Cecil Sharp the collector of English folk music, hailed Bolshevism as a new order of society "in which no one shall starve and no able-bodied person shall be idle," but on her first morning in the Soviet Union she passed a corpse lying in the snow.[15]

Again from the Soviet point of view, things went wrong in the case of Malcolm Muggeridge, a correspondent for the *Manchester Guardian* in the early Thirties. With the evidence of Soviet life under his eyes, he moved from initial sympathy to a lifelong opposition to Communism, all in his own inimitable and scornful humor. To him, political pilgrims were one of the wonders of the age, "travelling with radiant optimism through a famished countryside, wandering in happy bands about squalid, over-crowded towns, listening with unshakeable faith to the fatuous patter of carefully trained and indoctrinated guides, repeating like schoolchildren a multiplication table, the bogus statistics and mindless slogans endlessly intoned to them."[16] Muggeridge singled out Walter Duranty as the cynical epitome of this type, the greatest liar[17] of any journalist that he, Muggeridge, ever had met. English-born but the *New York Times* man in Moscow, Duranty said that the terror-famine killing millions in the Soviet Union was "mostly bunk," and the confessions in the show trials were genuine. Perhaps the Soviets had bought or blackmailed him, but Muggeridge thought that his support of the Soviet regime was "a response to some need in his nature"—as seems the case with political pilgrims one and all.

The visitor to Russia, advised Julian Huxley, the brother of Aldous Huxley, in his book *A Scientist Among the Soviets*, "must attempt to discard some of his bourgeois ideas about democracy, religion and traditional morality, his romantic individualism, his class feelings, his judgements of what constitutes success, and pick up what he can of the atmosphere in which the Russians live"[18]—a fancy way of saying Join the Party, which was the point of the whole exercise. J. D. Bernal, an early Communist, a physicist, and willing to accept an allowance from his mother while advocating revolution, was one of many scientists including Huxley holding the opinion that science was better in the Soviet Union than in capitalist countries. Its direction there, Bernal told a conference in Moscow of the World Federation of Scientific Workers (another front organization) was "in the hands of those whose only aim is to destroy and torture people." In that same speech, he greeted the "great leader and protector of peace and science, Comrade Stalin."[19] Forty-eight hours later, the Soviet Union tested its first plutonium bomb. Bernal received the Stalin Prize. Huxley became director general of UNESCO.

Intourist's practice was to shepherd the pilgrims into delegations on the correct psychological assumption that this was the way to get the participants to suspend their critical faculties, each contributing to the general mood of credulity and group-think. A standard example is contained in *Soviet Russia Today*, subtitled "Report of the British Workers' Delegation," and published in 1927 by the Labour Research Department. Those on this delegation were veteran Left-wingers, A. J. Cook of the Miners' Federation, Tom Mann, James

Maxton, and Fenner Brockway who was a Member of Parliament (later known on account of subsequent cause-mongering as the Member for Africa). As though shedding completely their long experience of politics and industrial relations in particular, these men now hoped to give British workers "new faith in their struggle against capitalism in Britain." In their view, it was ludicrous to suppose that those they met had been prepared to deceive them. Everyone looked healthy and well-fed, and their clothing was strong and warm. The peasants were contented and appreciative. Lefortovo was one of the grimmer secret police prisons, but they found the Governor "was personally of a kind and gentle temperament . . . prison life in Russia is better than the conditions that many British miners have to endure today."

Hugh Dalton was part of a Fabian study group of impeccable fellow-travelers in 1932, and just thirteen years later he was Chancellor of the Exchequer in the Attlee Government. "There were about fifteen of us including Graham Haldane, Margaret Cole, D. N. Pritt [a lawyer who was to write a book defending the Moscow show trials], Harry Weldon, a philosopher [Fellow of Magdalen College, Oxford], and Redvers Opie, an economist who spoke and understood Russian. I returned after five weeks of talk and travel immensely stimulated. I had caught a quick but vivid glimpse of a quite new world. And this remained with me as an abiding influence."[20]

Neither fame, intelligence, nor status protected pilgrims from making fools of themselves in full view of the world. In the summer of 1931, Bernard Shaw, then a public figure with an international reputation, spent nine days in the Soviet Union. Lady Astor, Lord Lothian, and others were with him. Shaw's "brutal frivolity," in Henry James's brilliantly exact pinpointing of the man, stamped the whole visit and its aftermath. At dinner, sitting next to Mrs. Chamberlain, wife of the *Daily Telegraph* correspondent, Shaw waved his hand at the excellent food and said, "Russia short of food? Look at this!" She told him that all winter she had not been able to buy milk for her four-year-old daughter. "Nurse her yourself!" said Shaw.[21]

A two-and-a-half-hour interview with Stalin charmed Shaw: "I expected to see a Russian working man and I found a Georgian gentleman." Stalin was not a dictator, but comparable to a Pope. In Leningrad the British Consul, Reader Bullard, had charge of him (previously in Jiddah, he had dealt with St. John Philby). At tea, Shaw said how much he despised British parliamentary government and how he admired Mussolini and the Soviet system. In a speech in the hall where the show trials were to be staged, he said that Communism was capable of leading mankind out of its crisis. That October in a broadcast on American radio, he compared Lenin to Jefferson, Stalin to Hamilton, and Lunacharsky (commissar for education) to Paine. He could prattle unselfconsciously about the secret police and "necessary shooting." A year later, he was writing, "Our question is not, to kill or not to kill, but how to select the right people to kill."

Reader Bullard had grown up in the East End of London, where his father was employed on the wharfs. Unlike Shaw, he could recognize cruelty and human suffering when he saw it. His diaries are an exceptional testimony to the horror of Soviet life. He had to sort out the disasters that befell British subjects staying in the Soviet Union because they were deluded enough to believe in Communism. It cost Shaw nothing to spout his embarrassing tripe but anyone who listened to him would have to pay a high price. One of Bullard's heartfelt diary entries seems aimed at him: "I would like to devise a quite special punishment for people who induce others to come to the Soviet Union to live."[22]

Still, the thick volume *Soviet Communism: A New Civilization* with or without a question mark, depending on the edition, is a monument to gullibility without equal in the language (though the many volumes which Professor E. H. Carr devoted to asserting that the Soviet system was an economic and social success as well as a force for peace is a worthy runner-up). Sidney and Beatrice Webb, the joint authors, had

had protracted political experience; the launching of the *New Statesman* and the London School of Economics were personal triumphs of theirs. For many years, they studied minutely official papers and reports, and drafted all manner of technical commentaries. A one-time cabinet minister, Sidney Webb was elevated to the House of Lords as Lord Passfield. At Passfield Corner, their country house, they entertained people like themselves including the Soviet ambassador. Problems about servants are a subject in Mrs. Webb's diaries and letters. She would say of herself, "I am the cleverest member of the cleverest family of the cleverest class of the cleverest race in the world."

Without knowledge of Russian, however, the Webbs had to depend for their research on whatever was available in English, French, or German. They spent three weeks in the Soviet Union. Potemkin had once constructed artificial villages to hoodwink Catherine the Great, and Soviet officials now did the same for them. Accustomed to test their cleverness on the ins and outs of British administration, they were unable to imagine that words did not correspond to Soviet reality, but on the contrary deliberately veiled it. For all their intelligence and experience, they were like people under hypnosis, their critical powers suddenly suspended. Because their guides told them so, they believed that Stalin was the duly elected representative of a Moscow constituency in the Supreme Soviet and therefore could not be a dictator. They believed that the White Sea Ship Canal, in fact dug by slaves who had died in great numbers, was "a triumph of human regeneration." They often refer approvingly to "the liquidation of the landlord and the capitalist," as though this was some benign natural process demanding no further inquiry. They believed that talk of penal settlements for "deported manual workers" was "incredible" to anyone acquainted with the economic results of the chain-gang, and they spoke warmly of the "constructive work of the OGPU," then the acronym for the secret police. These prize boobies were nonetheless the only couple in nine hundred years to be buried together in the same ceremony in Westminster Abbey.[23]

Edwina Mountbatten, the wife of Lord Mountbatten, member of the Royal Family and future Viceroy of India, returned to Moscow in 1936 during the Great Terror. "It's fascinating being here again and seeing the progress everything has made since 1929. . . . It's gone by leaps and bounds . . . I gather shorter hours, higher wages, *and* lower prices (not only from what Intourist tell one!!) and the people on the whole are contented and the young ones happy and enthusiastic."[24] At the Potsdam Conference at the end of the war, Lord Mountbatten was to tell Stalin that he had long been "an admirer of the Generalissimo's achievements not only in war but in peace as well." Penderel Moon was a Fellow of All Souls, the most prestigious of Oxford colleges, had a brilliant career in the Indian Civil Service, was knighted, and finally retained after independence by the government of India. Also in Moscow during the Great Terror, he told his father that Communism must certainly spread. In another decade the Soviet Union would be "as powerful as any state in the world and the standard of living immeasurably higher than in most." He toyed with the idea of collective farming in India.[25]

Communist front organizations were quick to single out potential admirers and sponsor their visits. After the war, the Society for Cultural Relations with the USSR paid for J. B. Priestley to come to the Soviet Union, and his repayment was *Russian Journey,* a pamphlet published in 1946, and a classic of the genre. Priestley presents himself as "an author whose recent novels and plays happen to be popular" in the Soviet Union, as though his invitation was a compliment or a coincidence, and nothing to do with the Socialist beliefs he had boasted all his life. As easily manipulated as Bernard Shaw, he too found that rations and luxury food were better than at home. Theatrical productions were of a "perfection that not all the money in America can buy." There were no secret police, he said with a flippancy that was particularly offensive, "unless they were disguised as sparrows." The Soviet Union dealt wisely with its own people and "glitters and hums with their dance and song," and therefore "is not fundamentally an aggressive power." At that moment the Red Army was in Warsaw, Prague, Vienna and Berlin, forcibly shaping the Soviet bloc.

Doris Lessing has left an account of her visit to the Soviet Union in 1952 to attend the Authors World Peace Appeal, the kind of event that Moscow devised to keep up appearances. This delegation was led by Naomi Mitchison, a particularly pertinacious fellow-traveler. Another fellow-traveler taking part was the writer A. E. Coppard, "as innocent as a babe" and who had fallen in love with Communism "as if he had been given a potion." Lessing herself had been instructed to delay her Party membership until this visit was over. As part of the usual agitprop formalities with Soviet functionaries, the delegation was taken to a collective farm. There an elderly peasant insisted on speaking out: "You must not believe what you are told. Visitors from abroad are told lies. You must not believe what you are shown. Our lives are terrible. You must go back to Britain and tell everyone what I am saying. Communism is terrible." Recollecting this act of extraordinary bravery, Lessing rightly supposes that the man knew he would be arrested and disposed of—in her genteel verb. Needless to say, at the press conference held on their return to London, none of these authors appealing for world peace thought fit to say what this man was prepared to die for.[26]

What emerges from this massive complex of deception and self-deception is the outline of a Soviet Britain. At all levels of society, an array of people took the Soviet Union as an ideal model to be imitated, and worked to the best of their abilities to establish Communism as the proper political destiny for the country. If the opportunity had arisen, they would no doubt have been ready to support a Soviet take-over and defend whatever measures were involved.

The prospect of such an eventuality evidently was what attracted the excitable Guy Burgess. He visited the Soviet Union in 1934, and had no choice but to live there unhappily after his treachery was detected and he had to flee. Anthony Blunt was the agent recruiting

Burgess and others for the Comintern, and in the following year he too did the Soviet tour.[27] His brother Wilfrid, an aesthete unconcerned with politics, accompanied him. (They were from a junior branch of the family of the Arabist Wilfrid Scawen Blunt.) The organizer was John Madge, a Communist and the brother of the poet Charles Madge. With them were Michael Straight, the rich young American who was also to become a Soviet agent; Charles Rycroft, an eminent psychiatrist; Charles Fletcher-Cooke, then a socialist, later a Conservative Member of Parliament; Michael Young, a sociologist who eventually wrote *The Rise of the Meritocracy*; the giddy bohemian Nancy Cunard who lived in Paris with her black lover; and Christopher Mayhew, a future Labour minister and blinkered Arabist. Mayhew reacted with the enthusiasm that the Soviet authorities aimed to implant. Years later he could feel "genuinely ashamed about my obtuseness on this Russian visit," but the explanation of it was that "Our British system of society seemed so detestable." In the event of a Soviet take-over, who among them would have collaborated and who resisted?

The motives of the cold and aloof Anthony Blunt remain inscrutable. The Britain he betrayed was also the country in which he was at home, a professor, a knight, honored by the Royal Family, his homosexuality accepted, his privileges and his comforts assured. When finally he was exposed, he was astute enough to make a deal with the British secret services to ensure that he did not have to live in the Soviet Union whose cause he had made his own. This psychological riddle is insoluble. Blunt's last favor to the Soviets was to ensure that Kim Philby got away to Moscow where he lived with a pension from his KGB masters. Philby evidently was proud that he had sent to their death would-be Soviet defectors as well as secret agents infiltrated by Western intelligence services into Communist countries. In spite of being a near alcoholic, he took great pains to screen his character, and none of his British colleagues have been able to provide insight into his motivation. "To betray, you must first belong. I did not belong," he told the journalist Murray Sayle, but this was special pleading to be seen as some sort of victim. His had been an insider's career, and the establishment up to the level of the prime minister had covered for him. He also said of himself that when the KGB proposed that he work for them he did not hesitate: "One does not look twice at an offer of enrolment in an elite force."[28] If so, he betrayed Britain much as his Arabist father had done, empowered by an exhilarating sense of getting one's own back on a world that had no idea what was going on.

People in many walks of life had an undeclared or cryptic role in shaping a Soviet Britain. One such was Christopher Hill. Born in 1912, he was the son of a solicitor in York. He won a scholarship to Balliol College, and went up to Oxford in 1931. It is not clear when he became a Communist, what exactly was the purpose of the year he spent in the Soviet Union in 1935 and whether the Soviet authorities suborned him. As a Russian speaker, he was recruited in 1940 to British Military Intelligence and then seconded to the department of the Foreign Office responsible for the Soviet Union. Hiding his membership of the Communist Party, he soon became head of the Russian desk, in a position to influence British policy towards the Soviet Union. At the Foreign Office he wrote books in praise of Lenin and Stalin such that even a Soviet historian might have blushed before putting his name to them. Stalin was depicted as a great humanitarian, and the Terror had been "non-violent." After the war Hill returned to Balliol and eventually became Master of that college. In his prolific writings he set out to show that the English Civil War had been a proto-Bolshevik revolution. A steadfast Marxist and at heart a closet Stalinist, at the end of his life he queried on television whether Gulag had really existed.

Among dubious figures employed by the Foreign Office was Geoffrey Wilson. Originally a barrister, he was personal secretary to Sir Stafford Cripps, appointed ambassador to Moscow in 1940, and himself teetering on the edge of fellow-traveling. When Wilson's tour of duty finished and he was back in London, he applied to return. "I want to get to Moscow again for a bit. My faith grows weak here and I find that it revives in Moscow and when I can wander about in Russia." Nikolai Tolstoy shows how Wilson exerted himself to influence British policy in a way that accommodated Stalin's principal aims. It is extraordinary that a man of his opinions was present at the Yalta conference drawing the geo-political map of the Cold War. As the Red Army consolidated the Soviet bloc, Wilson told a left-wing group that "we can do nothing but rejoice."[29]

James Klugmann has somehow escaped the attention he deserves. In the shadowy outline of a Soviet Britain he is a key figure. At Cambridge with the other traitors, he obtained a first class degree in French and German. "My commitment to the cause was for life," he declared. "We simply *knew,* all of us, that the revolution was at hand." He was present at a meeting with Blunt and Burgess when they recruited the hapless Michael Straight to be a Soviet agent. Denis Healey remembers passing a mysterious package to Klugmann who was then in Paris as secretary of the World Student Assembly, yet another Soviet front on the international stage. Before Douglas Springhall was imprisoned for spying, Klugmann cooperated with him in building the Young Communist League, and he helped to organize aid to Spain. Editor of *Marxism Today,* he was the keeper of the flame.

Through accidental introductions, he gained entry into SOE, Special Operations Executive, the wartime agency set up to operate in German-occupied Europe: "Security checks revealed nothing detrimental, due to the chance destruction of a mass of files including Klugmann's by a German incendiary bomb." From 1942 onwards Klugmann worked in the SOE section handling Yugoslavia. There his superior was Basil Davidson, reputed to be a British secret service agent but whose published writings before and after the war just happen to be monotonously pro-Soviet. Suborning superiors and squeezing out critics, these two manipulated the others in the small section.[30]

In a close assessment of the evidence available, David Martin leaves no doubt that Klugmann was an important Soviet agent. Initially British policy was to support Colonel Draja Mihailovich, who had mobilized armed resistance to the German occupation and intended post-war Yugoslavia to be a democracy under its restored monarchy. Klugmann doctored SOE intelligence and reports from the field, giving the false impression that Mihailovich was collaborating with the Germans, and crediting his military operations to his rival, the Communist Josef Tito. Acting on this disinformation, the British government dropped Mihailovich, and instead backed Tito, a switch that led directly to the Communist takeover of power. In the process of setting up their absolute state, the Communists made sure to execute Mihailovich and many others. Churchill went on record that this disastrous sequence of events resulted from the worst decision he had made in the war. Klugmann had in effect outwitted the prime minister.

Stalin envisaged incorporating the new Communist Yugoslavia into the Soviet bloc of eastern and central European countries under his control after 1945. On nationalist grounds, Tito refused to buckle under. Klugmann was the Yugoslav specialist available to condemn Tito, and under orders from the Party he did so in a book with the giveaway title *From Trotsky to Tito* (the English edition published by Lawrence and Wishart, of course). The fact that Klugmann was prepared to write a vicious polemic calling for a struggle to the death against the very man on whose behalf he himself had just betrayed his colleagues and his country is all anyone need know about him. Klugmann may have had more blood on his hands than Kim Philby. If his anticipated revolution in Britain had occurred, he no doubt would happily have had more still.

After the war, the Campaign for Nuclear Disarmament mobilized hundreds of thousands of adherents who cloaked themselves in a fatalistic slogan that they deemed idealistic, "Better Red than Dead." Every year CND mounted a much-publicized march to Aldermaston, the site not far from London of nuclear research and development. This was an outdoor version, so to speak, of the pre-war Left Book Club. Public personalities like Bertrand Russell and Labour Party leader Michael Foot were in the forefront. The general secretary of CND was Peggy Duff, whose autobiography *Left, Left, Left* is very much part of the times and a masterpiece of self-righteousness. She boasted that there were few towns in Britain to or from which she had not marched, and few military bases where she had not protested. For her, agitator was a term of unqualified approval. She depicted herself engaged in "a dual liberation of the oppressed of the Third World, and of the repressed of the developed world." A lot of people, then, were in need of the salvation she promised but was in no position to deliver. Had the campaign succeeded in persuading Britain and the United States to abandon the nuclear weapon, the balance of power would have swung in favor of the Soviet Union. In the sense that it was opening the way for Communism to be imposed on the Western world, CND was gambling with the lives of millions.

Communism in its turn offered various subsets, and one of these was participation on the Republican side in the Spanish Civil War. This began in July 1936 when General Franco staged a military uprising against the government of the Spanish Republic. Hitler and Mussolini supported him with troops and weaponry, while Stalin sent advisers to the Republic. The British government adopted a policy of non-intervention. A cause was born and instantly romanticized: Spain was to be the arena where Communism would confront Fascism and defeat it. "The immediate future of all humanity rests to no small degree in the hands of the workers of Britain." Unrecognizably exaggerated, this opinion of John Strachey's was widely accepted as fact. Educated men and women approved of Auden's poem "Spain," with its fist-clenching line "But today the struggle," advocating armed militancy. Communist and fellow-traveling intellectuals published incendiary appeals to fight Fascism; they signed manifestos and attended congresses; they paid for ambulances and sometimes even drove them.

Still a Communist at the time, Arthur Koestler covered the war for the *News Chronicle*. Sentenced to death when he fell into the hands of Franco's Nationalists, he was saved by a campaign on his behalf in London. In his autobiography he compressed the mood of those times into a telling quip: "'I believe I have seen you in Madrid,' became an opening gambit at Left-wing cocktail parties." Journalists made no pretense of objectivity. G. L. Steer of *The Times* used the bombing of Guernica by German planes as a pretext for Basque nationalism. Atrocities were in order so long as your side committed them. John Langdon-Davies, a prolific journalist, could describe how "simple-hearted working men and peasants in overalls" had shot thirteen fascist sympathizers in cold blood. "Ugly? Yes, but how natural; thanks to those who let loose the supreme horror of civil war." In other words, these thirteen and all their kind were responsible for their own deaths.[31]

The Communist Party recruited volunteers and, in order to circumvent the law prohibiting British citizens from fighting for foreign causes, sent them to an office in Paris run by Charlotte Haldane (Moscow had the same significance for her, she said, as Mecca for fanatical Muslims). This office arranged transport by railway to Spain. Their destination was a base at Madrigueras near Albacete. Here, one historian comments, was "an ensemble cast, of different classes, temperaments, and, to a degree, motivations, each trying to find and play his part." The Party sent its hard men to ensure that they were kept under political observation and control, condemning "bad elements" to gaol or just shooting them. The all-important commissars were David Springhall and Peter Kerrigan. The first military commander, Wilfrid McCartney, was accidentally shot and wounded by Kerrigan. His successor, Tom Wintringham, was one of the few in the battalion to have served in the First World War as an officer. A veteran Communist, he had been jailed for sedition in

1925. As a rule volunteers had no experience of warfare and they received the minimum training in handling weapons. The political cause was no substitute for discipline. Two specialists in the period give the figure of 2,762 volunteers enrolled in the British battalion of the International Brigade before it was disbanded in November 1938. They add that 543 were killed and 1,763 wounded.[32] Another authority puts the number of deserters at 298. The adventurous American journalist Virginia Cowles passed the battalion on its way to the front, and they struck her as "a pathetic group . . . many of them ill-suited to soldiering."[33] Hemingway was scathing, telling Maxwell Perkins, "The British volunteers in the International Brigade were the absolute scum of the Brigade. After the Jarama fight they deserted by whole companies; they were cowards, malingerers, liars and phonies and fairies. They were absolutely panic-ed [*sic*] by the tanks, and their officers, when they were brave, were so stupid that their stupidity was absolutely murderous."[34]

Julian Bell was killed driving an ambulance. The son of Vanessa Bell and therefore the nephew of her sister Virginia Woolf, he had been molded by Bloomsbury and its values. An undergraduate at Cambridge, he wrote to his mother that he had slept with Anthony Blunt, "certain you won't be upset or shocked by my telling you." In an article in the *New Statesman* in 1933 he spoke for pretty well all his friends and acquaintances: "It would be difficult to find anyone of any intellectual pretensions who would not accept the general Marxist analysis of the present crisis." John Cornford grew up in a very well-known Cambridge family, and went to the university there. His mother, Frances Cornford, was the granddaughter of Charles Darwin and herself a poet with an individual voice. At Stowe school, aged sixteen, he became a Communist. Writing to a friend just returned from the Soviet Union, he revealed his fanaticism (and knowledge of Communist slogans in German) when he described breaking off with a girl: "If one's ready to kill and be killed for the revolution, this kind of break shouldn't make too much difference. Heil, Rot Front!" Reader

Bullard quotes Cornford's aunt disparaging the change in her nephew. "[H]e thinks of nothing but his political religion. It seems to have affected every part of his life. He has hardly any affection for his family, his manners have deteriorated, and he is so dirty in his person that it is a trial to his friends to have meals with him." In one of his last poems, Cornford wrote, "Swear that our dead fought not in vain,/ Raise the red flag triumphantly/ For Communism and for liberty." Hard though it tried after he was killed, the Party was unable to manufacture a Byronic legend out of lines like these.

In his memoir, Wintringham lists those whose presence in Spain in his opinion added a touch of distinction and social range: Giles and Esmond Romilly (related to Churchill); Noel Carritt and his brother (from a socially prominent family of Communists); Malcolm Dunbar, son of Lady Dunbar; Ralph Bates, the novelist; Arthur Ollerenshaw, the musician; Miles Tomalin, the intellectual; Lewis Clive, descendent of Clive of India; David Mackenzie, son of an admiral; Clive Branson; Peter Whittaker; young Traill from Bloomsbury; "Maro" the cartoonist; R. M. Hilliard, the "Boxing Parson" of Kilkenny; Lorimer Birch, the scientist from Cambridge.[35] In his very comprehensive history of the British in this civil war, James K. Hopkins names some very different but no doubt more representative volunteers: Fred Jones, the assistant cook at an Unemployed Holiday Camp in Oxford; Thomas Gibbons, a building laborer; Johnnie Stevens, a Young Communist "in the fore of anti-fascist activity"; William Seal, a baker's roundsman; Steve Yates, an electrician "arrested and fined many times" for fighting against Fascism in his borough.[36] (Peter Kemp was one of a handful fighting for the Nationalists. He went "wrapped in a naïve, romantic day-dream," and his experience was much like that of those on the Communist side. He encountered James Walford, an artist, and an artilleryman by the name of Guy Spaey who had been at Cambridge with him; also a nurse, Pip Scott-Ellis, daughter of Lord Howard de Walden. Seeing the execution of prisoners from the International Brigade sickened him. Worse, on pain of being shot himself, he was ordered to shoot an English seaman with a hard-luck story that the Fascists disbelieved.)[37]

In the churchyard of Powerstock, a secluded hamlet in deepest Dorset, is the grave of John Pascal Rickman. He died in Spain in February 1937 and the inscription adds, "He gave his life in the cause of freedom." This is myth. In sober fact, he and all those killed were victims of Stalin's perfidy. Stalin cared nothing for the anti-fascist proletarian movement mobilized in the name of Communism. His objective was to expand Soviet power. Outright Soviet victory in Spain risked driving the democracies into a counter-balancing coalition with Hitler. If the fighting in Spain were to last for a long time, however, the democracies would eventually have to join with him, and he would then obtain a share of the spoils that nobody could challenge. To that end, he deliberately limited military aid to the Republicans. Playing both ends against the middle, he was simultaneously putting out feelers to Hitler. Meanwhile he made sure to achieve the lesser objectives of liquidating Trotskyites and other ideological enemies, while also getting hold of Spain's gold reserve. Through terror and murder and torture, the Soviet commissars, Comintern agents, and secret policemen in Spain set up a prototype of the post-war European police states of the Soviet bloc. Those like Rickman who lost their lives were not comparable to Philhellenes of the previous century fighting against an ancient despotism, but on the contrary deceived into fighting for a modern despotism.

A fairly recent obituary in the *Guardian* perfectly expresses the long-term determination of Spanish civil war survivors to cling to the self-flattering illusion that they had taken up arms in a noble cause, and so block out the sorry reality that they were pawns in the expansion of Soviet imperialism. "Girling, Elizabeth (Aytoun). 7 March 1913–24 March 2005. Peacefully at home in Edinburgh, surrounded by family to the sound of the 'Internationale.' Dearly loved wife of the late Frank, mother and grandmother. Lifelong social, political and peace activist, Old Labour, Spanish Civil War volunteer where she met Frank in 1938, founder of Partizan Coffee House."[38]

Revolting as the atrocities had been in Spain, those in the long-drawn experiment with Communism in China have proved far worse. No previous spasms of cruelty in the history of mankind had led to mass-murder on such a scale. Evidently a psychopath, Mao Tse-tung forced his nation to submit to whatever whim happened to be impelling him at the moment. Family, culture, tradition, and simple human pity were to count for nothing.

As established by the researches of Frank Dikötter, solely in the years of the tragically misnamed Great Leap Forward of 1958 to 1962, Mao Tse-tung is responsible for the deaths of forty five million of his fellow Chinese. Just as previously in the Soviet Union, so too Communists and fellow-travelers now rushed into China to defend the Party's violence and to participate in it. From the outset of the campaign to transform China into the People's Republic, the likes of Edgar Snow and Anna Louise Strong were well aware of witnessing the repeat of the revolutionary ordeals that had already ravaged the Soviet Union, but they made this out to be the way to a bright new future. Did the Chinese masses deserve to be the objects of such lying, such delusion, such contempt for their humanity?

In 1935, Julian Bell began a year's teaching in the National University of Wuhan. According to his biographers Stansky and Abrahams, he devoted himself to falling in love with a married Chinese lady, responding to the politics of the country with "diffidence and mild irritation." The news from Europe instead decided him to go to Spain, where he was to meet his death. William Empson taught in China from 1937 to 1939. As was usual with poets of the period, he was spell-bound by Auden and influenced by Marxism, though in his case mildly. The Nationalists of Chiang Kai-shek and the Communists were fighting one another as well as the invading Japanese, and in the confusion Empson tended to favor the former and to be skeptical of the latter, a number of whom were his students. Also in the late

1930s, Michael Lindsay, son of Lord Lindsay, Master of Balliol, taught in Beijing where he met and married his student Hsiao Li. They supported Communist resistance in Yenan, smuggling medical and radio supplies, and he broadcast and wrote propaganda for the Communists. An International Brigade member by the name of Joe Hinks fought in Mao's army. Having served his sentence for espionage, the former commissar David Springhall spent the rest of his life in China.

Rewi Alley was a New Zealander who came to China in 1927. He worked in Shanghai in the Fire Station and as a factory inspector. With other foreigners including a Comintern agent, he became a member of a Marxist-Leninist Study Group, and involved in the Communist underground. He seems always to have feared that his homosexuality would count against him. He and George Hogg, an Oxford-educated Englishman, set up a school in a remote province to spread cooperative ideas. For this and his work with refugees, Edgar Snow bizarrely compared him to Lawrence of Arabia and praised him as "one of the world's truly great people." After the Communist take-over, he put himself through what his biographer Anne-Marie Brady calls, "the necessary reconstruction of his public image from apolitical humanitarianism to outspoken supporter of Communism." To this end, he wrote a book *Yo Banfa! (We Have a Way!)* promising the Chinese "the glorious future that now faces their country." During the 1956 Suez crisis he spoke to a mass meeting of thousands, while at the same time two of his friends, Nan Green and Elsie Fairfax-Cholmeley, carried protest banners past the Embassy. Foreigners were forbidden to take part in the Cultural Revolution in 1968. Alley was "isolated and scared, unable to travel and frightened that he might be either arrested or deported."[39] He seems to have settled down as some sort of unofficial guide instructing fellow-travelers in correct thinking.

Nan Green had been in Spain with the International Brigade, and her husband had been killed there. Everything about Elsie Fairfax-Cholmeley makes her seem an identikit Communist who might have stepped out of the pages of a socialist-realist novel whose function is to edify the workers. Her father was a landowning squire in Yorkshire, and she had been privately educated. Drifting into the Institute of Pacific Relations, a front organization in New York, she came into contact with Chinese Communists and went to Hong Kong. After several years of wartime drama, she married Israel Epstein, a Jewish rolling stone originally from Poland, also thrown up in China. He too had attended a weekly Marxist discussion group. Living in Beijing, he carried out what he describes in his autobiography as "foreign-language publicity work for China" alongside Alan Winnington of the *Daily Worker* and the Australian Wilfred Burchett, both notorious for inventing American "war crimes." Epstein and his wife were also press-ganged to help build a dam and reservoir, taking their "muscle-wrenching but heart-warming turn in carrying heavy loads of earth in baskets slung from shoulder poles, and pushing and pulling wheelbarrows filled with stones uphill." Already aged fifty-three, Elsie would set off from the house, a towel at her belt, a pack with her bedding and a change of clothing on her back, "a picture of the pick-and-shovel labourer." During the Cultural Revolution this couple were both arrested, and each kept in solitary confinement for five years with no information of the other's fate. Deprived of education, their children were sent into the country. In language euphemistic to the point of comedy, he resumes what had happened as "an unwelcome shock," due to "the unveiling of erosion, in the revolutionary structure itself, of the post-Liberation spirit of simplicity and integrity."[40]

Born in London, David Crook came from a prosperous family. He was educated at Cheltenham, a good public school, and did a degree in New York at Columbia where he enrolled in the American Communist Youth League. He joined the International Brigade in Spain and was soon recruited as a Comintern agent in the campaign to liquidate Trotskyites and anarchists. It is said that later in life he regretted what can only have been a season of crime. Prepared by reading Edgar

Snow, he was sent to Shanghai to report to the Soviets on Trotskyites there. In 1940 he met Isabel, daughter of Canadian missionaries. Married, they did post-war research on revolution in a Chinese village, and were invited to stay in Beijing to teach English to elite students. He too served five years in solitary confinement at the time of the Cultural Revolution, but his wife said he never blamed China, always feeling "immeasurably enriched" by participating in the country's "great but tortuous revolution."[41]

Left-wing London refused to acknowledge that once again a revolution was devouring its children. The ubiquitous Victor Gollancz set up a China Campaign Committee, with Kingsley Martin, Dorothy Woodman (Martin's long-term mistress cultivated Asian dictators), and two Communists, John Allen and Arthur Clegg. Even by the standards set by Shaw, Wells, or the Webbs in the Soviet Union, the promotion of Communist China by fellow-travelers is mind-boggling. Already in 1953, as many as 672 prominent artist and scientists including E. M. Forster, J. B. Priestley, Doris Lessing, Augustus John, and Henry Moore gave the impression of mass hypnosis by signing a so-called "Message" to Chinese colleagues "to see an end to all the dissensions which at present threaten to separate us."

Basil Davidson, fresh from playing his part in putting the Communists into power in Yugoslavia, wrote *Daybreak in China.* The mainspring of the revolution, he thought, was the Chinese belief in "the good and peaceful destiny of mankind." At a time when there were twenty million and possibly twice as many more "enemies of the people" in *Lao gai,* the country's equivalent of Gulag, James Cameron visited the Beijing prison. In the eyes of this famous reporter, supposedly a hard-bitten observer of history in the raw, the gates were open, there was only one guard with a rifle, and the Chinese were getting the moral stigma out of imprisonment. For him, there were no signs of terror or sense of fear, "the element of personal acquisitiveness was at vanishing point," and Mao was "the Abraham Lincoln of China." A persistent fellow-traveler greatly indulged by the media was Felix Greene, cousin of Graham Greene, who thought, "No one can be in China for more than a few hours without sensing an almost tangible vitality and an enormous optimism." The ineffable Hewlett Johnson, the Red Dean of Canterbury, was as enraptured by Mao as he had been by Stalin: "He had the beautiful head of the portraits; at times of repose one saw evidence of past suffering; as he spoke his whole expression lit up with warmth and radiance." Why, Mao had even said goodbye to him, "lingering in the courtyard to point out a lovely flowering tree." The underside of this abysmal sentimentality was his conviction that the United States was using germ warfare in Korea.

Joseph Needham was a crank camouflaged as a scholar. Born in 1900, he was the son of parents who left him isolated but gave him a good education ending at Cambridge University where he became a biochemist. On the far Left since a teenager, he made sure to keep his private income and run an expensive car. Morris dancing was one of his fads, and another was nudism, with an interest in erotica. In 1935 he took the usual fellow-traveling tour to the Soviet Union. Lenin offered inspiration, he found, and the "genius" of Stalin put humanity in his debt. In 1942 he was sent to China—this was arranged by J. G. Crowther, head of the science department of the British Council, and himself author of a misleading book about Soviet science. A married man, Needham lived in a *ménage à trois* with a well-connected Chinese student. She introduced him to Mao and Chou Enlai who gave him the help he needed. (Cooperating with him, a British diplomat, Derek Bryan, campaigned so hard for the People's Republic that the Foreign Office got rid of him, whereupon he helped found a front organization, the Society for Anglo-Chinese Understanding.)

In the course of his life Needham wrote a series of volumes whose title *Science and Civilisation in China* is self-explanatory. Simon Winchester, the author of his biography entitled *Bomb, Book & Compass* (titled *The Man Who Loved China* in the United States), summarizes some of his frenzied political activities: "he joined, or spoke to, the

Progressive League, the New Left Review Club, the Tawney Society, and the British Peace Society; he contributed to the Scientists' Protest Fund; he co-founded Science for Peace. He marched to air bases and bomb plants with the Campaign for Nuclear Disarmament." Accusing the United States of biological warfare at the height of the Cold War, the Communists set up an International Commission with Needham at its head. He declared that he was thrilled to be able to support the party now in power in the People's Republic. Needless to say, the report asserted that the United States had used bacteriological weapons. Thus Needham's scholarship was at the service of deception and agitprop. He campaigned on behalf of the Rosenbergs; he supported the Cultural Revolution. Loaded with honors in England, he was Master of Caius College, Cambridge, for ten years. One obituary called him "an Erasmus for our times."[42]

Here is how *The Times* summed up the career of Dr. Tony Smith, its one-time medical correspondent: "He was passionate about Chairman Mao's China and would hear no criticism of it. He visited China with an official party in 1976 and came back full of praise for how much the regime had done for its people's health and convinced that all flies had been eliminated in China as well as sexually transmitted diseases." When Mao died, Anthony Wedgwood Benn, a hereditary viscount who renounced his title and became a socialist cabinet minister, paid a courtesy call to the Chinese Embassy. There he told the First Secretary how much he admired Mao, "the greatest man of the twentieth century." Idolization of mass-murder crossed boundaries. Valéry Giscard d'Estaing, the French president, found it in him to say that on Mao's death "a lighthouse of humanity" had just been extinguished.

The abasement of free people to the monstrosity of Chinese Communism is a cautionary tale about the degeneration of intellect and moral judgment. Norman Douglas is an author not much read except for his novel *South Wind,* but he should be remembered for saying, "There is no cause so vile that some human being will not be

found to defend it." Many in England agreed with Günter Grass, the
German novelist, that Latin America should follow "the Cuban
example," thus ignoring judicial executions, long-term prison sen-
tences for dissidents, and the flight into exile of refugees by the million. For Nelson Mandela, the murderous Che Guevara was "an
inspiration for every human being who loves freedom." Fellow-travelers visited North Vietnam—and were to remain indifferent to the
boat people who risked their lives escaping from victorious Communism. John Peet defected to East Germany in June 1950, when he
was thirty-four years old. He made a statement, "I simply cannot
consent to take part any longer in the warmongering which threatens
. . . the Soviet Union and the People's democracies." Publishing in
East Berlin an eight-page report every fortnight for over twenty
years, he was warmongering for the Soviets against real democracies.
Sir Reginald Hibbert of the Foreign Office and a Communist during
his wartime mission in Albania, wrote *Albania's National Liberation
Struggle,* to give credit for ending Fascist occupation in the war to the
Communists and not the Nationalists, sounding suspiciously like a
counterpart to Klugmann in Yugoslavia. Before upsetting Ayatollah
Khomeini with a novel taken to be blasphemous, Salman Rushdie
went to Nicaragua as the guest of the Sandinista Association of Cultural Workers. In a late flowering of classic fellow-traveling, he was
escorted round the country for just three weeks, after which he
could conclude that the Sandinistas were "emphatically" not dictators: "they struck me as men of integrity and great pragmatism."[43]
George Galloway, then a Labour Member of Parliament, appeared on
television at the time of the first Gulf War to praise Saddam Hussein
for his "courage" and, even more insinuating in the circumstances, his
"indefatigability."

The vileness of Malcolm Caldwell exceeds even these examples.
The son of a Scottish miner, he became a university lecturer in Lon-
don, and was in his thirties when he took up the cause of the Khmer
Rouge and Pol Pot. That regime was responsible for the deaths of at

least two million people, or about a third of Cambodia's population. A thorough liar, Caldwell had no interest in facts, and worse, no interest in human beings. For him, this mass-murder had not occurred, and if it did then it was part of a world-wide revolutionary shift "holding out the promise of a better future for all." In December 1978 he had a private audience with Pol Pot. Some hours afterwards, a gunman shot him dead. Quite possibly Pol Pot had had him murdered, which would be poetic justice of a sort. The crime remains unsolved, as mysterious and murky as Caldwell's psychology.[44] What seems common to these various defenders of tyranny is a disposition to violence and cruelty, leading them to admire vicariously whoever has the requisite will and power to dispense with every moral restraint in pursuit of some enormity.

A young man named Andrew Anthony has described in a rather mournfully honest autobiography, *The Fall-Out,* how at his comprehensive school in London he was taught by a Maoist who looked like a "gothic or pre-Raphaelite hippy." This woman carried round a copy of Mao's *Little Red Book,* spoke of the coming revolution as inevitable, and was "permanently angry about the state of the world." As soon as he had absorbed her outlook, the Nicaragua of the Sandinistas seemed to offer him "a politically and morally straightforward issue." In that country, in 1988, he joined what was called the Margaret Roff brigade, named after a Manchester City councilor and lesbian rights campaigner who had died in a fire in a Nicaraguan hotel. His associates were "an assortment of hard-core communists, Trotskyists, softish socialists, liberals and Christians," while confronting them was "Western imperialism and injustice." That is the composition, the mind-set and the randomness of the throng today traveling expensively and far in a state of permanent anger in the track of some cause or other, about climate change, say, globalization, or a G20 summit. In a tradition that is well established by now, such people continue to recast the real world in the image of their inner disturbances and fantasies.

Epilogue

George Orwell earned a lasting place in the canon of English literature by evoking with such intuition the danger of foreign ideological causes. Writing during the Second World War, at a moment when rival ideological causes were fighting to the death, he predicted that the intellectuals who hoped to see England Russianized or Germanized would be disappointed. The country and its national culture might change out of recognition but "England will still be England, an everlasting animal stretching into the future and the past." His image of an everlasting animal speaks for itself, but it is very much of its time. Dying in 1950 at the age of forty-six, Orwell did not live long enough to witness the process of change under way across the world. British people had done more than their fair share of breaking up other empires by promoting nationalist causes within them, and now it was the turn of the British Empire to be destroyed by the nationalism of its subject peoples in Asia and Africa.

Britain might have won the war, but seemingly there was nothing to show for it except loss. The actual losers were Germany and France, since the latter's claim to the status of victor could not wipe away the humiliating surrender of 1940. Governing circles in both those countries were inclined to blame their calamitous and century-long enmity on nationalism and began to devise structures to replace it. Nationalism was right and necessary for the peoples of the emerging Third World, then, but in the case of sophisticated Europe the traditional nation state would have to become obsolete. Under compulsion to adapt to an imaginary transnational status, the man on the street might object, but Jean Monnet, the Frenchman who was the principal architect of the coming future, had the answer to that: "Europe's nations should be guided towards a super state without their people understanding what is happening. This can be accomplished by successive steps each disguised as having an economic purpose, but which will eventually and irreversibly lead to federation."

Whatever the intention may have been in abolishing the European nation state, in practice yet another ideological cause was born. Britons who had previously backed causes from the French Revolution to Communism had done so voluntarily, as private citizens banding together. Membership of the European Union is a cause that British government and its servants have pursued as policy. In keeping with the founding father Monnet's advice, they have disguised their purposes. The motivation has as much to do with psychology as politics. Irrational passions, post-colonial guilt, loss of confidence in self-rule, illusions about human nature, some sort of national panic have prevented British governments and opinion-makers from taking measured decisions in the national interest. Moreover, the whole project is contrary to other contemporary movements of world-historical importance, of which Third World nationalism is only one example. The Soviet Union had always proclaimed itself a supranational empire of the kind that Europe was aiming at, but it had failed to correspond to profound questions of identity and nationhood, and therefore vanished into thin air.

These factors were clear from the beginning. In the event of joining this European experiment, Britain would have to give up things defining its identity and nationhood, moreover things that have made it very different from continental Europeans. Lord Kilmuir, the Lord Chancellor in 1960, warned the cabinet:

I must emphasise that in my view the surrenders of sovereignty involved
are serious ones, and I think that, as a matter of practical politics, it will
not be easy to persuade Parliament or the British public to accept them.[1]

Lord Denning, the Lord Chief Justice in 1974, was speaking
about European law "flowing up the estuaries of England ... like a
tidal wave bringing down our sea walls and flowing inland over our
fields and houses" but his elegiac simile is descriptive of almost every
other sphere of national life.[2]

The sole prime minister acting from genuine conviction that
Britain should join Europe no matter what the cost was Edward
Heath. Sir Con O'Neill, the official negotiating entry on his behalf,
summed up Heath's approach, "Swallow the lot, and swallow it
now."[3] To have his way, Heath was furtive in the approved style of
Monnet, deceiving the electorate into believing that they were to
enter a common market, and nothing more. He obliged an unfortunate minister, Geoffrey Rippon, to lie to Parliament about the terms
of entry into what was already a proto-federal Union. In all the years
that the European Union has been taking shape, the British have been
allowed just one referendum, and it was carefully manipulated to
reach the decision pre-ordained by the Heath government.

The Franco-German alliance set up its capital in Brussels, built
gigantic palaces of glass to serve as institutions of command and control, accumulating and monopolizing power. A self-appointed and
tax-free nomenklatura consisting of many thousands of bureaucrats
has appropriated the function of initiating and legislating a constant
flow of regulations, directives, recommendations, opinions and reso-
lutions that have changed former ways of doing things out of all
recognition, imposing standardization irrespective of national prac-
tices or context. This bureaucracy has now taken over the greater
part of what used to be the function of legislation in Westminster and
every other European parliament. In Brussels, there is neither sepa-
ration of powers nor accountability. In spite of its name, the

European Court of Justice has the specific political purpose of promoting European integration.

The force of events, Lord Denning's tidal wave, has carried other
prime ministers headlong in the surrender of sovereignty, sometimes
against their will but apparently powerless to decide on any other
course of action, perhaps too blind or too cowardly to do so. The
usual pressure groups and organizations have been formed to promote the European Union; they are mostly subsidized from Brussels,
also aided and abetted by the media, above all the BBC. Defending
the construction and the performance of European Union, civil servants are the up-to-date version of fellow-travelers. Representative
of the Foreign Office is Sir Oliver Wright, who as ambassador in
Germany used to go round that country speechifying, *"Ich bin ein
Eurofanatiker,"* without "provoking even a flicker of an eyebrow in
Whitehall."[4] Fear that the defense of separate national interests is
likely in a time of crisis to lead to violence that bursts apart the
supra-national fiction is carefully stifled.

Forsaking the party of war-time victors and associating with the
party of war-time losers, the British are invited to think about themselves in quite different ways. They are now subjects of the European
Union, which has a president whose relationship to the British
monarchy remains undefined for the time being. They have acquired
the trappings of enforced identity that comes with their new state-
hood, a flag that is not the Union Jack, an anthem that is not "God
Save the Queen," a passport common to four hundred million people
whose languages, law, traditions, history, and in some cases religion
they do not share. More by luck than judgment, they have so far
avoided the European currency, but have nonetheless decimalized the
pound. Metrication has replaced almost all imperial weights and
measures. In his futuristic nightmare *1984,* Orwell happens to treat
the memory of the pint as a symbol of the England that could once be
taken for granted, but has since been volatilized by ideologues. Much

more of Jean Monnet's legacy, and the transfer of loyalties to a foreign cause will be complete, and there will no longer be the Britain
of the past to betray.

Acknowledgments

Niccolò Capponi, John Clare, the late Amos Elon, Amanda Foreman, Jonathan Foreman, the late John Gross, Ben Macintyre, Noel Malcolm, answered my questions or put me on the track of relevant material. Douglas Matthews has done the index with his customary professionalism. Roger Kimball is the supportive publisher of whom authors usually can only dream. Special thanks go out to all of these for their help.

Notes

Chapter One: The Revolution of the World

[1] Mary Moorman, *William Wordsworth: A Biography*, p. 22.

[2] Bernard Bailyn, quoted in David A. Wilson, *Paine and Cobbett*, p. 40.

[3] Craig Nelson, *Thomas Paine*, p. 140.

[4] John Keane, *Tom Paine: A Political Life*, p. 126.

[5] Quoted in Robert Middelkauff, *The Glorious Cause*, p. 108.

[6] John C. Miller, *Origins of the American Revolution*, p. 185 and p. 204.

[7] J.G.A. Pocock, quoted in Jack Fruchtman, *Thomas Paine: Apostle of Freedom*, p. 3.

[8] A. Owen Aldridge, *Thomas Paine's American Ideology*, p. 193.

[9] Middelkauff, p. 258.

[10] Paul Johnson, *A History of the American People*, p. 133.

[11] Fruchtman, p. 183.

[12] Keane, p. 311.

[13] J. M. Thompson, Ed. *English Witnesses of the French Revolution*, p. 129.

[14] Keane, p. 430.

[15] Keane, p. 436.

[16] Nelson, p. 287.

Chapter Two: The Mighty Projects of the Times

[1] Robert and Isabelle Tombs, *That Sweet Enemy*, p. 96.

[2] Constantia Maxwell, *The English Traveller in France*, p. 149.

[3] Maxwell, p. 156.

[4] *The Works of John Moore*, vol. IV, p. 1.

[5] J. M. Thompson, p. 4.

[6] J. M. Thompson, p. 99.

[7] Tombs, p. 186.

[8] Namier, quoted in E. Tangye Lean, *The Napoleonists*, p. 216.

[9] Alfred Cobban, ed., *The Debate on the French Revolution*, p. 39.

[10] Albert Goodwin, *The Friends of Liberty*, p. 502.

[11] G. P. Gooch & Ghita Stanhope, *The Life of Charles Third Earl Stanhope*, p. 87.

[12] David O. Thomas, *The Honest Mind*, p. 330.

[13] Claire Tomalin, *The Life and Death of Mary Wollstonecraft*, p. 2.

[14] Tombs, p. 192.

[15] Carola Oman, *Britain Against Napoleon*, p. 13.

[16] Deborah Kennedy, *Helen Maria Williams and the Age of Revolution*, p. 53.

[17] Goodwin, p. 284.

[18] Niall Ferguson, *Cash Nexus*, p. 79.

[19] F. M. Todd, *Politics and the Poet*, p. 51.

[20] Wilbur George Meyer, *Wordsworth's Formative Years*, p. 5.

[21] Meyer, p. 89.

[22] Mary C. Moorman, *Wordsworth: A Biography*, p. 220.

[23] Gooch & Stanhope, p. 96.

[24] Gooch & Stanhope, p. 241.

[25] Philip Anthony Brown, *The French Revolution in English History*, p. 91.

[26] Stella Tillyard, *Citizen Lord: Edward Fitzgerald*, p. 139.

[27] Tillyard, p. 222.

[28] Tillyard, p. 241.

[29] Oliver Knox, *Rebels and Informers*, p. 153.

[30] J. G. Alger, *Englishmen in the French Revolution*, p. 98.

[31] Tristram Stuart, *The Bloodless Revolution*, p. 295.

[32] Stuart, p. xxv.

[33] David Erdman, *Commerce des lumières*, p. 96.

[34] Stuart, p. 308.

[35] Erdman, p. 90.

[36] Erdman, p. 8.

[37] Deborah Kennedy, p. 57.

[38] Deborah Kennedy, p. 59.

[39] Deborah Kennedy, p. 97.

[40] Deborah Kennedy, p. 101.

[41] Helen Maria Williams, *Letters on The Events which have passed in France since the Restoration in 1815*, p. 1.

[42] Claire Tomalin, *The Life and Death of Mary Wollstonecraft*, p. 178.

[43] David A. Wilson, p. 148.

[44] Cobban, p. 372.

[45] Henry Weissar, *British Working-Class Movements and Europe 1815–1848*, p. 4.

Chapter Three: "The God of My Idolatry"

[1] E. Tangye Lean, *The Napoleonists*, p. 140.

[2] Lean, p. 20.

[3] Tombs, p. 229.

[4] Oman, p. 146.

[5] Oman, p. 138.

[6] Lean, p. 62.

[7] Kennedy, p. 177.

[8] Stuart Semmel, *Napoleon and the British*, p. 2.

[9] Semmel, p. 161.

[10] Semmel, p. 47.

[11] For William Roscoe, see A. C. Grayling, *The Quarrel of the Age*, p. 191.

[12] Lean, p. 9.

[13] Semmel, p. 137.

[14] Grayling, p. 17.

[15] Grayling, p. 172.

[16] Andrew Roberts, *Napoleon and Wellington*, p. 194.

[17] Roberts, p. 195.

[18] Grayling, p. 193.

[19] Lean, p. 99.

[20] Lean, p. 105.

[21] Lean, p. 112.

[22] Semmel, p. 155.

[23] C. M. Woodhouse, *The Philhellenes,* p. 62.

Chapter Four: "We Are All Greeks"

[1] Elie Kedourie, *Nationalism,* p. 1.

[2] Elie Kedourie, *The Chatham House Version,* p. 6.

[3] William St. Clair, *That Greece Might Still Be Free,* p. 27.

[4] Terence Spencer, *Fair Greece, Sad Relic,* p. 237.

[5] Gary J. Bass, *Freedom's Battle,* p. 72.

[6] St. Clair, p. 59.

[7] St. Clair, pp. 17, 19.

[8] St. Clair, p. 66.

[9] David Brewer, *The Flame of Freedom,* p. 78.

[10] St. Clair, p. 92.

[11] St. Clair, p. 81.

[12] J. M. Hussey, ed., *The Letters and Journals of George Finlay,* vol 1, pp. 12, 21.

[13] David Cordingly, *Cochrane the Dauntless,* p. 301.

[14] E. M. Church, *Sir Richard Church in Italy and Greecei,* p. 2.

[15] Church, p. 321.

[16] Douglas Dakin, *British and American Philhellenes,* p. 198.

[17] St. Clair, p. 32.

[18] Iris Origo, *The Last Attachment,* p. 39.

[19] Leslie Marchand, *Byron: A Biography,* vol. III, p. 1094.

[20] C. E. Vulliamy, *Byron,* p. 239.

[21] Harold Nicolson, *Byron: The Last Journey,* p. 91.

[22] Lean, p. 269.

Chapter Five: That Sound That Crashes in the Tyrant's Ear

[1] Weissar op. cit. p. 18.

[2] Edward M. Brett, *The British Auxiliary Legion in the First Carlist War in Spain 1835–1838,* p. 35.

[3] D. B. Horn, *British Public Opinion and the First Partition of Poland,* p. 69.

[4] Weissar, op. cit., pp. 32, 51.

[5] Adam Zamoyski, *Holy Madness,* pp. 93.

[6] John Howes Gleason, *The Genesis of Russophobia in Great Britain,* p. 68.

[7] Gleason, op. cit., p. 123.

[8] Otto Zarek, *Kossuth,* p. 265.

[9] A. J. P. Taylor, *The Trouble Makers,* p. 58.

[10] *Authentic Life of His Excellency Louis Kossuth, Governor of Hungary* (1851), p. 12

[11] Eva H. Haraszti, *Kossuth as an English Journalist,* p. 42.

Chapter Six: Imperishable and International Poetry

[1] DNB, quoting Mrs. J. R. Swinton, *A Sketch of the Life of Georgiana, Lady de Ros,* p. 44.

[2] Margaret C. W. Wicks, *Italian Exiles in London 1816–1848,* p. 78.

[3] Frances Winaver, *The Immortal Lovers,* p. 213.

[4] Lucy Riall, *Garibaldi: The Invention of a Hero,* p. 79.

[5] For Colonel Forbes, see G. M. Trevelyan, *Garibaldi's Defence of the Roman Republic,* p. 349.

[6] Zamoyski, p. 366.

[7] G. M. Trevelyan, *Garibaldi and the Thousand,* p. 125.

[8] Winaver, p. 290.

[9] For *The Times* and Swinburne, see Raleigh Trevelyan, *Princes under the Volcano,* p. 180.

[10] For Forbes and Meuricoffre, see Riall, pp. 229–230.

[11] For fan mail, see Riall, pp. 299–300.

[12] For Peard, see Christopher Hibbert, *Garibaldi and His Enemies,*
p. 272. Also G. M. Trevelyan, p. 492.

[13] Hibbert, p. 271.

[14] Raleigh Trevelyan, p. 185.

[15] Riall, p. 345.

[16] Martin Thom, *Times Literary Supplement,* 17 June 2009.

Chapter Seven: Pasha Inglesi

[1] Woodhouse, p. 151.

[2] For the Circassian committee, see Zamoyski, p. 421.

[3] Karl Marx, quoted in Geoffrey Nash, *From Empire to Orient,* p. 46.

[4] Nash, p. 45.

[5] *Times* letter, quoted in Andrew Ryan, *Last of the Dragomans,* p. 17.

[6] John Howes Gleason, p. 153.

[7] Nash, p. 43.

[8] Adolphus Slade, *Records of Travels in Turkey 1854,* p. 225.

[9] Adolphus Slade, *Turkey and the Crimean War,* p. 20.

[10] Anne Taylor, *Laurence Oliphant,* p. 8.

[11] Margaret Oliphant, *Memoir of the Life of Laurence Oliphant,* vol. 1,
p. 249.

[12] G. M. Trevelyan, *Garibaldi and the Thousand,* p. 174.

[13] Margaret Oliphant, p. 276.

[14] Taylor, p. 51.

[15] Dorothy Anderson, *The Balkan Volunteers,* p. 5.

[16] Dorothy Anderson, p. 73.

[17] Edward Vizetelly, *The Reminiscences of a Bashi-Bazouk,* p. 48.

[18] Vizetelly, p. 56.

[19] Vizetelly, p. 345.

[20] Aubrey Herbert, *Ben Kendim,* p. xiv.

[21] Margaret FitzHerbert, *The Man Who Was Greenmantle,* p. 5.

[22] Herbert, p. 24.

[23] Herbert, p. 157.

[24] Herbert, p. 207.

[25] FitzHerbert, p. 117.

[26] Edith Durham, *High Albania,* p. xii.

[27] FitzHerbert, pp. 122–123.

[28] John Fisher, *Gentlemen Spies,* p. 18.

[29] FitzHerbert, p. 221.

Chapter Eight: "Those Poor Armenians"

[1] Elie Kedourie, *The Chatham House Version,* p. 286.

[2] J.A.R. Marriott, *The Eastern Question,* p. 325.

[3] Peter Balakian, *The Burning Tigris,* p. 36.

[4] John T. Seaman, Jr., *A Citizen of the World,* p. 79.

[5] Balakian, p. 119.

[6] G.W.E. Russell, ed., *Malcolm MacColl: Memoirs and Correspondence,* p. 264.

[7] Oliver Baldwin, *The Questing Beast,* p. 45.

[8] Baldwin, p. 80.

[9] Baldwin, p. 168.

[10] Baldwin, p. 107.

Chapter Nine: "To Heal This Ancient Nation"

[1] Tudor Parfitt, *The Lost Tribes of Israel,* p. 37.

[2] Victoria Clark, *Allies for Armageddon,* p. 56.

[3] Victoria Clark, p. 66.

[4] Bruce Westrate, *The Arab Bureau. British Policy in the Middle East,* p. 173.

[5] Robert Blake, *Disraeli,* p. 66.

[6] *The Satirist,* quoted in Christopher Hibbert, *Disraeli,* p. 143.

[7] Blake, p. 538.

[8] Hibbert, p. 263.

[9] Mark Sykes, *Dar-ul-Islam,* p. 171.

[10] Isaiah Berlin, *Chaim Weizmann,* p. 27.

[11] Isaiah Berlin, in *Chaim Weizmann: A Biography by Several Hands,* ed. Meyer Weisgal, p. 37.

[12] N. A. Rose, ed., *The Diaries of Blanche Dugdale*, p. 91.

[13] Rose, p. 15.

[14] Rose, p. 132.

[15] Christopher Sykes, *Orde Wingate*, p. 85.

[16] John Bierman and Colin Smith, *Fire in the Night*, p. 63.

[17] Sykes, p. 110.

[18] Tom Segev, *One Palestine, Complete*, p. 430.

[19] Bierman and Smith, p. 128.

[20] Sykes, p. 215.

[21] Sykes, p. 311.

[22] Sykes, p. 315.

[23] Bernard Wasserstein, *The British in Palestine*, p. 52.

[24] John Lord, *Duty, Honour, Empire*, p. 394.

Chapter Ten: "Every Englishman's Idea of Nature's Gentleman"

[1] Jason Thompson, *Edward William Lane*, p. 26.

[2] Thompson, p. 44.

[3] Thompson, p. 333.

[4] A. H. Layard, *Autobiography and Letters*, vol. ii, p. 138.

[5] E. B. Soane, *To Mesopotamia and Kurdistan in Disguise*, p. 330.

[6] Soane, p. 317.

[7] Fawn M. Brodie, *The Devil Drives*, p. 34.

[8] Brodie, p. 50.

[9] Richard Burton, *A Pilgrimage to El-Medinah and Meccah*, vol. I, p. 2.

[10] Kathryn M. Tidrick, *Heart-Beguiling Araby*, p. 208.

[11] Elizabeth Longford, *A Pilgrimage of Passion*, p. 214.

[12] Longford, p. 215.

[13] Roger Owen, *Lord Cromer*, p. 26.

[14] W. S. Blunt, *My Diaries 1888–1914*, p. 792.

[15] Claire Sheridan, *Arab Interlude*, p. 89.

[16] Lady Evelyn Cobbold, *Pilgrimage to Mecca*, p. 194.

[17] Cobbold, p. 102.

[18] Peter Clark, *Marmaduke Pickthall*, p. 12.

[19] Elie Kedourie, *The Chatham House Version*, p. 33.

[20] Richard Aldington, *Lawrence of Arabia*, p. 206.

[21] Polly A. Mohs, *Military Intelligence and the Arab Revolt*, p. 162.

[22] Westrate, p. 4.

[23] *The Letters of Gertrude Bell*, p. 572.

[24] Private information. The late Professor J. B. Kelly calculated that Philby misappropriated the equivalent today of £30,000, taking into account variations in currencies and exchange rates.

[25] Elizabeth Monroe, *Philby of Arabia*, p. 108.

[26] Anthony Cave Brown, *Treason in the Blood*, p. 85.

[27] Cave Brown, p. 99.

[28] Cave Brown, p. 231.

[29] Geoffrey Furlonge, *Palestine Is My Country*, p. 85.

[30] Frances Newton, *Fifty Years in Palestine*, p. 127.

[31] Newton, p. 293.

[32] Freya Stark, quoted in Rory Miller, *British Anti-Zionism Then and Now Covenant*, vol. 1, issue 2 on covenant@idc.ac.il

[33] For Aubrey Lees, see Richard Griffiths, *Patriotism Perverted*, p. 138.

[34] Benny Morris, *The Road to Jerusalemi*, p. 251.

[35] Trevor Royle, *Glubb Pasha*, p. 451.

[36] Royle, p. 405.

[37] Henry Hardy and Jennifer Holmes, eds., *Isaiah Berlin: Enlightening. Letters 1946–1960*, p. 50

[38] Benny Morris, *1948*, p. 434.

[39] For deserters, see Morris, p. 107.

Chapter Eleven: Germany Calling

[1] James Sexton, ed., *Aldous Huxley. Selected Letters*, p. 158.

[2] Stephen Koss, ed., *The Pro-Boers*, p. xxvii.

[3] Koss, ed., p. xxxiii.

[4] Seaman, p. 187.

[5] For Campbell-Bannerman, *Clarion,* and Hobson, see Bernard Porter, *Critics of Empire,* pp. 62, 103, 128.

[6] F. M. Leventhal, *The Last Dissenter,* p. 2.

[7] John Hall, *That Bloody Woman,* p. 63.

[8] Hall, p. 169.

[9] Hall, p. 258.

[10] Adrian Weale, *Patriot Traitors,* p. 73.

[11] Weale, p. 87.

[12] Geoffrey G. Field, *Evangelist of Race,* p. 27.

[13] Field, p. 32.

[14] Field, p. 2.

[15] Lucy Davidowicz, *The War Against the Jews,* p. 16.

[16] Biographical details and quotations are from Brigitte Hamann, *Winifred Wagner.*

[17] Stephen Dorril, *Black Shirt,* p. 343.

[18] Guy Liddell, *Diaries,* vol. I, p. 72.

[19] Richard Griffiths, *Fellow Travellers of the Right,* p. 136.

[20] Dorril, p. 339.

[21] Dorril, p. 247.

[22] For John Warburton, see *Daily Telegraph,* 12 September 2004.

[23] Biographical details and quotation are from Trevor Grundy, *Memoirs of a Fascist Childhood.*

[24] For Olive Baker and Elsie Orrin, see Sean Murphy, *Letting the Side Down,* p. 31.

[25] For Norman Piggott, see Andrew Roberts, *The Spectator,* 23 January 1993.

[26] Dorril, p. 23.

[27] Lean, p. 292.

[28] Dorril, p. 389.

[29] For Lord Lothian, see Richard Griffiths, p. 154.

[30] John Marlowe, *Late Victorian,* p. 355.

[31] Ian Kershaw, *Making Friends with Hitler,* p. 171.

[32] Robert Rhodes James, ed., *Chips: The Diaries of Sir Henry Channon,* pp. 105–113.

[33] Maurice Willoughby, *Echo of a Distant Drum,* p. 206.

[34] For Rachel Fenwick, see Patrick Marnham, *Wild Mary,* p. 45.

[35] For Michael Burn, see his memoir *Turned Towards The Sun.*

[36] For Sir Reginald Goodall, see *Sunday Telegraph,* 13 May 1990.

[37] Rebecca West, *The New Meaning of Treason,* p. 4.

[38] Peter Martland, *Lord Haw Haw,* p. 24.

[39] Martland, p. 161.

[40] For the Funkhaus and personnel, see Nigel Farndale, *Haw-Haw,* pp. 132–4.

[41] For Leonard Brown, see Marquis de Slade, *Yeomen of Valhalla,* p. 49.

[42] For Pearl Vardon, see Martin Doherty, *Nazi Wireless Propaganda,* p. 22.

[43] For Susan Hilton, see Murphy, p. 80.

[44] Adrian Weale, *Patriot Traitors,* p. 190.

[45] David Faber, *Speaking for England,* p. 281.

[46] For Stranders and other Legionaries, see Marquis de Slade, *Yeoman of Valhalla* and Weale.

[47] For Eddie Chapman, see Ben Macintyre, *Agent Zigzag.*

Chapter Twelve: There Are Many Wicked Men in the World

[1] Arthur Ransome, quoted in *Times Literary Supplement,* 21 August 2009.

[2] Kevin Morgan, *Harry Pollitt,* p. 153.

[3] Victor Gollancz, *Reminiscences of Affection,* p. 42.

[4] Andrew Thorpe, *The British Communist Party,* p. 43.

[5] Figures from James Eaden and David Renton, *The Communist Party of Great Britain since 1920,* p. 62.

[6] For Gollancz, see John Lewis, *The Left Book Club,* pp. 20–21.

[7] G.D.H. Cole quoted in Tombs, p. 610.

[8] Lean, pp. 319–320.

[9] C. H. Rolph, *Kingsley,* p. 220.

[10] *Daily Telegraph,* 15 February 2009.

[11] See Peter Stanford, *C. Day-Lewis. A Life,* pp. 140–164.

[12] Thomas Schuttenhelm, ed., *Selected Letters of Michael Tippett,* p. 124.

[13] *Dylan Thomas. The Collected Letters,* new edition, ed. Paul Ferris, p. 72.

[14] Paul Ignotus, *Political Prisoner,* p. 6.

[15] For Evelyn Sharp, see *Times Literary Supplement,* 7 August 2009.

[16] Malcolm Muggeridge, *Chronicles of Wasted Time,* vol. I, p. 244.

[17] S. J. Taylor, *Stalin's Apologist,* p. 2.

[18] *A Scientist Among the Soviets,* p. 24.

[19] Andrew Brown, *J. D. Bernal: The Sage of Science,* p. 308.

[20] Hugh Dalton, *The Fateful Years,* p. 84.

[21] *Inside Stalin's Russia: The Diaries of Reader Bullard 1930–1934,* eds. Julian and Margaret Bullard, p. 83.

[22] Bullard, p. 193.

[23] Kitty Muggeridge and Ruth Adam, *Beatrice Webb: A Life,* p. 257.

[24] Lady Mountbatten, quoted in Elie Kedourie, *Commentary,* December 1985.

[25] Clive Dewey, *Anglo-Indian Attitudes,* p. 227.

[26] Doris Lessing, *Walking in the Shade,* pp. 56–82.

[27] Miranda Carter, *Anthony Blunt,* pp. 131–133.

[28] Kim Philby, *My Silent War,* p. xix.

[29] Nikolai Tolstoy, *Stalin's Secret War,* pp. 291–294.

[30] David Martin, "James Klugmann, SOE Cairo and the Mihailovich Deception" in *Deception Operations,* eds. D. A. Charters and M.A.J. Tugwell, pp. 53–84.

[31] John Langdon-Davies, *Behind the Spanish Barricades,* pp. 80–81.

[32] Peter Stansky & William Abrahams, *Journey to the Frontier,* p. 365.

[33] Anne Sebba, *Battling for News,* p. 98.

[34] Ernest Hemingway, *Selected Letters,* p. 505.

[35] Tom Wintringham. *English Captain,* p. 330.

[36] James K. Hopkins, *Into the Heart of the Fire,* p. 361.

[37] Peter Kemp, *Mine Were of Trouble,* p. 31.

[38] For Elizabeth Girling, see *Guardian,* 5 May 2005.

[39] Anne-Marie Brady, *Friend of China,* p. 84.

[40] Israel Epstein, *My China Eye,* passim.

[41] For David Crook, see *Guardian,* 18 December 2000.

[42] *Daily Telegraph,* 27 March 1995.

[43] Salman Rushdie, *The Jaguar Smile,* p. 70.

[44] Michael Ezra, "Pol Pot's Apologist," *Democratiya,* 16 Spring/Summer 2009.

Epilogue

[1] Christopher Booker, *The Great Deception,* p. 122.

[2] Booker, p. 355.

[3] Booker, p. 168.

[4] *The Times,* 9 September 2009.

Index